THE STORY OF MYSTICISM

THE STORY OF
MYSTICISM

HILDA GRAEF

DOUBLEDAY & COMPANY, INC., GARDEN CITY, NEW YORK, 1965

Nihil obstat: Daniel V. Flynn, J.C.D.
   Censor Librorum

Imprimatur: Terence J. Cooke, V.G.
   Archdiocese of New York

The nihil obstat and imprimatur are official declarations that a book or pamphlet is free of doctrinal or moral error. No implication is contained therein that those who have granted the nihil obstat and imprimatur agree with the contents, opinions or statements expressed.

Library of Congress Catalog Card Number 65–19934
Copyright © 1965 by Hilda Graef
All Rights Reserved
Printed in the United States of America
First Edition

CONTENTS

PREFACE

The present book is not meant to be an exhaustive study of mysticism; this is impossible to give in a moderate-sized volume. Hence a selection had to be made, and if I have left out certain mystics my readers would have liked to find in it, in the interests of ecumenism and catholicity I have deliberately included some less well-known ones, especially those of the Eastern Church. Wherever possible I have given the most important biographical facts as well as the main points of their teaching, but I have rarely gone into the more intricate problems of mystical theology, since the book is meant to provide an introduction to this fascinating subject for the lay reader, not a discussion of mystics and mysticism for the expert. On the other hand, I have made use of modern scholarship, including modern psychology, to explain certain phenomena, but I have tried to avoid technical terms as much as possible.

Oxford,
Advent 1964.   HILDA GRAEF

A concise, comprehensive, and popularly written survey of mystical experience from the pre-Christian era to the twentieth century.

I A BRIEF SURVEY OF
NON-CHRISTIAN MYSTICISM

It is very difficult to arrive at a proper definition of mysticism, especially if we include in this term not only the Christian, but all other mystical experience. And it can hardly be doubted that there is also a genuine mysticism outside Christianity, or at least the aspiration towards genuine mystical experience. All religions believe in a power or powers beyond man, greater than man, who are feared or loved, and in any case worshiped; and in most religions, especially in the Eastern ones, there exists an elite who do not content themselves with merely worshiping these powers, but aspire to unite themselves with them in a more intimate manner. This desire for union with the divine, the absolute, the powers beyond, or however else this superhuman goal of the mystical aspiration may be called, is generally believed to rest on a special vocation, a call from above, and involves an often very strenuous preparation, a turning away from the visible world and its enjoyments and, in most cases, severe physical austerities.

SHAMANISM

In a survey as short as the present introductory chapter, only a few forms of extra-Christian mysticism and their principal features can be indicated,[1] to form the backdrop, as it were, against which the great spiritual pageant of Christian mysticism will be shown. Just as we distinguish the so-called primitive from the higher religions, so we may also speak of a "primitive" and a

[1] For further information see the Bibliography.

"higher" mysticism. The former can best be studied in what modern scholars call shamanism, a term derived from the word for seer or prophet, "shaman," used by the Tunguses of Siberia. It denotes a kind of mystical religion in which trance-states play a central part, and which is also found among other primitive tribes, for example the Eskimo and the Australians. In these trances or ecstasies the seer reaches the sphere of the divine and communicates with it; he develops paranormal faculties such as clairvoyance, foretelling of the future, even bilocation (being, or rather appearing, in two places at once) and the gift of healing. The acquisition of these faculties requires a long training, given by an older shaman who plays a part similar to that of the spiritual director in Catholic spirituality. The practices in this training period, too, are akin to those of the purgative stage of the mystical way: fasting, vigils, solitude play an important part in the preparation of the shaman for ecstasy. They are, however, frequently carried so far as to lead to a veritable disintegration of the personality, symbolizing, as the French expert on the subject, Mircea Eliade, has shown, the return to the primeval chaos, from which the world emerged. This, says Eliade, "is the sign that the profane man is about to dissolve and a new personality is going to be born."[2] The "folly" of the neophyte is the necessary precondition of the emergence of the fully fledged shaman, who is in contact with the world beyond and capable of exercising preternatural powers. Primitive man, with his magical view of the world full of spirits and mysterious forces, wishes to come into contact with that invisible world and to be protected from its evil influences, and the shaman is the man set aside to effect this communication through his own first-hand knowledge of the world beyond normal experience. The magical rites he uses have a purifying effect on him, so that he is able to reach this world, indeed to become part of it, and thus to give others a share in it.

[2] "Le symbolisme des ténèbres dans les religions archaiques" in *Etudes Carmélitaines*, Polarité du Symbole, 1960, p. 22.

HINDUISM

While the mystical aspirations of the primitive religions are surrounded by magic, those of the higher religions rest on far more elevated philosophical and spiritual foundations. Of these, Hinduism, and its offspring, Buddhism, have developed the most subtle forms of Eastern mysticism. Hinduism has produced a mystical literature of a very high order in the Upanishads, the Bhadgavad-Gita and the Vedanta. The Upanishads (i.e. secret teachings), dating probably from the eighth to the fifth centuries B.C., are a collection of instructions, mostly in the form of question and answer. Their basic teaching is that everything in the world is Spirit, "atman," which is also the Self, the deepest essence of man. But at the same time this is also Brahman, the mysterious power whose expression is the universe, for atman, the self, and Brahman, the underlying essence of the world, are one, so that the teachers of the Upanishads can say of everything in this world: *Tat twam asi*—this is thou; man and the universe in which he lives are fundamentally one.

Yet this is not acutally pantheism; for Brahman does not equal the universe, rather is it the supreme reality immanent in, yet transcending it. Atman, which is also Brahman, is concealed in the heart of all things, for "He is the all-pervading, all-filling inner self of all beings, the Overseer of all activities," as one of the Upanishads expresses it. For a Western mind, brought up in the dualistic Jewish-Christian world view, in which God the eternal Creator is strictly separate from the temporal creation which he governs by his providence, this Indian tendency to identify the inner and the outer, to let the divine and the human selves merge into one, is difficult to understand and even more difficult to explain. This is perhaps one of the reasons why many writers on mysticism hold that the fundamental mystical experience of union is the same in all religions, that basically the experience of the Hindu does not differ from that of the Christian mystic. The following chapters will show that this is an erroneous view, that there is a profound and essential difference between the experience of the Indian sage and the Christian saint; but in order to make this clear we must try to penetrate a little more deeply into the teaching of the Upanishads.

Although these have passages which speak of the "Lord of lords" and "the one God," this being is never really separated from the world; for the universe is at least part of him; indeed, "there is nothing in this world that is not God." The goal of the mystic, therefore, is to find this God, to become aware of the divine presence in the world and in himself, a presence which is hidden from ordinary men, to unite himself to it and thus—a very important aspect of Eastern mysticism—to be delivered from the sufferings of this world. In Hindu thought these are linked with the doctrine of metempsychosis, the transmigration of souls into other bodies, either human or animal, according to man's actions. This is the law of "karma." The teaching of the Upanishads aims at delivering man from this cycle of rebirth by finding his true, immortal self (atman) and thus becoming united to the divine self of Brahman. This goal can only be attained through strenuous ascetical practice, by which the mystic turns away from all activities and all desires of this earth. For these spell duality and difference, death and decay, and prevent him from reaching the desired state in which he does not perceive the "other" at all, but "everything is one self." Then the Brahman, the great Self, is fully known and thus the cycle of rebirths is broken. Man has attained immortality, the eternal atman in him has become one with Brahman, the universal Self.

The one-sided intellectualism of the Upanishads with its rejection of a loving, active concern with this world could not completely satisfy the aspirations of many Hindu mystics, and some time between the first and second centuries B.C. another mystical work made its appearance. This was the Bhagavad-Gita, the "Song of God," destined to become the most influential religious book in India. The framework of this poem was provided by the story of an Indian prince, Arjuna, who had to lead an army against his fellow countrymen in a civil war. Before the battle on which depended his succession to the throne he was tormented by doubts and asked the advice of his charioteer, Krishna, who is an incarnation of Brahman. Krishna told him to fight, because such was his duty as a prince and warrior. Arjuna, however, was not satisfied with this answer, but wanted to know how it could be reconciled with the teaching that the knowledge of Brahman transcends all action. Krishna replied that there are two ways leading to Brahman: the way of contemplation (as taught in the Upanishads) and the way of action, not, indeed, of ordinary activity, but a special kind of action, which is done for the sake of God, as an act of worship, and quite disinterested in its results. This is the way of *bhakti*, variously translated as "personal devotion" or "loving faith."

The theological foundation of the Bhagavad-Gita is by and large the same as that of the Upanishads. Brahman is the supreme being and atman the universal spirit immanent in man which, however, is seen as more individual in the Gita than in the Upanishads. The divine spirit is present in every man in the depth of his being, but in varying degrees of consciousness. In Krishna it is completely conscious, and the disciple of the Gita is called to realize this consciousness in himself so that he, too, may attain *nirvana*, the blissful state of perfect tranquillity, or Brahman. While also retaining the way of knowledge taught by the Upanishads, the Gita recommends particularly the way of *bhakti*, the devotion offered to Krishna as the most perfect manifestation of Brahman, a devotion which purifies a man and prepares him for union with Brahman. This latter also needs the practice of yoga (a Sanskrit word meaning union), mentioned already in the Upanishads. It is a technique of concentration designed to exclude all sense perception. The follower of *bhakti*, united in his heart to Krishna, to whom all his actions are offered, and purified from all earthly attachments by the practice of yoga, will finally himself become Brahman.

Both the teachings of the Upanishads and of the Bhagavad-Gita were later (from the eighth to the twelfth centuries A.D.)

given a philosophical foundation in the Vedanta, a work of several philosopher-mystics. Their conception of the mystical union is largely one of complete identity. In it the human soul knows that it is itself the universal Spirit, Brahman himself. Only Brahman is real. The visible and perishable world is unreal; it is the veil of "maya," hiding reality. When a man has achieved the mystical unity with Brahman he realizes that the whole world of ordinary experience is an illusion, for in his mystical experience he is himself Brahman; hence, all contrary experience of individuality and multiplicity must be deception. To this sphere of ordinary experience belongs the idea of a personal God and of many gods, which are, however, recognized to be necessary as long as man has not yet shed the veil of maya, but which are incompatible with the experience of identity granted to the mystic.

So Hindu mysticism is based on the belief in the fundamental unity of the self with the Absolute, which is the essence of its mystical experience, while the outside world and all experience relating to it are seen only as a deceptive veil hiding Brahman. Hence, in the last analysis, all reality is Brahman and all reality is also the self: *Tat twam asi*—this is thou. This mysticism of identity rules out any authentic transcendence and at the same time also any real sense of history, because history, too, belongs to the veil of maya.

BUDDHISM

Buddhism, the other great Indian religion, is an offspring of Hinduism, and hence shows similar trends, especially in one of the many forms into which it developed, the so-called Mahayana Buddhism, which again is split up into several schools. One of its basic tenets anticipates the conception of the maya of the Vedanta (the Buddhist scriptures date from about 200 B.C.) in that it teaches that our world of space and time is an illusion. According to one school of thought the ultimate reality is the

Void, the "Sunya," about which nothing can be affirmed, but which can be attained in mystical experience; according to another it is "suchness," something that is above and beyond anything we can conceive, that is neither existence nor non-existence, or any other of the opposites in which we are wont to think, but supreme reality.

This supreme reality is also the "eternal Buddha"; not the historical figure of Gautama Buddha, but the Buddha-nature, the *dharmakaya*, that is the body of truth or reality, the Absolute that transcends all human thought and perception but is not, as the Jewish-Christian God, conceived as personal. For the *dharmakaya*, though being above all things, is at the same time identical with their being and embraces them, so that all are united in it. Those who have attained to this realization of the identity of all things, for which there is neither the self nor the other because both are the same, are called *bodhisattvas*. They have reached the state which fits them for entering nirvana, but have voluntarily delayed their entrance in order to help their fellowmen to reach the same goal. The doctrine of the underlying identity of all beings leads naturally to an ethics of love and compassion and the complete suppression of self, for this is really non-existent. So the *bodhisattva* will identify himself with others even in their guilt in order to set them, too, on the way to *nirvana*.

This goal of fitness for nirvana is reached only after years of strenuous asceticism through the "eightfold path," the stages of which are called right understanding, right resolve or thought, right speech, right action, right effort, right meditation or mindfulness, right concentration. The latter two will lead to trance-states or raptures culminating in a state of perfect serenity, in which the mystic has become wholly indifferent to either pleasure or pain.

The mystical thought of both Hinduism and Buddhism is extremely subtle and at the same time frequently ambiguous, difficult to grasp especially for the Western mind accustomed to think in more clearly defined categories. Here only the rou....

sketch could be given, but one fundamental element common to both Hindu and Buddhist mysticism will have emerged: being based on the idea of the essential unity of all beings and the denial of all separateness, the goal of the mystic way is not union with Another, but merging into the One with the consequent loss of all personal identity.

NEOPLATONISM

Whereas neither Hindu nor Buddhist mysticism have had any direct observable influence on the mystical teaching of the great monotheistic religions of Judaism, Christianity, and Islam, Neoplatonism has played an important part in all three of them. Neoplatonism is a pronouncedly mystical development of the philosophy of Plato (427–347 B.C.); its foremost representative is Plotinus (c. 205–270 A.D.). He was a native of the Egyptian town of Lycopolis, and studied in Alexandria under Ammonius Saccas, a Platonic philosopher. Later Plotinus traveled to Persia, to acquaint himself more closely with Eastern thought, which he had probably met already in Alexandria, the intellectual and spiritual center of the Hellenistic world. At the age of forty Plotinus settled in Rome; there he wrote his famous *Enneads,* so called because his disciple Porphyry arranged the fifty-four treatises of which they consisted in groups of nine (Greek *enneas*).

Neither the thought nor the style of Plotinus are easy to understand; hence, he has been interpreted in various ways. His system is based on a triad whose members, however, are neither equal nor are they persons. The highest member is the One, or the Good, the first principle of being, incomprehensible in itself, transcending all categories of human thought such as existence or essence. Nevertheless, the transcendence also has an element of immanence, because it contains all; and so the thought of Plotinus has sometimes been interpreted as being pantheistic, whereas others have regarded it as approaching theism. The second member of his triad is *Nous*, which is variously translated

as Mind, Intelligence, or Spirit. Perhaps the best translation is
that by Professor Hilary Armstrong, who defines it as "intuitive
thought which is always united with its object." This *Nous*
has been engendered by the One, and in its turn engenders
Psyche, the World Soul, which links the perfect intellectual
world of *Nous* to the imperfect world of time, space, and matter
as we know it, which this soul has created and which it is order-
ing. Hence, the Plotinian soul has a twofold aspect: on the one
hand it reaches up into the world of *Nous*, while on the other
it is responsible for, and actually identical with, the lower world
of our cosmos, which includes the world of individual human
souls. Hence, says Plotinus, "the soul in all the several forms of
life is one Soul, an omnipresent identity." But this unity of individual souls does not mean that they are actually completely
identical, for it allows of variety; so that, because of our unity,
we can share our experiences, but because of our variety, these
experiences differ. On the other hand, that part of the World
Soul that reaches up into the world of *Nous* has its counter-
part also in the soul of the individual.

This Plotinian teaching on the higher part of the soul is immensely important for mystical theology, for it is this part of
the soul which is capable of contemplation and which is, indeed,
eternal and incapable of evil. Evil has its cause in matter, which
for Plotinus is the absence of order and indeed of "being," resembling the Indian conception of the veil of maya. Hence, the
way to union with the One involves, like the Indian way, complete detachment from all material things and a withdrawal into
one's own self. In this life of recollection even separate ideas
and discursive reasoning will gradually disappear, until the soul
reaches a state of ecstasy, the "flight of the alone to the Alone," ·
the vision in which a man sees "the Supreme . . . as one with
himself," knowing his own Godhead. In this life such a state of
"deification" is transitory, because the soul is still hindered by
the body; but when it will be freed from its fetters in death it
will enjoy this vision permanently in the unity of the One.

SUFI MYSTICISM

One of the three great monotheistic religions, Judaism, Christianity, and Islam, the last seems the one least fitted to encourage the development of mysticism, because of its uncompromising insistence on the absolute transcendence of God, which should rule out any possibility of a union between him and the believer. Nevertheless, so deep is the desire of truly spiritual men in every religion that Islam, too, has produced its quota of mystics in the Sufis, so called from the white woolen habit they wore. What distinguishes Sufism as well as Jewish and Christian mysticism from the Indian schools of mysticism is the emphasis on love. In Indian mysticism this is present only in *bhakti*, and even there only in a rather rudimentary form. For love is possible only between persons; it cannot exist where the I is held to be identical with the Thou. Mohammedans, on the other hand, believe in a personal God and are exhorted by the Prophet to surrender to him completely and to remember him not only in formal prayer but at all times. Despite the emphasis on the divine transcendence this constant occupation with God must bring about a relationship between him and his worshiper within which a mystical life can develop. Moreover, Islam has been strongly influenced by Christianity as well as by Neoplatonism, which have considerably contributed to the evolution of mysticism within it.

Sufism developed and attained its height in Persia between the ninth and thirteenth centuries of our era; Al Hallaj in the tenth century, Al-Ghazzali in the eleventh and Jalal al-Din Rumi in the thirteenth were among its finest representatives. The Sufi way to the goal, that is to say union with God, is divided into many stages and needs a teacher, corresponding to the Western spiritual director. Preparation for the mystical life proper begins with conversion from worldly pleasures to the service of God, leading to detachment and poverty, which includes not only physical poverty but indifference also to fame, insults, and other experiences which normally agitate the minds of men. From

there the Sufi aspirant is led to the sometimes very painful exercise of patience, because, though detached from worldly desires, he has not yet reached God, whom he loves. He therefore
surrenders himself completely to the good pleasure of God and
thus achieves perfect contentment with all God wills for him. He
is thus prepared for the mystical life of union with God, which
again is divided into various stages, culminating in contemplation and "certainty." Al-Ghazzali, the great mystical theologian
of Islam, used the Christian image of the soul as a mirror that
has to be cleansed to reflect the divine light. It is done by meditation and recollection, by which men draw near to God in love
and finally experience the divine presence in ecstasy. This he
describes as a state in which the Sufi is so absorbed in God that
he feels neither his own body nor anything happening around
him, nor his own thoughts, but is overwhelmed solely by the
divine glory. As in Christian mysticism, this state is likened to
inebriation, in which the "self" is lost in God. Because this is a
union of love the Sufis often use erotic language to describe
their experience, in the same way as the imagery of the Song
of Songs is used by the Christian mystics. But, unlike the latter,
the Sufis believed that they could really see God's essence; for
what prevents this vision is the self, and when this has died a
mystical death, God will appear.

To induce this vision many Sufis used special practices such as
singing and dancing; another practice, the so-called *zikr* or "remembrance," consisted of repeating over and over again the for-
mula of the Mohammedan faith: There is no god but Allah—a
practice closely resembling that of the fourteenth-century Hesychasts in the Eastern Church who used the Jesus-prayer for the
same purpose (cf. Chapter X).

MYSTICAL ELEMENTS IN JUDAISM

The mystical element in Israel's religion, which also stresses
the utter transcendence of God, is evident already in the early
books of the Old Testament. Indeed, in the very first chapters

of Genesis the foundation is laid for later mystical developments, for they teach that man was made in the image of God. Thus there is in man's nature as it were a sphere which provides a meeting place between him and his Maker, which was disturbed, but not destroyed by the fall. For God told the serpent, the symbol of the evil one, that he would put enmity between him and the woman, whose seed would bruise his head, a saying which is interpreted as the promise of the Messiah who would restore the original relationship between man and God.

But even before the coming of the Messiah God did not deprive man entirely of communion with him. There were certain men whom he called to enjoy a very special relationship with him, for example Abraham, the patriarch of Israel, to whom God appeared several times, whether in dreams or in vision, promising to make a great people of him. Then there is Jacob, to whom he renewed the promises made to Abraham and who saw a ladder reaching from heaven down to earth, on which angels were ascending and descending, a symbol of the connection that exists between mortal men and the transcendent powers of the spiritual world. The most striking expression of the Jewish idea of man's relationship with God, however, occurs in the narrative of Exodus, where it is said of Moses, the great Lawgiver of Israel: "And the Lord spoke to Moses face to face, as a man is wont to speak to his friend" (33:11). This is an entirely new and unique way of religious thinking, which presupposes a conception of God and of man such as we have not so far found except in Mohammedanism, which, however, is much later than Judaism and Christianity and has borrowed from both. It presupposes not only a wholly transcendent God, ruling out even the slightest vestige of pantheism, but also the capacity of man for reaching this transcendence in a way which leaves the human personality itself completely intact. God is the almighty Creator and man is his creature, but both God and man are personal beings capable of entering into communion with one another. There is no question of a "mystical death" or of man being absorbed into God, even less of God being in any way identified with man and his world; but the divine and the human are capable of being "friends," because God himself has given man this possibility through the mysterious likeness to himself that he established in the human spirit.

This conception of God and his relationship to man is sometimes considered unduly anthropomorphic, especially by contemporary thinkers who refuse to accept the idea of God as a person and prefer to think of him as an impersonal force permeating the universe, the life force or some similar concept. But if the notion of a personal God seems to them to put God on an equal level with man, the idea of an impersonal force would place him even below man, for a person is superior to a force. To give but a crude example: this life force is sometimes compared to something like electricity. Now man can, indeed, use electricity, but electricity cannot use man, hence electricity and any other impersonal force must be lower than man, and so God would be beneath man. Neither can a force give orders or enter into communion with a person, whereas another person can do just this. But this idea of a personal God is frowned on particularly because it seems to limit God, because we can think of persons only as limited beings, whereas forces seem to us far less limited, being able to penetrate this world. But a divine Creator Person is not limited in a way a human person is, because he is capable of entering into communion with created persons in a far more intimate way than these can do with each other. Neither Brahman nor atman nor the "eternal Buddha" are personal beings capable of entering into genuine communion with man, they can only absorb man into themselves. The God of Abraham, Isaac, and Jacob, the God of Moses is a Person, union with whom is not a union of absorption, but a union of love, even though he is an infinite and man is a finite person.

The stories of Moses and the Patriarchs were edited in the eighth and seventh centuries B.C. by men influenced by the so-called prophetic movement of that time, among whose chief representatives are Hosea, Isaiah, and Jeremiah. Though these prophets did not teach a mystical way like the Mohammedan

Sufis, they themselves had mystical experiences, and the attitude to God which they taught might well lead others to the same. Isaiah's great inaugural vision of the Lord sitting on a high throne surrounded by seraphim crying "Holy, Holy, Holy, the Lord God of hosts, all the earth is full of his glory" (6:1) is an experience both of the transcendence and the authentic immanence of the personal God of Israel. He is not far removed from the earth, which is full of his glory, he is not a God "up there" or "out there," as the traditional Jewish-Christian conception of God is sometimes misrepresented today. He is the God who both reigns in heaven, that is to say in the world of the spirit beyond space and time, and who fills the temporal world of men with the awareness of his presence. And because man is aware of this presence and is conscious of its holiness, the prophet who receives this vision cries out: "Woe is me for I am undone; because I am a man of unclean lips."

This is the classic reaction of man to a genuinely mystical experience: the awareness of the divine Presence calls forth the corresponding awareness of man's own unworthiness and his need for purification, present also, as we have seen, in the mysticism of the East which demands a strict ascetical preparation from the disciple who would attain to union with Brahman. What is noteworthy in the vision of the prophet, however, is that this purification is not achieved by his own efforts, but through the intervention of one of the seraphim who touches his lips with a live coal, by which the prophet's iniquities are taken away. The ultimate purification is the work of God, and its effect is, in the case of Isaiah, to make him ready for the work of bringing God's message to man.

This message, though often couched in terms of threats and prophecies of doom, because of the people's frequent disobedience, is yet essentially a message of love, and its charter is the famous *Shema* (Hear), so called from the first Hebrew word of Deuteronomy 6:4f: "Hear, O Israel, the Lord our God is one Lord. Thou shalt love the Lord thy God with thy whole heart, and with thy whole soul, and with thy whole strength."

The Book of Deuteronomy, written probably in the seventh century B.C., had been strongly influenced by the prophetic movement and its emphasis on the love relationship between the transcendent God and man. The eighth-century prophet Hosea described Jahweh as the lover and husband of Israel: "And it shall be in that day . . . she [i.e. Israel] shall call me, my husband . . . And I will espouse thee to me for ever" (2:16–19). When in the following centuries, just before, during and especially after the Exile (598–c. 525), the religion of Israel became more personal, this command of love was interpreted as addressed not only to the people as a whole, but also to individuals: Jeremiah, the prophet of the Exile, calls out to God in his distress: "Thou hast beguiled me, Jahweh, and I am beguiled" (20:7), and the prophesies that a time will come when the Lord will write his law no longer on tablets of stone, as Moses had done, but in the very hearts of men (3:31ff). For God is omnipresent: "Am I a God at hand, saith the Lord, and not a God afar off? . . . Do not I fill heaven and earth, saith the Lord" (23:23f). And because he "fills heaven and earth," man, too, can be "filled" with God, having his law of love, the *Shema*, in his very heart. For this is precisely the mystery of the God of both Jews and Christians, that he is, indeed, a Person over against us whose law men must obey, but that at the same time he also dwells in us by love, an indwelling which most believers accept by dark faith, but of which those we call mystics also become aware experimentally, because they respond to this indwelling with their whole heart.

The great vision of Ezekiel 1:4–28, in which the prophet sees the divine chariot with the four mysterious living creatures and above it the sapphire throne of the glory of Jahweh, expressed particularly the transcendence of the omnipotent God. The living creatures which go wherever the spirit goes and which are full of eyes symbolize God's omnipresence and his omniscience, from which nothing is hidden. They are, however, not God himself, who seems farther away from the world than in the vision of Isaiah, even though this has very probably influenced the vision of the later prophet. Ezekiel's vision, however, had a far-reaching importance for Jewish mysticism, as we shall see presently.

The interior presence of the transcendent God is most clearly and beautifully expressed in some of the Psalms, most of which were written after the Exile. Almost the whole of Psalm 138(139) is one loving praise not only of God's omnipresence in the world but also of his most intimate relationship with the poet: "O Lord, thou has searched me and known me . . . thou understandest my thought afar off . . . If I take the wings of the morning and dwell in the uttermost parts of the sea: Even there shall thy hand lead me, and thy right hand shall hold me." Psalm 62(63) passionately asks that God make his presence felt: "My soul thirsteth for thee, my flesh longeth for thee . . . for thy loving-kindness is better than life . . . My soul shall be satisfied as with marrow and fatness," and in Psalm 41(42) the Psalmist compares his thirst for God to the thirst of the hart for water: "so panteth my soul after thee, O God," and yet another praises God's continual presence with him, for Jahweh is all in all to him: "Whom have I in heaven but thee? And there is none upon earth that I desire beside thee" 72(73).

These poems express the most urgent longing of man for the intimately felt presence of his God, a longing that can only be called mystical, as it is the desire of the human person to be united with—not, it should be noted, to be absorbed into—the divine Person. In the Wisdom literature this mystical trend of the Jewish religion took a slightly different aspect.

Partly no doubt under the influence of Gentile thought with which the Jews who had emigrated to Alexandria became acquainted, their uncompromising monotheism absorbed certain new elements, more particularly the conception of wisdom. In the Book of Proverbs, which seems to have received its final form in the fourth century B.C., wisdom is not regarded as an abstract, but almost as a person. In the famous eighth chapter she is introduced as crying at the gates of the city: "The Lord possessed me in the beginning of his ways . . . when there were no depths, I was born . . . When he prepared the heavens, I was present . . . I was at his side as a master workman: and was delighted every day, playing before him at all times, playing in the world, and my delights were to be with the children of men." Wisdom is not God himself, but a very nearly personal power born before the world was made and present at its creation, indeed, playing in it, a link as it were between the transcendent God and his creatures. This function of wisdom becomes even more evident in the biblical book that bears its name and which was probably written by an Alexandrian Jew of the second century B.C., though it has been dated even as late as the first century A.D. There wisdom is described as "more active than all active things . . . For she is a vapour of the power of God and a certain pure emanation of the glory of the almighty God . . . the unspotted mirror of God's majesty" (7:24–26).

The idea that there are "emanations" of God was soon to play an important part in the development of Jewish mysticism, for it bridged the gulf between the inaccessible Divinity and his creation.[3] The mysterious "wisdom" does not only deliver the just from their enemies, but enters the very soul of the saints; she is the indwelling power of the transcendent God. For "being one, she can do all things; and remaining in herself the same, she reneweth all things, and from generation to generation passeth into holy souls" (Wisdom 7:27). At the same time Wisdom is identified with the Word, "For," says the author of the Wisdom Book, "While all things were in peaceful silence . . . thy almighty word leapt down from heaven from thy royal throne" (18:14f). Beside Wisdom and the Word there is a third divine power mentioned in the Old Testament, the Spirit. This

---

[3] The concept of "emanations" was one of the main elements of Gnosticism, from Greek gnosis=knowledge, a collective name for different systems of religious thought professing a fundamental antagonism between God and the world. This was bridged by a number of graded intermediate beings called emanations, or aeons, which connected the inaccessible highest God with the world of matter and were arranged in pairs such as the male Nous and the female Sophia. Gnostic ideas have influenced mystic teaching in various ways, as will be seen in the course of this study.

Spirit of God fills the prophets; he is frequently mentioned in Ezekiel and twice called the "holy spirit," whom the Psalmist begs God not to take away from him (50[51]:13) and who is grieved by the sins of Israel (Isaiah 63:10). The full revelation of the divine Word and the Holy Spirit was reserved to the New Testament and is, as we shall see, at the base of Christian mysticism; but their partial revelation in the Old Testament also nourished later Jewish mysticism.

Though this also underwent Neoplatonist and other influences, it had its roots firmly in the Old Testament. One main school of it was the so-called Merkabah (=chariot) mysticism, based on Ezekiel's vision of the chariot of Jahweh. To become a "Merkabah rider" meant to reach a state of ecstasy in which man came into contact with the unseen world; from the early Middle Ages all kinds of artifices and even magic were used to induce such a state. In the Merkabah as well as in other forms of Jewish mysticism the angels play an important part as mediators between God and men, especially the angel Metatron, in whom the essence of the Deity exists, because the numerical value of the Hebrew letters of his name (the Hebrew letters served also as figures) equaled that of God's name Shaddai= Almighty. This is a typical example of rabbinical mysticism, which centered in the divine name and in numbers. Metatron, who was also called the "Prince of the Presence" (i.e. of God) or the "Prince of the World," represented God's active presence in the world; he was also regarded as the special intercessor for Israel.

Another, more subtle conception of the divine Presence in the world is the Shekhinah. The word derives from *shachan*= dwell and means the indwelling God, the Father of Israel. Jahweh dwells in Israel as a whole as well as in the individual Israelites, but this indwelling can be experienced only after stringent purification. When perfect purification has been achieved the Shekhinah can be perceived even by the senses: it can be heard, seen and even smelt. In the Kabbalah (i.e. tradition), a mystical movement with a strongly theosophic flavor, which reached its peak in the later Middle Ages, the Shekhinah is regarded as the feminine element in God. Here the Gnostic influence is evident. The Kabbalists distinguish between the hidden God, the *Deus absconditus,* and the "living God" who manifests himself in creation, revelation, and salvation. Their intense meditation on these two aspects of God led them to conceive the world of the "Sefiroth," a divine world of immense complexity underlying this material world and present and active in it. The Kabbalists aimed to know both the God as manifested in the world and the Bible and also the hidden God "in the depths of his nothingness," a paradoxical manner of expression we shall also meet in certain Christian mystics.

Another form of Jewish mysticism, which developed in Germany about the middle of the twelfth century, was Hasidism, which stressed the immanence of God and taught the practice of interior tranquillity as a kind of spiritual defense during the persecution the Jews suffered at the time of the Crusades. While not neglecting the external glory of Jahweh as it appears in the mystic visions of the Merkabah, the Hasidim of the Middle Ages laid particular emphasis on the interior glory, the Holy Spirit, by which God speaks to the soul.

The Platonic influence was strongest in Philo (c. 20 B.C.– 50 A.D.), the famous Alexandrian Jew who attempted to synthesize Hellenistic thought with rabbinic theology, and who is mentioned out of chronological order at the end of this chapter, because he had hardly any influence on Jewish mysticism but considerable importance for the development of Christian mystical theology. His thought is developed mainly in commentaries on Genesis and Exodus, which he interprets not literally, but allegorically, a common practice at the time, which was also adopted by St. Paul in his letter to the Galatians (4:24). Philo stresses the transcendence and complete incomprehensibility of God, and his problem, too, is to bridge the gulf between him and the world. For Philo the principal connecting link is the Logos, the Word, whom he describes as an attendant on the One Supreme Being, or even as the first-born Son of God. He was responsible for the divine image in man, he guided the patriarchs, he spoke to Moses in the burning bush, and he intercedes with God on behalf of men. Philo even calls him a "second Deity," subordinate to the transcendent God who is above virtue, above knowledge, even above the Good. The highest knowledge man can have of God is to "comprehend that God is incomprehensible." The way to this negative mystical knowledge leads from a life of virtue through the renunciation of all creatures and of self to ecstasy, which is a divine gift in which man is brought into direct contact with the Uncreated.

Jewish mysticism is, as it were, the prelude to Christian mysticism, as the Old Testament is the preparation for the New. The oneness and transcendence of God are always present to the mind of the Jewish mystic, and the problem of the relation of the one transcendent and perfect Creator to this world of multiplicity and imperfection is clearly seen. The later Old Testament authors and the Jewish mystics attempted to solve it by assuming certain divine powers, whether angels or emanations, subordinate to the one inaccessible God, yet somehow inherent in him as well as in the world, who made the connection between the two. Through their meditation the mystic could in some way meet God himself in ecstasy.

II MYSTICISM IN THE
NEW TESTAMENT

As we have seen, men have at all times and in all religions groped for some way to unite themselves to the Divine; they had never dared to hope that God would unite himself to them in such a perfect and unique way as to become man himself. When this happened it was something so overwhelming that it seemed foolishness to the pagans, but to the Jews it was something even worse: it was a scandal and a stumbling block to them (cf. I Corinthians 1:23). It was one thing to believe that the inaccessible Jahweh was related to the world through some intermediary beings, whether angels or aeons—it was quite another to assert that God himself had come to earth as a real man to live, suffer and die as a man. For Philo, the Word, the Logos of God, was a being inferior to God himself, manifesting himself in the world in various ways; whereas St. John could write in his Gospel: "The Word was God. The same was in the beginning with God . . . and the Word was made flesh and dwelt among us" (1:1f;14).

After nineteen hundred years of Christianity these statements are so familiar to us that we hardly realize their tremendous impact, much less understand what they must have meant to the men and women who first heard them. For, according to the Gospel, the Logos was not only a power of God, but was God himself, a statement which, to the Jew, seemed to imply there were two Gods, since St. John in some way distinguished him from God when he wrote that the Word was God, but was also "with God." But, what seemed even more "scandalous" —both to Greeks and to Jews—was the further, to them unbelievable, statement that this mysterious God-Word had been made "flesh." They might have understood if the Evangelist had written that he "appeared" as man, as the Greek gods frequently did and as in the Old Testament Jahweh or his "angel" had appeared to Abraham (Genesis 18); but to make any such interpretation impossible John insists that the Word was God himself and that he was not only made man but actually "flesh," a man with a body like our own. To the intellect this seemed inconceivable. How could the absolute, eternal, completely self-sufficient divine Being become a limited human being of flesh and blood? St. John himself gives the answer: "God so loved the world that he gave his only-begotten son." The divine love is strong enough to bridge the chasm between Creator and creature; there is no necessity to assume intermediate beings, because God's own being is not, as it were, a monolithic structure, but a living society of the Father, the Son he has eternally generated, and the Spirit of love that unites them, three divine Persons in one divine Nature, as the later Fathers of the Church worked out the mystery of the Trinity. Of these Persons the Son, or the Word, as he is called in the Prologue of St. John's Gospel, is particularly concerned with the creation of the world, for "all things were made by him," and so he also bridges the gulf between God and man by becoming man himself. God the Father retains his transcendence, but he becomes accessible through his Son, because the Son is one with him: "He that hath me seeth the Father also" (John 14:9); "I and the Father are One" (John 10:30).

The importance of the Incarnation for the mystical life can hardly be exaggerated, and this is what makes Christian mysticism radically different from all other forms of mysticism. This essential difference is very often denied by writers on the subject, who hold that the mystical experience is basically the same in all religions, a view which is lent some substance by the misleading language of some of the Christian mystics themselves. Nevertheless, the mystical experience in a religion based on the Incarnation must differ fundamentally from any other, for it is inescapably linked to a historical fact, to something that has actually happened in this world of space and time. Indian mysticism is farthest removed from this, because it considers this world as a complete illusion and attempts to escape from it into a mysterious *nirvana*; while even Mohammedan and Jewish mysticism had to assume certain manifestations of God, like the pre-existent Mohammed, the Chariot or the Shekhinah which, however elevated, yet were neither God himself nor entered the world of men as a human being.

Christian mysticism, on the other hand, rests on the fact that at a certain accurately defined movement of history, "in the fifteenth year of the reign of Tiberius Caesar, Pontius Pilate being governor of Judea, and Herod being tetrarch of Galilee . . . the word of the Lord was made unto John" (Luke 3:1f) and the God-man, "made of a woman," as St. Paul says in his Letter to the Galatians (4:4), began his ministry. God himself is spirit, but in becoming man he entered the world of sense, and through entering it he hallowed the material things he had created, so that now water could not only cleanse man's body, but also his soul and his whole being, and bread and wine could become not only man's material, but also his spiritual food and drink. It is obvious that this sanctification of matter must have had a tremendous influence on the mystical life; for matter was now no longer something the mystic must renounce as evil in itself; indeed, if rightly, that is to say sacramentally, used it became for him a way to God. More, because God himself had become flesh and voluntarily subjected himself to all the limitations and sufferings this entailed, which is what St. Paul means when he writes in his Letter to the Philippians that Christ "emptied himself" (2:7), therefore the Christian mystic cannot legitimately strive to rid himself of the body and of his emotions, so that he no longer feels hunger or cold, sorrow, or joy, as the Indian mystics and the Greek Stoics tried to do. For by becoming man Christ willed to share in all this; we know that

he wept at the death of Lazarus (John 11:35), that he felt compassion and even anger (e.g. Matthew 3:7), and that he loved
some of his friends more than others (cf. John 11:5, 13:23 and
elsewhere). So it cannot be the aim of the Christian mystic to
render himself insensitive; on the contrary, we shall see that it is
just the mystics who become increasingly sensitive as they progress in their life of union with God. Finally, their ultimate
goal can never be the "flight of the alone to the Alone," even
though some of them may feel called to the hermit life. For
man is no lonely spirit; Christ surrounded himself with the
apostles and other disciples, he founded his own community,
the Church, and proclaimed that the second commandment of
love "thou shalt love thy neighbour as thyself" is equal to the
first, "thou shalt love the Lord thy God with thy whole heart"
(Matthew 22:37–39). Therefore Christian mysticism can never
renounce the duty of loving one's neighbour; it will always
essentially be a mysticism in community; man approaches God
not as an isolated individual, but as the member of a body.

This becomes quite clear in the teaching of St. Paul, himself
a mystic of the highest caliber. His fundamental experience,
which changed the ardent young Pharisee from a violent per-
secutor of the nascent Jewish-Christian community into the
great apostle of the Gentiles, took place on the road from
Jerusalem to Damascus, where he was going to round up the
Christians and "bring them bound to Jerusalem" (Acts 9:2).
As Paul and his party were nearing Damascus, the future apostle
suddenly saw a light from heaven surrounding him, and from
this light came a voice saying: "Saul, Saul[1] why persecutest thou
me?" The experience was so tremendous that it threw him to
the ground; but he retained sufficient consciousness to ask:
"Who art thou, Lord?" and received the answer; "I am Jesus

[1] St. Paul's Jewish name which he later abandoned, using only his Roman
name, Paul.

whom thou persecutest. But arise, go into the city, and there it shall be told thee what thou must do."[2]

In some respects this vision resembles the so-called inaugural visions of the Old Testament prophets like Isaiah and Ezekiel; as in their case, Paul receives a revelation and at the same time a call to act. Yet there are also profound differences. The very setting of the vision is remarkable. The prophets received their vocation in the temple; St. Paul on the public highway. They saw the throne of Jahweh and the worshiping angels in impressive detail—Paul merely saw a light and heard a voice. But though the experience itself was apparently so simple, its effect was far greater than that of the visions of the prophets, for it turned Paul's whole life upside down, it changed his very religion, and the same man who had been obsessed by the one desire to destroy the small Christian communities because they seemed to endanger his Jewish religion, from now on devoted all his energies to spread this Christian faith throughout the world.

The words Christ spoke to him were as simple as the setting in which Paul heard them, yet they contained the germ of his most characteristic doctrine. "Why," asks the Lord, "persecutest thou me?" Now Paul had never persecuted Jesus personally; he had only persecuted his followers. This question implied that Christ identified himself with his faithful; whoever persecuted them, persecuted him—an identification which recalls Christ's words in the description of the last judgment: "As long as you did it to one of these my least brethren, you did it to me" (Matthew 25:40). And Paul dared to write later to the Galatians: "I live, now not I: but Christ liveth in me" (2:20).

We have just spoken of "identification"—do not these passages bear out the opinion of certain writers that the mystical experience is basically the same in all religions? Do we not have here a teaching on the identity of God with men resembling that of Hindu and Buddhist mysticism? The answer to this

[2] This is the original Greek text; the longer version of the Douay Bible follows an inauthentic addition.

question is less difficult than might be expected: the seeming resemblance is simply due to the poverty of the language, which uses the same word "identity" for metaphysical as well as moral unity. The unity between the Divine and the essence of man in the Indian religions is a metaphysical identity: man is really of the same substance as Brahman. But when Christ identifies himself with the least of his brethren, and when St. Paul writes that Christ liveth in him, the identification is a moral, we might even say a mystical one: the Christian who nurses the sick and visits the prisoners because he sees Christ in them does not assume that they are really Christ himself; but because Christ became man we are now able to see his humanity in the humanity of our fellowmen and to treat them as we would treat him. And if Paul says: "Christ liveth in me," he immediately explains: "I live in the faith of the Son of God, who loveth me and delivered himself for me." Again, the unity of Christ and the apostle is a unity of faith and love, of mutual surrender, which always leaves intact the frontier between the human and the divine, however close their relationship.

This union is not only the union of the alone with the Alone. It is the union within the society of Christ which is so closely knit that Paul can call it the "body of Christ," because Christ himself had identified himself with his persecuted followers. Now this "body of Christ" is not just a metaphor, it is something very real, and its members must undergo a death and a birth. To most Christians today baptism is no more than a rite by which the child or, in rare cases, the adult, becomes a member of the Church. To St. Paul and the early Christians it was much more, it had a profound mystical significance. You are "buried with him (Christ) in baptism," St. Paul writes in his letter to the Colossians, "in whom also you are risen again by the faith of the operation of God who hath raised him up from the dead. And you, when you were dead in your sins and the uncircumcision of your flesh, he hath quickened together with him, forgiving all offences" (2:12f). So baptism is a true mystical death and resurrection, symbolized by the immersion in water and the coming up again cleansed, re-enacting sacramentally the death and the resurrection of Christ, with whom the newly baptized person is clothed (symbolized by the white garment) as Paul writes to the Galatians "As many of you as have been baptized have put on Christ" (3:27). This profound interpretation of the baptismal rite shows quite clearly that the identification of the Christian with Christ, his incarnate God, is always on the sacramental and mystical level, and it should be noted in this context that in the first centuries of our era the term mystical meant sacramental—the early Christians made no difference between the sacramental and the mystical life, which to them were one.

This is particularly noticeable in St. Paul's teaching on the Eucharist, the sacrament par excellence, which the Greek Fathers also called the mystical bread or the mystical table. The Christian who has mystically died and risen again in baptism needs a spiritual food to sustain his new supernatural life, just as he needs material food to sustain his natural life. In the Eucharist he participates in the sacrifice of Christ on the Cross: "The chalice of benediction which we bless," writes St. Paul to the Corinthians, (I, 10:16), "is it not the communion of the blood of Christ? And the bread which we break is it not the partaking of the body of the Lord?" The Christian who receives Holy Communion is therefore literally incorporated into Christ, he becomes, as it were, one body with him. Such a sacramental communion between God and man was not unknown among the pagans; in the Persian cult of Mithras, for example, which had become very popular among the Roman soldiers of the first centuries of our era, there was a sacrament of bread and water mixed with wine by which men were believed to partake in the life of Mithras. The similarity of this and other pagan rites with the Christian Eucharist might have dangerous consequences, hence St. Paul had to warn his converts in the strongest possible terms against mixing up the two: "You cannot drink the chalice of the Lord and the chalice of devils: you cannot be partakers of the table of the Lord and of the table of devils" (I Corinthians 10:21). For the Christian, Holy Communion is not a human invention: it rests on the historical fact of the Last Supper of the God-man with his disciples; but the similarity of the rites is perhaps to be explained by the universal desire of religious men for the closest possible union with the unseen powers, which was actually fulfilled in the communion with his flesh and blood Christ gave to his faithful.

Again, this union with Christ in and through the Eucharist is not only a union of the individual with his God, though it is also that; for St. Paul continues his explanation of the bread and the chalice as communion with the body and blood of Christ with these words: "For we, being many, are one bread, one body, all that partake of one bread." So the Eucharist has the further, most important effect also of uniting Christians with each other, just as the great Christian commandment of love concerns not only God, but also our fellowmen. Thus for St. Paul the mystical life is life within the Body, that is to say the Church, of which Christ is the head, so that, as he says in his letter to the Colossians, "we may in all things grow up in him who is the head, even Christ" (4:15).

Now this growth is a growth in charity, which is the essence of the mystical, as it is the essence of the Christian life in general. Paul's converts in Corinth were not exactly model Christians. He had to reprimand them because there was drunkenness and lack of charity towards the poorer members of the community at their love feasts which preceded the celebrations of the Eucharist, and they also were particularly addicted to the more striking phenomena of the Christian life such as the performance of miracles, the speaking "in tongues," graces of healing, and such like. In his famous chapter I Corinthians 13, the apostle instructs them that these marvels are actually of very little importance compared with the one great essential: charity—or perhaps we should rather call it love, because charity has assumed in our language the meaning of organized good-doing. "If I speak with the tongues of men and of angels, and have not love, I am become as sounding brass, or a tinkling cymbal. And if I should have prophecy and should know all mysteries and all knowledge, and if I should have all faith, that I could remove mountains, and have not love, I am nothing." And he goes on to explain that love is patient and kind, that it is neither jealous nor ambitious, is slow to anger and endures all things, that it never falls away, but still is gloriously existent when our earthly knowledge has become meaningless in eternity.

The Corinthians, however, seem to have taken little notice of this teaching, for in his second letter to them St. Paul had to reprimand them because they had let themselves be taken in by some false apostles who had dazzled them with sensational experiences while condoning their moral laxity. As Paul, on the other hand, had never boasted of ecstasies and seems moreover not to have been a brilliant orator, the Christians in Corinth turned away from his teaching and followed the "false apostles." Therefore Paul decides, though with the greatest reluctance, to allow his converts a glimpse of his own mystical life; "I know a man in Christ," he writes, "above fourteen years ago (whether in the body, I know not, or out of the body, I know not: God knoweth) such a one caught up to the third heaven. And . . . he was caught up into paradise and heard secret words which is not granted to man to utter" (II, 12:2–4).

It is an extremely, perhaps even disappointingly brief description of a very exalted mystical experience; nevertheless it is of the utmost importance for the understanding of authentic Christian mysticism. First of all, the apostle does not like to speak of such an exalted and intimate experience at all—he does it only because the boastings of the false apostles force him to present the credentials of his own apostleship. Mystical experiences are not for the market place; they belong to the "inner chamber" to which Christ bids us retire when we pray (Matthew 6:6) and are to be divulged only if there is a very good reason to do so. And so Paul speaks of himself in the third person—he cannot bring himself to say "I" when recounting this most sacred secret of his inner life. But he calls himself "a man in Christ," an expression very dear to him and containing in four words the essence of Christian mysticism. For the Christian mystic is truly a "man in Christ." He has not lost his own personality in another nor does he feel himself merged into the ground of the universe; but his own indestructible person lives wholly in another, divine-human Being, and as such, as a "man in Christ" he is raised in ecstasy to another, divine sphere. To this he gives the names of third heaven and paradise, the first being probably an astronomical term familiar to his Gentile converts, the latter the biblical expression more intelligible to his Jewish Christians. He was "caught up," which is the translation of a Greek word meaning "violently seized," which corresponds well with the apostle's statement that he did not know whether his spirit was at that time still in his body or out of it—because his whole consciousness was suddenly and forcibly riveted on the ineffable mysteries he learned, those "secret words" which cannot be expressed in human language. This impossibility of communicating it is a characteristic of the most exalted form of mystical experience, which St. Paul distinguished from other "visions and revelations of the Lord" which he evidently enjoyed fairly frequently. But all these experiences he kept secret, for he wanted to be judged by his normal behavior, not by these extraordinary graces—an attitude shared by all genuine Christian mystics. For the foundation of the mystical life is the life of virtue involving a certain amount of asceticism—a fact well known, as we have seen, also to non-Christian mystics, though apparently not to certain modern would-be adepts who believe that mystical experiences can be induced by the use of drugs, and who confuse the super-conscious state of ecstasy with the subconscious state of trance. There is, however, one fundamental difference between the asceticism of the Indian and that of the Christian mystic, even though their practices may be similar. Again St. Paul provides the clue: "But I chastise my body," he writes to the Corinthians (I, 9:27) "and bring it into subjection, lest perhaps, when

I have preached to others, I myself should become a castaway."
This means that he disciplines his body in order not to fall into
any sin—for no other purpose. As we shall see in the following
chapters, the ascetical practices of the mystics sometimes had
an influence on the development of their mystical experiences,
but with few exceptions, these practices were never undertaken
in order to bring the experiences about, whereas in other religions asceticism was deliberately practised to induce abnormal
states of consciousness. For the Christian mystic aims at one
thing only: as perfect a union with God as is possible to him.
If the way to this union involves visions, ecstasies and similar
phenomena he will accept them—but he will not consciously
provoke them. St. Paul chastises his body not in order to induce
strange experiences but to keep himself on the safe and narrow
road; for to him there is only one goal: union with Christ in
love of his body, the Church.

ST. JOHN THE EVANGELIST

Love is also the key word of the other great New Testament
mystic, St. John the beloved disciple. He belonged to those
Israelites who were dissatisfied with the ordinary religious life
of their people. He had joined John the Baptist who preached
to necessity of a profound change of heart and announced the
coming of One whose shoes he himself was not worthy to
loosen and who would baptize them with the Holy Spirit and
with Fire. Then, one day as John and Andrew, his fellow disciple,
were standing with their master, the Baptist suddenly pointed
to a man who was walking along and said: "Behold the Lamb
of God." He had said before that the Messiah was the Lamb
of God who would take away the sins of the world (John 1:29);
now, when he pointed Jesus out to them they lost no time, but
immediately put themselves under his authority. John then also
brought his brother James, and Jesus gave the two brothers the
significant name "Boanerges, which is Sons of Thunder" (Mark
3:17). They deserved this name, for both John and James were

men of violent temper; once they even asked Jesus to let them call down fire from heaven to destroy a city whose inhabitants refused to receive their master, and Jesus had to rebuke them: "The Son of man came not to destroy souls, but to save" (Luke 9:56).

It is often believed that mystics are by nature very gentle people, living in another world far removed from the passions of ordinary men. Nothing could be farther from the truth. They are, on the contrary, mostly men and women of very strong emotions, whose serenity is achieved only after a severe struggle against their ardent nature and whose union with God is the measure of their tremendous capacity for love directed to one supernatural end. John, the young Son of Thunder, had just this capacity for love, which was purified and refined in the short time of his intimacy with the Master who also loved him in a very special way, and which was brought to perfection in the long years of contemplation after Christ had ascended and the Holy Spirit had come down on the young Church. John's as yet unpurified love for his Master expressed itself in the request, made through his mother, that he and his brother might have privileged places in Christ's kingdom. Jesus told them that they knew not what they asked; for they evidently still regarded his kingdom as an earthly realm, and he continued: "Can you drink the chalice that I shall drink"?—the cup or chalice being a Hebrew term for destiny. They at once declared themselves ready; but instead of rewarding their devotion with the promise of a special place Jesus tells them that they shall, indeed, drink his chalice, that is to say share his sufferings, "but to sit on my right hand or left hand is not mine to give to you, but to them for whom it is prepared by my Father" (Matthew 20:23).

It was an answer that was intended to teach John and his brother a lesson: their love of Christ must be for him alone, without regard to any special favors—a lesson which all future mystics have to learn, and which John himself learned to perfection, being the only one of the apostles who did not flee when his master died on the cross. More, when on the morning of the Ressurrection he arrived first at the tomb, he did not enter it, but restraining his own impatience waited for Peter to go in first. Again after the Resurrection, John was the first to recognize the Lord in the miraculous draught of fishes, yet he did not keep his knowledge to himself but at once told Peter, who threw himself into the lake and swam to Christ who was standing on the shore, while John humbly followed in the boat with the others. For John, the man of intuition, submitted willingly to the authority of Peter, to whom Christ had entrusted the guidance of the Church; indeed he later stressed Peter's authority in his own Gospel by recounting the Risen Lord's threefold command to Peter to feed his lambs. For, contrary to the opinion of many modern writers on mysticism, the mystic is not a natural rebel against authority; in fact, he submits to authority perhaps more readily than others because he knows the dangers of relying exclusively on his own personal experience. On the other hand, the intuitions of the mystic are necessary to the Church, which might otherwise fall into sterile dogmatism and authoritarianism. The first chapters of Acts show Peter and John, the man of authority and the man of vision, side by side, preaching together, performing miracles together, going to prison together, for one is as necessary to the well-being of the Church as the other.

Traditionally, both the Apocalypse and the Fourth Gospel have been attributed to the beloved disciple, and we here follow this tradition. For though we are well aware of certain differences of style and outlook in both biblical books, these may be accounted for by the fact that the Apocalypse was written some time before the Gospel, and belongs to a different literary category, while the similarities between the two books seem to us much more important. From the mystical point of view it would seem that the earlier book belongs to a phase of the spiritual life in which the imagination still plays an essential part, while the Gospel is the work of a mature contemplative, who has penetrated through signs and symbols to the very essence of the religion of Christ.

In both books Jesus is seen as the pre-existent Word of God and as the Lamb who takes away the sins of the world by his sacrificial death. The Apocalypse was written during a time of persecution, probably under the Emperor Domitian, and the sufferings of the Christians from the cruelty of the pagan powers merge in the seer's vision with the sufferings that will overtake the world at the end of time. The imagery of the visions resembles that of the Old Testament prophetic and apocalyptic literature: God is seated on a magnificent throne surrounded by a rainbow, immovable in majesty, while Michael, the archangel, is fighting with the dragon and casts him out of heaven. But "in the midst of the throne" there appears a figure unknown to the Old Testament books: "a Lamb standing, as it were slain" (5:6). When the Baptist had first shown Jesus to St. John he had called him "the lamb of God," and when the apostle stood under the Cross he saw him as a lamb that was slain. And now, when he sees him again in his glory he is still the Lamb that was slain, but a Lamb full of power, before whose wrath men tremble (6:16). For he shares the throne of God himself (22:1,3), and he is also the "Word of God," the "King of Kings and the Lord of Lords" (19:13,16), expressions which show that John has fully understood the divinity of Christ through which he is equal to the Father, and which he expresses even more clearly in the Prologue to his Gospel: "And the Word was God."

For at the beginning of his revelations Christ himself had appeared to the apostle, and this vision introduced him perhaps even more deeply into the mystery of Jesus whom he had once known so intimately: "I saw seven golden candlesticks, and in the midst of the seven golden candlesticks, one like to the Son of man . . . and from his mouth came out a sharp two-edged sword. And his face was as the sun shineth in his power. And when I had seen him, I fell at his feet as dead. And he laid his right hand upon me saying: Fear not. I am the First and the Last, and alive, and was dead. And behold, I am living for ever and ever and have the keys of death and of hell"

(1:12ff). The vision had a similar effect on John as the experience on the road to Damascus had on Paul: he fainted. It is a phenomenon that occurs frequently in the lives of the mystics: the impact of the divine is too strong for a human nature not yet accustomed to such visitations, and results in a momentary weakness which resembles a swoon; for even the beloved disciple was not yet able to bear the sudden full revelation of Christ's divinity, and was comforted with the words Jesus had so often spoken during his life on earth: "Fear not."

The Fourth Gospel, the "spiritual Gospel" as Clement of Alexandria first called it, has been beloved by Christian mystics throughout the ages. For it shows Christ not so much as he was seen by simple fishermen and presented in the catechetical instructions given to new converts, but rather as he appeared to a great contemplative after a relatively short time of personal contact and a lifetime of reflection. Further, at the time that St. John wrote his Gospel and the brief letters bearing his name, certain heresies had already made their appearance, notably those of the Ebionites who denied the divinity of Christ and of the Docetists, who, on the contrary, held that the divine Christ only appeared as a man, but had no real human nature. Thus St. John had to defend the great mystery that Christ is both true God and true man, which to him was not only a theoretical conviction, but a living mystical experience as he writes in his first Letter: "That which was from the beginning, which we have heard, which we have seen with our eyes, which we have looked upon and our hands have handled, of the word of life. For the life was manifested: and we have seen and do bear witness and declare unto you the life eternal, which was with the Father and hath appeared to us" (1:1,2). The apostle almost goes out of his way to make it quite clear that Jesus Christ was a real human being, perceived by sight, hearing, and touch; the Christian mystical experience rests in the last analysis on the evidence of the senses of the apostles; if their hands had not handled the Word of life made flesh, there would be neither a Christian faith nor a Christian mysticism. This historical, indeed physical fact is their basis; but neither faith nor mystical experience can remain content with stressing only the true humanity of Christ, for this must become transparent to let the divinity shine through.

To express this, John likes to use signs and images, which are worked out in the great "discourses" of his Gospel. The first of these, the conversation of Christ with Nicodemus in chapter 3, treats of the water of baptism, which is a symbol of the divine light; in the early Church baptism was also called enlightenment or illumination. For St. Paul it showed forth the burial and Resurrection of Christ, for John it is above all the rebirth from the Spirit: "Unless a man be born of water and Spirit he cannot enter into the kingdom of God." Water is the sign of the Spirit, a word which in Greek and Aramaic also means wind, and Jesus plays on this double meaning when he says, "The wind blows where it will, and you hear its voice, but you know not whence it comes and whither it goes. So is every one that is born of the Spirit." This means that to the "natural man" the Christian who lives by the Spirit is incomprehensible; for both his beliefs and his actions obey the law of the Spirit, "because the light is come into the world and men loved darkness rather than the light." If this incomprehensibility applies even to ordinary Christian men and women, how much more to the mystics, who live so much more perfectly under the guidance of the Spirit whom they have received in the waters of baptism.

The mystic symbolism of water is further developed in the conversation of Christ with the woman of Samaria in the next chapter. To her Jesus speaks of the "living water," which will quench the thirst of the man who drinks it not just temporarily, as does ordinary water, but for ever. The reference is again to the baptismal water, which will be to man "a fountain of water, springing up into eternal life." Neither the learned Nicodemus nor the simple Samaritan woman could quite understand this extraordinary merging of the material with the spiritual in the teaching of Christ. For the Indian mystic the world of matter was a total illusion; for the Jew water has, indeed, ritual cleansing powers; when Christ, the Incarnate Word through whom all things were made, himself entered the world of matter as man, he brought out the hidden spiritual potentialities of it and made matter into the vehicle of Spirit.

This becomes even more evident in the great eucharistic chapter 6, which begins with the miraculous feeding of the multitude with five loaves and two fishes. Christ, who himself ate and drank in the normal way, knew man's material needs and did not hesitate to satisfy them even by a miracle. But bread, like water, has also a spiritual significance; it could become nothing less than the flesh of Christ himself. John is the only Evangelist who does not record the institution of the Eucharist at the Last Supper, no doubt because this was sufficiently well known to all Christians at the time he wrote his Gospel. He makes good this lack in the present chapter by stressing most forcibly both the reality and the spiritual efficacy of the sacramental meal. In answer to the Jews who demand another sign from him, quoting the manna, the "bread from heaven" which Moses had given their fathers to eat in the desert, Jesus denies that this was really "bread from heaven": "For the bread of God is that which cometh down from heaven and giveth life to the world." When his hearers then ask for this bread he says to them: "I am the bread of life . . . If any man eat of this bread, he shall live for ever; and the bread that I will give is my flesh, for the life of the world . . . Amen, amen, I say to you: unless you eat the flesh of the Son of man and drink his blood you shall not have life in you . . . He that eateth my flesh and drinketh my blood hath everlasting life: and I will raise him up in the last day . . . He that eateth my flesh and drinketh my blood abideth in me, and I in him."

Perhaps we know these words too well to be able to realize how deeply they must have shocked those who first heard them, especially if we remember that the Jews were strictly forbidden to eat blood. But even many Christians throughout the ages have found this realistic language repellent and tried to interpret it symbolically. Here again we have this interpenetration of the spiritual and the material, which is the result of the Incarnation and hence the distinguishing characteristic also of Christian mysticism, and it is not as paradoxical as it sounds that the most "spiritual" Gospel is also in a certain sense the most "material" and certainly the most "sacramental" one. For Christianity is a religion for the whole man, and teaches not only the survival of the soul, but the resurrection of the body, as Jesus himself promises as the effect of eating his flesh: "And I will raise him up in the last day." It is unfortunate that so often spiritual writers—including even great mystics—speak of men as "souls," which lends a certain unreality to their teaching. But the mystic, too, lives in the body and will be reunited with it on the last day; therefore he too, must be nourished by the Body and Blood of Christ. The eucharistic communion not only ensures eternal beatitude, it is also an "abiding" of Christ and the Christian in each other; therefore many of the greatest mystics have had throughout their life a veritable hunger for the Eucharist. The word "abiding" which St. John uses signifies the mutual indwelling which is the most intimate union with, yet never an absorption of man into the Divinity, a union which is not transitory but lasting, and which literally "nourishes" the mystical life from its very beginnings even to the "mystical marriage" which is the highest stage of it.

Baptism is the entrance door to the mystical "enlightenment," the Eucharist the food on the way to union with God. But apart from the divine action in the sacraments man, too, has to make his contribution to reach the goal. True, St. Paul "buffeted" his body, but the royal road he taught was the road of charity. St. John's teaching is almost the same. It is given at the most solemn moment, at the Last Supper, the Testament of the Lord to his disciples. "Before the feast of the Passover, Jesus knowing that his hour was come that he should pass out of this world to the Father, having loved his own who were in the world, he loved them unto the end . . . He riseth from supper and layeth aside his garments and . . . putteth water into

a basin and began to wash the feet of the disciples . . . Then he said to them: Know you what I have done to you? You call me Master and Lord. And you say well: for so I am. If then I the Lord and Master have washed your feet, you also ought to wash one another's feet . . . A new commandment I give unto you: that you love one another, as I have loved you, that you also love one another. By this shall all men know that you are my disciples, if you have love for one another" (John 13:1–35).

A very simple symbolic action, a very simple "new commandment." Is this all that "mysticism" is about? It may not be "all," but it is certainly the essence of it. For Christian mysticism begins with the love of Christ for his own, and the answering love of men expresses itself in keeping the new commandment of loving each other "as I have loved you"—that is with a love that seeks not its own (as St. Paul said to the Corinthians), but the good of the other. For "if you love me, keep my commandments" (John 14:15); there can be no authentic Christian mysticism without this.

Now this may sound to many of our contemporaries rather flat. The practices of yoga or exotic drugs like mescalin seem to lead to "mystical" experiences so much more easily and excitingly. But, as we have seen, even non-Christian mysticism as far as it is authentic requires a lifetime of moral and ascetical effort to reach the goal of union or unity with the Absolute. Only the teaching of Christ lays the greatest emphasis on mutual love—and this is in fact more difficult, if less "glamorous," than ascetical practices. For these, however arduous, involve only oneself; but love involves a "thou," and this thou may often be repulsive to our feelings. Christ does not require from us, as the Upanishads ask from the Indian mystic, to reach a stage where we perceive no more difference between ourselves and all else that exists. To the Christian this is inconceivable. Christ asks from us much more: to recognize fully the "otherness" of our neighbors, with all their shortcomings, even their hostility to ourselves, and yet to love them as God himself loves them.

To do this without divine help is impossible: "I will ask the Father," says Christ to his disciples, "and he shall give you another Paraclete, that he may abide with you for ever: the spirit of truth, whom the world cannot receive, because it seeth him not . . . But you shall know him; because he shall abide with you and shall be in you . . . In that day you shall know that I am in my Father; and you in me and I in you" (John 14:16–20). The Paraclete, the Holy Spirit, is that Person of the Holy Trinity who is most deeply concerned with the sanctification of those redeemed by the Son. "He shall be in you," a mysterious power who "shall teach you all things and bring to your remembrance all that I said unto you." He is the same spirit whom Isaiah called "the spirit of wisdom and of understanding, the spirit of counsel and of fortitude, the spirit of knowledge and of godliness . . . the spirit of the fear of the Lord" (11:2, 3) the Spirit of these seven gifts which rule the Christian and which are brought to their full development in the mystical life. The indwelling Spirit teaches man and brings him his gifts; and as the Spirit is never separated from the Father and the Son, they, too, will come to the Spirit-taught man and make their abode with him, as Christ has promised his disciples. This union of man with the divine Trinity begins in baptism, it is perfectly lived only in the beatific vision of eternity; but its fullness is anticipated on earth in the mystical union to which some of God's friends have been raised.

ST. STEPHEN

Though the martyrdom of St. Stephen took place before St. Paul's conversion and long before the writing of the Apocalypse and St. John's Gospel, it is being discussed here because it is the first instance of what we would call the "mysticism of martyrdom," which will be treated more fully in the next chapter.

Stephen was not an apostle, he was not even a priest. He was a deacon, an office introduced a few years after the first Pentecost to relieve the apostles of such duties as the distribution of alms, but which also included preaching and baptizing. Foremost among the first seven men chosen was Stephen, "a man full of faith and of the Holy Spirit" (Acts 6:5). He was also "full of grace and power" (6:9) and did great miracles; besides, he had such wisdom and learning that his opponents did not know how to answer his arguments. He anticipated St. Paul by teaching that the temple worship would be superseded and that the traditions of Moses had been abrogated by Christ. Some of the Hellenistic Jews who heard his discourses were so incensed against him that they misrepresented his teaching and accused him before the court of the Sanhedrin—before which Christ, too, had been arraigned—of speaking against the Holy Place and the Law. When asked by the High Priest whether this was true, he summarized the history of Israel, showing that the prophets themselves acknowledged the temporary nature of the temple worship and finally accusing his hearers of having murdered the Just One, whose coming the prophets had foretold. When he had finished, "he, being full of the Holy Spirit, looked up steadfastly to heaven, saw the glory of God and Jesus standing on the right hand of God. And he said: Behold, I see the heavens opened and the Son of man standing on the right hand of God." We cannot tell with certainty from this brief account whether St. Stephen was actually "a mystic" in the ordinary sense of the word, though this may be inferred from the words that he was "full . . . of the Holy Spirit." What is certain is that at the supreme moment of his life he was granted a mystical experience of a high order; he was given a glimpse of the glory of God and of Jesus "standing on the right hand of God"—expressing the closeness of the humanity of Christ to his Father. Stephen was the first martyr of the Church, and his experience was to be repeated in the lives of many who succeeded him. The mystical union is, as it were, a foretaste of heaven; and the mystical experiences of the martyrs imme-

diately preceding their death are evidently given them to
strengthen them in their ordeal. So close was the union of
Stephen with Christ and so powerful the grace accorded to him
that his own last words echo the words of Jesus from the Cross:
"Lord, lay not this sin to their charge." For true mystical experiences are not like dreams that come and go without leaving
a trace in the human consciousness. They have, on the contrary,
a profound effect on the whole personality of the recipient, increasing in him the Christlikeness first given to him in baptism.
This effect, moreover, is very often not restricted to his own
life, but may affect the well-being of the whole Church. The
chapter in Acts narrating Stephen's death ends with the words:
"And Saul (who was guarding the outer garments of those engaged in stoning St. Stephen) was consenting to his death."
There can be little doubt that the mystical experience of St.
Paul on his way to Damascus was psychologically prepared by
his assistance at the death of Stephen, that is to say that the
profound impression which the first martyrdom in the Christian
Church must have made on the sensitive mind of Paul opened
a channel through which he himself could receive a revelation.
"If Stephen had not prayed," writes St. Augustine, "the Church
would not have gained Paul" (Sermon 315).

III THE AGE OF
THE MARTYRS

The connection between mysticism and martyrdom has rarely
been so strikingly expressed as in the letters of Ignatius, bishop
of Antioch, who was thrown to the beasts in the arena of the
Colosseum in Rome about the year 110, in the reign of the
Emperor Trajan. We know nothing of his earlier life, but both
his teaching and his character emerge quite clearly from the
seven letters he wrote to various Christian communities on his
last journey from the Syrian town of Antioch to Rome.

Ignatius is one of the greatest lovers of Christ of the early
Church: "There is only one Physician," he writes to the Ephe-
sians, "both of flesh and of spirit, born and unborn, God in
man, true life in death, from Mary and from God, first passible
[i.e. capable of suffering] and then impassible, Jesus Christ our
Lord." Christ is at the center of his spiritual life, a Christ who
is both wholly human and wholly divine; and Ignatius stresses
particularly his humanity and the historical reality of his life,
because these were being denied by the Docetists, and because
he realized that they are at the very center of the Christian
faith: "Stop your ears, therefore," he tells the Trallians, "when
anyone speaks to you something other than Jesus Christ, who
was from the house of David, the son of Mary, who was truly
born and ate and drank, was truly persecuted under Pontius
Pilate, was truly crucified and died, while the powers in heaven,
on earth and under the earth looked on." The threefold "truly"

shows what importance Ignatius attached to the reality of
Christ's humanity; it was not only a doctrine assented to by
faith, but a living truth that had taken possession of the whole
man; and so he cries out: "If, as some unbelievers say, He suffered only in appearance . . . why am I in chains? Why do
I even pray that I may fight with the wild beasts? Then I would
die in vain. Then my witness would be a lie about the Lord!"
The life of union with Christ and the death of martyrdom are
inescapably linked to the reality of the human nature of the
Son of God. For if the human life and death of Jesus were
only a phantom, then, says Ignatius: "I am also in chains as
a phantom. When then have I given myself over to death, to
fire, to the sword, to wild beasts? But no; to be near the sword
is to be near God; to be with the beasts is to be with God;
only let it be done in the name of Jesus Christ. To suffer with
him I endure all things, if he, who is perfect man, strengthens
me."

For Ignatius martyrdom is the perfection of the mystical life:
to be with the beasts in the arena is to be with God, because
to suffer in this way is to suffer in the company of Christ, who
himself truly suffered, because he was truly man. But this mystical life is not a lonely, individualistic life; the second bishop
of Antioch after Peter sees his mystical martyrdom in the liturgical setting of the Church: "Grant me nothing more," he
writes to the Christians of Rome, frightened that they might
intervene to save his life, "than that I may be poured out as
a libation to God while an altar is yet prepared. You ought to
form a choir of love and sing to the Father in Jesus Christ,
because God has graciously summoned the bishop of Syria to
come from the rising of the sun in the East to its setting in
the West. It is wonderful to 'set' from the world unto God, that
I may rise again unto him." He wishes his death to be a sacrificial
offering accompanied by the chant of the Christian community,
giving thanks that the bishop from the East follows the setting
of the sun in order to rise again, like the sun, in the East to
the light of eternity.

For death is to him but the consummation of his mystical life with God. While still alive he is longing for death, for Christ, his great love[1] has been crucified and he is no longer on fire with the craving for earthly things: "But there is in me a living water speaking within me and saying: 'Come to the Father.' I do not delight in the food of corruption nor in the joys of this life. I long for the bread of God, that is the flesh of Christ who is the seed of David, and for drink I desire his blood, that is incorruptible love."

This very closely-knit text is a perfect example of the sacramental mysticism of the early Fathers. The "living water" is, of course, the baptismal water of which Christ spoke to the Samaritan woman, which is so potent within Ignatius that it urges him to be united to the Father. No corruptible food nor any earthly delights can satisfy his longing, which is for "the flesh of Christ who is of the seed of David"—again the insistence on the humanity of Christ and on the reality of his "flesh" which is the "bread of God," that is to say the Eucharist. "And for drink I desire his blood, that is incorruptible love." This, too, is sacramental, but at the same time it belongs to the mystical sphere: for this blood represents the unending love of Christ. The same identification of the blood of Jesus with his love occurs several times in the Ignatian epistles; the most striking one is perhaps that in the letter to the Trallians, where he writes: "Therefore put on gentleness and revive yourselves in faith, which is the flesh of the Lord, and in love, which is the blood of Jesus Christ." So here, at the very threshold of the patristic age, there exists already the mysticism of the blood of Christ, which is so often regarded as a specifically medieval Western devotion. Ignatius even writes to the Philadelphians: "This Church I salute in the blood of Christ"—the exact phrase St. Catherine of Siena used so frequently more than twelve centuries later, and he congratulates the Smyrneans because they

---

[1] This translation of *Eros* in chapter 7 of his letter to the Romans is based on the evidence of the Eastern Fathers as against the translation of some modern authors as "earthly desire."

are "well established in love through the blood of Christ." Because the pouring out of his blood for the redemption of mankind was the most telling sign of Christ's love, his blood and his love were identified. As blood is, as it were, the life-juice of the flesh, so love is the force that causes the faith to live. To call faith "the flesh of the Lord" seems a very strange expression, but it is readily explained by the martyr's insistence on the reality of the Incarnation, literally the "enfleshing," against the heresies of the time. To him faith is above all faith in the true humanity of the Son of God; and this leads him to the bold identification of the two.

Like St. Paul, Ignatius had received high illuminations which he attributed to the fact that he suffered for Christ, for he writes to the Trallians: "I am in chains and able to comprehend heavenly things and the angelic ranks and the orderings of principalities, things visible and invisible"; but he adds immediately: "nevertheless I am not for this reason a disciple." Just like St. Paul, Ignatius too plays down the extraordinary graces he has received.

Their content seems strange to the modern reader: they concern the angelic world and evidently were not imaginary visions but intellectual illuminations. Since immediately afterwards he warns his correspondents against heresy, it seems probable that he meant to contrast his infused mystical knowledge of the heavenly hierarchies with the Gnostic fables about aeons; the strange expression in the following paragraph, "They [the heretics] weave Jesus Christ into their web" would confirm this, since the Gnostics made Christ one of their aeons, so that their otherwise pagan speculations received some Christian coloring from this incongruous mixture. Ignatius also claimed supernaturally received knowledge about the state of the churches which he had visited on his way; so he writes to the Philadelphians: "I also pray for all those among whom I spoke . . . For even though some wanted to deceive me according to the flesh, nevertheless the Spirit is not deceived . . . I cried out, when I was with you, with God's own voice: Give heed to the bishops and to the presbyterys and to the deacons. Some, however, suspected that I said this because I had known before-hand of divisions caused by some. But he for whose sake I am in chains is my witness that I did not know it from human flesh, but that it was the Spirit who said these things: Do nothing without the bishop" (6,7).

As we shall also see in the following chapters, the experiences of the mystics are almost invariably colored by their own personalities, because the Holy Spirit does not work in a vacuum, he respects and makes use of the human spirit. Now in all his letters Ignatius places the strongest emphasis on the authority of the Christian ministry, especially of the bishops, for which reason Protestants from the times of Calvin onwards rejected them as spurious until, in 1644, the Anglican Archbishop Usher of Armagh established their authenticity, which is now universally accepted. It is therefore very probable that in the passage just quoted natural and supernatural elements are mixed: Ignatius' knowledge of the divisions in the Christian community of Philadelphia may indeed have been divinely infused; the remedy, to do nothing without the bishop, was in perfect accordance with his own views on episcopal authority, which is of divine institution and therefore also consonant with God's will. This delicate mixture of natural and supernatural elements makes the mystical experience difficult to interpret, not least for the mystic himself; and so it is no slur on either the great martyr of Antioch or on later mystics to point out the possibilities of natural factors coloring this experience.

Ignatius went to his death in an ecstasy of mystical love. There exists no reliable account of his actual martyrdom; but one passage of his letter to the Romans in particular gives a vivid picture of his state of mind: "Suffer me to belong to the beasts, through which I attain to God. I am God's wheat, and through the teeth of the wild beasts I am ground that I may be found Christ's pure bread." The martyr himself becomes a eucharistic bread through his sufferings, which achieve a union between God and man that is both sacramental and mystical and leads directly to the eternal union in the only true life after death; "My birth is imminent. Forgive me, brethren; do not prevent me from coming to life; do not wish me to die." As Christ called himself the life, so for the mystic and the martyr's true life begins only when he is perfectly united to his Lord in heaven, where his personality is not dissolved but fulfilled in a new birth, for "when I have arrived there, I shall be [truly] a man."

ST. POLYCARP

We have no reliable account of Ignatius' own martyrdom, but there are some authentic Acts of early martyrs which show that they had mystical experiences immediately before their death, just like St. Stephen, the first martyr. The earliest description of a martyrdom we possess is that of St. Polycarp, who was probably appointed bishop of Smyrna by the apostle John. Ignatius addressed one of his letters to Polycarp in which he instructed him on the duties of a bishop. When he was already well over eighty years old Polycarp undertook the long, irksome journey to Rome to discuss with Pope Anicetus the date of Easter, which was kept in Asia Minor on Nisan 14, regardless of the day of the week, and not, as in the rest of the Church, on the following Sunday. The question was left undecided, each part of the Church continuing to follow its own practice for the time being. Shortly after his return to Smyrna a persecution broke out there, and though Polycarp wanted to remain in the city his people persuaded their aged bishop to hide in a nearby farm. There he remained in prayer, and three days before his arrest he had a vision and saw his pillow on fire, which he interpreted as foretelling that he must be burned alive. He was eventually betrayed by two servants under torture, and when he was brought before the proconsul he heard a voice from heaven, urging him to be strong and courageous; for the proconsul tried to persuade him to swear by the genius of Caesar and speak against Christ; he evidently did not consider it prudent to kill the most reverend bishop in Asia Minor. But Polycarp refused saying: "Eighty-six years have I been his servant, and he has done me no wrong. How then can I blaspheme my King who has saved me?"

Then Polycarp was tied to the stake "like a noble ram . . . a burnt sacrifice . . . acceptable to God," and before it was lit he offered a prayer which, if it was not uttered by himself, at least expressed to perfection his state of mind: "O Lord God Almighty, the Father of thy beloved and blessed Son Jesus Christ, through whom we have received the knowledge of thee, the God . . . of all creation . . . I bless thee for that thou hast granted me this day and hour, that I might receive a portion among the number of martyrs in the cup of Christ unto resurrection of eternal life, both of soul and of body . . . May I be received . . . as a rich and acceptable sacrifice . . . For this cause, and indeed for all things. I praise thee, I bless thee, I glorify thee, through the eternal and heavenly High-priest, Jesus Christ, thy beloved Son, through whom with him and the Holy Spirit be glory both now and for the ages to come. Amen." "And when he had offered up the Amen," continues the author, "the firemen lighted the fire." This last prayer of the great martyr is mystical in spirit and liturgical in form; the Amen is the great Amen that ends the Canon of the Mass; it expresses the union of the martyr with the eternal High Priest, as Christ is presented in the Epistle to the Hebrews. The flames did not consume the martyr, but made a kind of wall around him so that he seemed like gold refined in a furnace and was finally killed by the thrust of a dagger: "after the pattern of the Gospel of Christ." For if the mystical life is the life of union with Christ, the martyr's death is its final consummation. Visions are a by-product; its essence is the union with and imitation of Christ in the supreme sacrifice of man's life for him, which is therefore most intimately related also to the liturgy. In these early days of the Church the mystical and liturgical life were still inseparably joined and so they cannot be treated separately, as will be possible later, though even then the connection will never be entirely lost.

OTHER MARTYRS

In other authentic descriptions of early martyrdoms the mystical element is equally present. In the Acts of Carpus, Papylus, and Agathonica, who were most probably killed in the reign of Marcus Aurelius (emperor 161–180), Carpus laughed after being nailed to the cross, and when asked what made him laugh he answered: "I saw the glory of the Lord, and I was glad." Sometimes the ecstasy of the martyrs during their torture was so deep that they were not at all conscious of their pains. In the letter of the churches of Vienne and Lyons on the martyrdom of their saints in 177–78 we are told that one of them, Alexander, uttered no sound at all, but communed in his heart with God, while Blandina, an ugly little slave woman, after being whipped and scorched was placed in a net and tossed by the bull, "having no further sense of what was happening because of her communing with Christ, was herself also offered up."

STS. PERPETUA AND FELICITAS

A particularly touching account is that of the two young women, Perpetua and Felicitas, and their companions, who were martyred in the arena of Carthage in Africa on March 7, 203, during the persecution of the Emperor Septimus Severus. Perpetua was a well-born lady, about twenty-two years of age, with a few-months-old baby, who herself wrote down an account of her experiences immediately before and during her trial, which was completed by an eye witness report of her death and probably edited by the great African theologian Tertullian, who had joined the Montanist sect.[2] Perpetua was still a catechumen

[2] Montanism had arisen in Phrygia in the latter half of the second century. Its adherents believed in an early descent of the Heavenly Jerusalem, preceded by a spirit of prophecy which the prophets and prophetesses of the movement claimed to have received. By the time Tertullian joined the sect, about 206, it

when she was put under surveillance by the civil authorities. Her father who was a pagan, visited her several times, trying to persuade her to give up her faith; at one of these meetings he lost his temper so much that he hit her in the eye. After that he did not come again for several days, and during that time Perpetua was baptized. At her baptism "the Spirit told me to ask nothing from the water except endurance of the flesh" —evidently a reference to a mystical experience. A few days later Perpetua, Felicitas, a slave girl eight months pregnant, Saturus, a young man, and several others were arrested and thrown into jail. "I was terrified," writes Perpetua, "because I had never experienced such darkness." The heat in the overcrowded prison was overpowering; besides Perpetua was wrecked with anxiety for her baby; so two deacons obtained for her for a few hours each day a transfer to a better part of the prison where her little boy was brought to her so that she could feed him. One day her brother, knowing that she was always in close communion with Christ, begged her to ask the Lord whether they would have to die or if they were going to be released. The next night she had a dream vision in which she saw a ladder reaching to heaven; instruments of torture were fastened at its side, and under it lay a dragon which tried to prevent them from climbing. Saturus, who later gave himself up voluntarily, climbed first, then Perpetua stepped on the dragon's head and climbed up too. At the top of the ladder was a beautiful garden, where an old man sat milking his ewes; he gave her a piece of cheese made from the milk, the sweet taste of which she still felt in her mouth when she awoke from her dream.

This is evidently a blending of the biblical and early Christian representation of Christ as the Shepherd with eucharistic elements. The dream prophecy was fulfilled when Saturus actually

---

had developed an excessively austere morality, forbidding among other things second marriages and flight in persecution. Its stress on the visions of its prophetesses may have influenced Tertullian to publish the martyrdom of Perpetua and her companions, in which visions play an important part.

died before her. After Perpetua's father had once more pleaded unsuccessfully with his daughter, she and the other Christians were tried at the forum. The procurator, too, attempted to persuade her to deny that she was a Christian for her child's sake; when she refused again he condemned her to be thrown to the wild beasts. While waiting for this in prison she remembered to pray for her brother Dinocrates, who had died unbaptized when he was only seven. He appeared to her in a vision, dirty and wounded, thirsting for water which was just out of his reach. After that she prayed more urgently for him, and after a few days she saw him again, this time in clean garments and drinking his fill. "Then I understood that he had been removed from his punishment." Immediately before being sent to fight with the beasts she had yet another dream vision, in which she fought with the devil and conquered him.

In the meantime the slave girl Felicitas had also been condemned; but as she was pregnant the execution of her sentence would not be carried out until after the birth of her child. She urgently wanted to die together with her friends, so she prayed that she might give birth at once. God heard her prayer, but she had a very painful birth and wailed and lamented, so that one of the prison wardens asked her what she would do when she was thrown to the beasts, since she screamed so much with this perfectly natural pain. She replied: "Now it is I who suffer what I suffer, but then another will suffer for me, because I am to suffer for him." In suffering and death for Christ the martyr is so intimately united to him that it seems Christ himself who suffers and who communicates his strength to the martyr— whereas in her childbirth Felicitas was left to herself, without this mystical union that would support her.

On the day of her martyrdom, Perpetua "followed with a shining face, like a true spouse of Christ." When she was tossed on the horns of a savage cow she fell on her hip; her tunic was rent, but she had sufficient strength to draw it over her side, so as not to appear immodest. Then she helped Felicitas to get up, after she had also been tossed. After that even the hardened spectators of these horrible shows had had as much as they could bear and shouted that the two young women should be taken away. But "Perpetua . . . being roused from what seemed like sleep, so completely had she been in the Spirit and in ecstasy, began to look about her, and said to the amazement of all: 'When we are to be thrown to that heifer, I cannot tell.' When she heard what had already taken place she refused to believe it till she had seen marks of ill-usage on her body and dress." She was finally killed by the sword.

This detailed first-hand account is clear evidence of how closely martyrdom and mystical experience are related. How much in some of the dream visions of Perpetua was due to her own imagination and how far they were genuinely supernatural is difficult to say. This is particularly true of the vision of her brother Dinocrates, the first of many visions of the dead reported in the lives of the mystics. But most of her other experiences obviously communicated supernatural strength to her, which Felicitas, too, was confident she would receive in her hour of need. Perpetua's final ecstasy, no longer a dream vision, was deep enough to make her oblivious even of the severest pain, yet left her sufficient power to help her friend.

The martyrdom of the two young mothers, who left even their babies for the sake of Christ, is perhaps the most touching and the most human story in the annals of the Early Church. It also shows that virginity had not yet come to play such an important role in the Church as it did in the following centuries.

CLEMENT OF ALEXANDRIA

This is also borne out by the writings of a very different person, Clement of Alexandria, head of the famous catechetical school of Alexandria and the Father of so-called Alexandrian theology. Clement, too, worked out his mystical teaching in the atmosphere of martyrdom; indeed, he had to flee from Alexandria during the very persecution in which Perpetua was killed. He was probably a native of Athens, of pagan parentage, had traveled extensively and studied both Christian and pagan authors. From the latter half of the second century many highly educated men had become Christians, and they were quite naturally concerned with making their faith palatable to pagan thinkers and to enter into discussion with them. Moreover, as has been mentioned before, various systems of "Gnosis" (knowledge) had entered into competition with the teaching of the Church, maintaining that Gnosis and faith are diametrically opposed to each other. Against them Clement wanted to show that, on the contrary, faith and Gnosis complement each other; indeed, the perfect Christian is the only true "Gnostic."

In his *Stromateis*, literally "patchwork," meaning "Miscellaneous Studies," especially in Book 7 he outlined this ideal, which comes very near, indeed, to what we mean by "mystic." With his description of the Gnostic he had also an apologetic end in view: he wanted to make the pagans realize that it was stupid to persecute the Christians, who were admirable men even according to the ideas of the Greek philosophers, and in no way "atheists," as they were accused of being, because they did not worship in the pagan temples. For, says Clement, the Gnostic worships the true God in a way that is worthy of him. His vision is that promised by Christ to the pure of heart. He approaches God through "the great High Priest" and becomes like him as far as he is able. This assimilation of the mystic, or Gnostic, to God is based on the image doctrine of Genesis and of the Pauline Epistles, where Christ is called the image of God, into which we, too, are to be transformed (cf. II Corinthians 3:18 and 4:4). For Clement writes that Christ, the image of the Father, impresses on the Gnostic the seal of perfect contemplation, after his own image, so that there is now another image of God, because God is enshrined in the Gnostic. His "converse with God," which is Clement's definition of prayer, is uninterrupted and penetrates his whole life.

Such a close union with God cannot, of course, be achieved in a day; it needs a long preparation. Clement describes it in Stoic terms: the would-be Gnostic must achieve a balance of mind where nothing disturbs him, he must be "passionless," the ideal of Stoic philosophy, which was taken over by Clement and greatly influenced a certain school of Christian mysticism. So Gnosis, knowledge, is a development of faith, and in its turn leads to love and hence to the inheritance of eternal life. "In my view," writes Clement, "the first saving change is that from paganism to faith . . . and the second, from faith to knowledge. The latter terminates in love, and thereafter gives the loving to the loved, that which knows to that which is known." Here is the first adumbration of the famous threefold mystical way of purification (through faith), illumination (through knowledge), and union (through love). This does not mean, of course, that the Christian of "simple faith" does not also have knowledge and love; for the love of God and one's neighbor is the prerequisite of every Christian life, as is the knowledge of one's faith. What Clement means here by knowledge and love is not ordinary, but mystical knowledge and love. Though he does not use the term "infused" and, like many Greek theologians, represents the mystical life somewhat more as a result of man's own efforts than the later Latin authors with their emphasis on grace, he makes it nevertheless clear that such heights are not reached without God's help; for, he says, when the Gnostic has done all that depends on him, he will be perfected by God: "For in this consists the perfection of the gnostic soul, in its being with the Lord, where it is directly subject to him."

This perfection can be reached also in the married state; for "He surpasses men, who, disciplined by marriage, procreation of children and care for the house, without pleasure or pain [i.e. "passionless"], has been inseparable from God and withstood all temptation" [*Stromateis* 7.12]. The view that marriage itself with all its duties can be a discipline profitable for attaining mystic heights was, as we shall see, soon to be abandoned both in the East and in the West; but with the increasing realization of the importance of the role of the laity in our own days it may be of particular interest to put on record that one of the

earliest and most influential Church Fathers did not consider
the heights of the mystical life beyond the reach of married
Christians.

ORIGEN

Origen (c. 185–254), the son of devout Christian parents, was
born in Alexandria. His father Leonidas himself taught him the
Scriptures, much of which he knew by heart as a young boy; for
he had to recite to his father a number of verses from them
every day. The church historian, Eusebius (c. 260–c. 340), says
that even at that early age Origen had come to be convinced that
the biblical narratives must contain a deeper sense than the obvious, "literal" one, a view which he developed in his later life
so that he became the father of the allegorical or "mystical"
Christian interpretation of Scripture. He was later sent to the
catechetical school, where he studied under Clement, and became acquainted with pagan literature and thought. While Origen's master fled from Alexandria during the persecution of Sep-
timius Severus his father suffered martyrdom. Origen himself
was so anxious to imitate him that his mother hid his clothes
to prevent him from leaving the house. For he was the eldest
of her seven sons and her only support after the death of his
father. He did not fail her, but supported the large family by
giving lessons. When the persecution had ceased the young man
of about eighteen years was appointed Clement's successor as
head of the catechetical school. He immediately sold all his pagan books, gave up his other teaching and threw himself whole-
heartedly into the study of Scripture. About this time he took
a step which he was greatly to regret later. In his youthful zeal
he took literally and acted on the words of Christ that there
are "eunuchs who have made themselves eunuchs for the kingdom of heaven" (Matthew 19:12). Perhaps this unhappy literal
application of a metaphorically meant text also contributed to
his later exaggerated allegorical interpretation of Scripture,

though this had, indeed, been the fashion in Alexandria ever since Philo.

During his first years at the catechetical school Origen devoted himself entirely to teaching, in which he was very successful. He also undertook several journeys. About 212 he went to Rome and three years later to Palestine to avoid the persecution of the Emperor Caracalla. There two bishops asked him to preach. His own bishop, Demetrius, however, regarded this as a breach of discipline and recalled him. From about 220 he also began to write, at the suggestion of a wealthy convert of his who placed stenographers and copyists at his disposal. In 230 he traveled again to Palestine, and there the same bishops who had asked him to preach ordained him priest despite his self-mutilation. These irregular proceedings infuriated Demetrius, who held two synods in 230 and 231, which deposed him from his teaching office and his priesthood and excommunicated him from the church of Alexandria. He therefore went to Caesarea, where he founded a school similar to that in Alexandria and continued his teaching and his literary work. In the persecution of Decius (250) he was imprisoned and underwent prolonged torture, the effects of which hastened his death a few years later.[3]

Origen was one of the most original thinkers the Church has ever had and also one of its greatest mystical teachers; indeed, in his Introduction to his translation of Origen's *Commentary on the Song of Songs*, R. P. Lawson calls him "a master mystic" (Ancient Christian Writers 26). His own life was entirely devoted to the study of the Scriptures, prayer and teaching; he describes it in his picture of the ideal Christian teacher in his Commentary on St. Paul's Letter to the Romans, though he would not admit that he himself was its perfect representative: "If therefore," he writes, "we want to know anything about the secret and hidden things of God . . . we must search faithfully and humbly for those judgements of God that are more deeply

[3] At the Council of Constantinople in 553 some of his doctrines were condemned as heretical, but as these have little connection with his mystical theology they need not be discussed here.

hidden in the divine writings. That is why the Lord said: Search the Scriptures. For he knew that such secrets are not discovered by those who, occupied with other things, hear or read them superficially, but only by those who penetrate more deeply into the divine Scriptures with a straight and single heart, with the yoke of labour and constant vigils, of whom I well know that I am not one."

Origen's mystical doctrine is based on the image-relation between God and man. The foundation of the soul's beauty, he teaches in his *Commentary on the Song of Songs*, that biblical book beloved by all mystics, is its creation in the image of God. It was spoiled, however by man's first sin, so that there are now two images, that which man received from God, and the "earthly" image which he assumed when he was cast out of paradise, as Origen explains in his homilies on Luke. When the soul approaches the Word of God she receives back the beauty that belonged to her original state. This happens in baptism, which is the beginning and source of God's gifts. It is a washing of both body and soul, and Origen has complete faith in its perfect efficacy. "For since not only the soul is called to salvation," he writes in a fragment from his Commentary on St. John's Gospel, "but also the body, which the former uses as an organ for its activities, this too, must be sanctified . . . and this baptism is called divine, for it is no longer mere water; it is sanctified by a mystical invocation . . . For they must first be made disciples learning the doctrines of truth, then keep what has been commanded them concerning the moral virtues, and thus be baptized into the name of the Father and of the Son and of the Holy Spirit. How then could this be mere water that has been received together with these, having participated in the power of the holy Trinity and been joined to moral and intellectual virtue?" From this and many other passages it emerges that Origen lays great stress both on doctrinal rectitude and moral virtue—they are the precondition of the Christian and hence of the mystical life. From there begins the spiritual ascent which Origen works out in terms foreshadowing the classical tripartite way of purification, illumination, and union. He writes in his *Commentary on the Song of Songs:* "This book comes last so that a man may come to it when his manner of life has been *purified* and he has *learned to know* the difference between things corruptible and things incorruptible; so that nothing in the metaphors used to describe the *love* of the bride for her heavenly bridegroom—that is of the perfect soul for the Word of God—may cause him to stumble."

In section 14 of the same commentary Origen describes the mystical way in greater detail. The purgative way is the "winter of the soul," when she is still in the thick of temptations and receives neither consolation nor a higher understanding from the study of the Scriptures—a pursuit which for Origen is inseparable from the spiritual life. If she has survived this time safely spring will come, when the bride-soul will enjoy a period of calm and rest. Then God calls her not only to renounce all carnal vices—this has already been achieved through the "winter"—but also to give up any occupation with visible things in order to hasten to what is invisible and eternal. After this she is led to the last stage, when the bride-soul contemplates the things that are wholly spiritual and eternal.

In this state the soul is filled with mystical knowledge, which is received from God direct without any human or angelic intervention. Origen was a biblical scholar, a great intellectual, hence his mystical teaching lays great stress on the illumination of the intellect. He interprets the kisses of the bridegroom in the *Song of Songs* as "divine teachings and meanings revealed in our heart without instructors' help," and he considers the knowledge imparted by the Holy Spirit as the greatest of the spiritual gifts. "The supreme function of knowledge," he writes, "is to know the Trinity; and, in the second place, to know God's creation"; so despite his assertion that at one stage of the mystical way the soul must turn away from all visible things Origen does not consider the knowledge of creation unnecessary. And of all created things it is most necessary that the soul should know itself. For unless it knows itself created in the image of God and appreciates its original beauty it cannot achieve union with Christ. This knowledge must probe very deep. Indeed, Origen suggests an "examination of conscience" that sounds surprisingly modern. "She [the soul] should know, for instance, whether she is of a good disposition or not, and whether or not she is upright in intention; and, if she is in fact of an upright intention, whether, in thought and in action, she has the same zeal for all virtues, or only for necessary things and those that are easy; furthermore, whether she is making progress, and gaining in understanding of things, and growing in the virtues; or whether perhaps she is standing still . . . and whether what she does serves only for her own improvement; or whether she can benefit others also." Nor is this all; Origen requires an extraordinarily subtle psychological self-knowledge from his "bride-soul"; for she is to ask herself whether she only controls her anger with some people but gives it free reign with others; whether she indulges in melancholy and bad temper only at times or always or never, whether she is easily carried away by eloquence without paying attention to the truth of what is being said, whether she quickly reacts to praise or reproach. All this meticulous self-examination is necessary to the soul so that she, "contemplating the beauty which she received at her creation in God's image, may judge how it may be renewed and restored."

When the soul is so fully purified and enlightened by self-knowledge that she is united to God, she receives wisdom and brings forth the "fruits of the spirit—joy, love, peace and the rest." Then, also her spiritual senses will be fully developed. Origen was the first to teach that just as the body has five senses, so the soul has, too. In his work against the pagan philosopher Celsus he states this doctrine, which, he says, he has found in the Scriptures. There is a divine sense of sight by which a man can see the angels, a hearing which distinguishes inaudible voices, a taste which enjoys the living bread that descended from heaven, a spiritual smell that perceives with Paul the "good odour of Christ" (II Corinthians 2:15) and a touch which, like John, can handle the Word of life (I John 1:1). In his *Commentary on the Song of Songs* he enlarges on this, explaining how Christ satisfies all the senses of the soul: "He is called the true light, so that the soul's eyes may have something to lighten them. He is the Word, so that her ears may have something to hear. Again, he is the bread of life, so that the soul's palate may have something to taste. And in the same way, he is called the ointment, that the soul's sense of smell may apprehend the fragrance of the Word. For the same reason he is said also to be able to be felt and handled, and is called the Word made flesh, so that the hand of the interior soul may touch concerning the Word of life. But all these things are the one, same, Word of God, who adapts himself to the various moods of prayer . . . and so leaves none of the soul's faculties empty of his grace."

There is then, in every human soul a capacity for experiencing divine things through faculties corresponding to the five senses of the body. This capacity is brought into play by the divine Word, who gives fulfillment to all the "senses" of the soul. It is a mystical experience corresponding for example to the words of the Psalmist: "Taste and see that the Lord is sweet" (33:9). It does not, however, refer to any imaginary experiences in which a man would hear, see, smell and so on things that are not there. Origen himself explains that these senses "are acquired by training, and are said to be trained when they examine the meaning of things with more acute perception." For Origen's mystical experience is inescapably linked to knowledge. Now as knowledge of the outer world comes to us by our ordinary senses, so knowledge of the spiritual world comes by the senses of the soul, when, as Origen says, "the Word of God takes possession of their hearing, their sight, their touch, and their taste as well," for "he who has reached the peak of perfection and beatitude will be delighted by the Word of God in all his senses." The full development of the senses of the soul belongs to the perfection of the mystical life; when the divine Word has satisfied them they will lose their desire for all else.

A person in this state has received the "wound of love." "If there is anyone," Origen writes, "who has at some time burned with this faithful love of the Word of God . . . so that he yearns and longs for him by day and night, can speak of nought but him . . . can think of nothing else, and is disposed to no desire nor longing nor yet hope except for him alone" he can truly say with the bride in the *Song of Songs:* "I have been wounded by love." He is completely under the empire of God who will lead him wherever he wills. But man must prepare himself for this, and apart from practicing the virtues as a matter of course, this is done through prayer. In his short treatise on prayer Origen sketches a pattern of it which sounds surprisingly modern. At the beginning we should glorify God through Christ in the Holy Spirit; after that we should thank God for all the benefits we have received from him, and this should be followed by a confession of our sins and a prayer for forgiveness. Only then should we ask God for his gifts. Origen would have us ask only for spiritual gifts. For he explains the petition in the Our Father, generally translated as "daily bread," as meaning "supersubstantial" (the Greek word *epiousios* is extremely rare and difficult to translate exactly) in keeping with his general trend towards a spiritualizing exegesis. For, he writes, "the supersubstantial bread is that which is most adapted to the rational nature . . . bringing to the soul health and well-being and strength, and giving to him that eats of it a share of its own immortality. For the Word of God is immortal." So the "supersubstantial bread" is "the Word of God"—but what is the exact meaning of it in this and in many other passages in Origen's work is not easy to determine. Here it seems to refer to the Eucharist; but it may also refer to the Word incarnate, or even to the Word of God in Scripture, for it is one of the most striking characteristics of Origen's mysticism that he attaches an almost sacramental efficacy to the words of Scripture, which for him is truly a food on which the mystical life is nourished.

In his *Commentary on the Song of Songs* Origen had written that a man must learn the difference between corruptible and incorruptible things. In his "Exhortation to Martyrdom," composed for two friends who were imprisoned in the persecution

of Maximin Thrax (c. 235), fifteen years before he himself had
to suffer for the faith, he wrote that God's favors far outweigh
the sufferings of the martyr; indeed, martyrdom is for him the
consummation of the mystical as it is the consummation of the
Christian life in general. For it is the final fulfillment of the
mystic's desire for complete union with God: "I believe that
they love God with their whole soul who, because of their great
desire to be united with him without distraction or disturbance
. . . undergo separation from the body of their lowliness." For
"he who bears witness to someone"—and martyr means literally
witness—"especially in a time of persecution and trial of faith,
unites and joins himself to him to whom he bears witness." This
ultimate union therefore also carries with it special mystical
illuminations, so Origen can console his friends with the promise
that now especially they are "worthy to see more of the mysteries
of God, you have a deeper and richer understanding . . . For
you the point is that your goal should be accomplished . . . My
wish is that it be accomplished through the greater sublimity and
fuller understanding, transcending all human nature, of God's
words and wisdom."

Thus Origen presents the mystical way of man, made in the
image of God, from its beginning in baptism through the purgative "winter" and the illuminative "spring" of the soul to its
final surrender to God in the perfection of the mystical life and
of martyrdom. The influence of Origen's teaching on later mysticism was tremendous; but when after his death the persecutions gradually ceased another element was added which made a
decisive impact on its development: this was the steady growth
of the ascetical life in the Church.

IV THE GROWTH OF THE ASCETICAL LIFE

The growth of the ascetical life of hermits, monks, and virgins is not unconnected with the spirituality of martyrdom. The prospect of having to suffer for Christ produced a considerable detachment from worldly concerns, the readiness to give up riches, family, friends, health, and life itself. Those who followed the advice of Christ: "When they shall persecute you in this city flee into another" (Matthew 10:23) would go into the desert as the safest place and there lead of necessity a life of great austerity. Besides, the ideal of virginity, already outlined by St. Paul in chapter 7 of his First Letter to the Corinthians, implied withdrawal from the ordinary daily life, and as virgins like hermits and monks were wholly devoted to prayer their communion with God led to mystical experiences as much as the self-sacrifice of the martyrs.

Indeed, in the first great Christian treatise on virginity, *The Symposium* of Methodius, written between 270 and 290, we are told that the virgins are true martyrs, "because they had the courage all their lives not to shrink from the truly Olympic contest of chastity" (7,3). Of Methodius' own life practically nothing is known, beyond the fact that he was an ascetic and a teacher, perhaps a bishop, and that he may have died a martyr. He lived in Lycia; perhaps also in Pamphilia, on the southern coast of Asia Minor. Methodius, unlike Clement of Alexandria, equates the perfect Christian life with virginity. In his opinion married chastity is very inferior, for he writes: "They also practise it who live chastely with their wives: they bring forth as it were little shoots around the trunk of the tree of chastity . . . not coming high enough as we do [i.e. the virgins] to touch its mighty branches, but they, too, produce shoots of chastity however small."

Though Methodius admits that chastity must be accompanied by the other virtues, he nevertheless places it higher than all the others, even charity, for he says that "nothing is superior to chastity in its power to restore mankind to paradise," indeed he seems to equate it with grace itself when he writes that "the Law was not at all adequate to free mankind from corruption, until virginity, succeeding the Law, held men in thrall to the commands of Christ." Hence it is not surprising that for him virginity is the basis of the mystical life. For only the virgin is the spouse of Christ, as the Church is his spouse par excellence. Methodius, too, bases the spiritual life on the image of God in which man was created and which was restored in baptism, for "those who are baptized in Christ become, as it were, other Christs by a communication of the Spirit, and here it is the Church that effects this transformation into a clear image of the Word." But men themselves must nurse this image to its full beauty, and this is precisely what the consecrated virgins do. They leave the world of sense, being constantly occupied with the things of the world beyond, which Methodius presents as a meadow full of marvelous flowers. It is doubtful whether he means by this a genuinely mystical experience or only a deliberate exercise of the imagination; for he writes soon afterwards that when the virgins die, angels will "escort them to the meadow we spoke of, which they had longed to enter before, picturing them in their imaginations from afar." So it is more likely that these virgins were taught a form of meditation intended to wean them from any attachment to created beauties, in order to make them receptive for the beauty of heaven. This is described in the language of Plato who presented the world of ideas as the real world, of which we can only see the shadows, like men living in a cave, on whose walls appear the shadows of the things outside. So Methodius writes that "There," that is in heaven, "is Justice itself, and Love itself . . . and all the other flowers and plants of Wisdom . . . of which we in this world see merely ghostlike shadows . . . because in this world there is no clear image of them, but only faint copies." Nevertheless, through the practice of virginity we can achieve a state where we touch heaven even though still walking on earth, because through it we imitate Christ, who preserved his flesh incorrupt in virginity. For the virgin, free from earthly cares, rises above feelings of pleasure and pain on "the wings of the soul," a conception which played an important part in later mystical teaching. She has preserved her five senses intact for Christ alone whom she will meet as her Bridegroom on the day of the general resurrection, which Methodius thought was quite near. This may account for his scorn for marriage though he did not, of course, in any way condemn it. Chastity, however is, according to him, the best preparation for the glory of immortality. Methodius does not describe an actual "mystical marriage" on earth, this is left to the next world, for which virginity is one long preparation. This appears clearly from the beautiful hymn sung by one of the virgins towards the end of the treatise, and which is based on Christ's parable of the Ten Virgins. Its refrain is: "Chastely I live for thee, and holding my lighted lamps, My Spouse, I go forth to meet Thee." The virgin has not yet been completely united to Christ, she has only prepared herself for the ultimate union for she sings: "For thee, my king, have I refused a mortal marriage . . . and I have come to thee in immaculate robes that I may enter with thee thy blessed bridal chamber."

ATHANASIUS: LETTER TO THE VIRGINS

Many of the ideas of Methodius found their way into later works on virginity. One of the greatest Doctors of the Church, St. Athanasius (d. 373) was a vigorous advocate of the virginal life. He is best known for his defense of the divinity of Christ against Arius, who taught that the Son of God was not eternal, but had been made by the Father as an instrument of creation and been raised to divine dignity by him. Athanasius was a native of Alexandria and most probably educated at its catechetical school, of which Clement and Origen had been such prominent teachers. He was one of the principal speakers at the Council of Nicaea (325), where he defended the orthodox doctrine of the divinity of Christ against Arius, and in 328 became bishop of Alexandria. But because of his opposition to Arianism, which had powerful adherents at the imperial court in Constantinople, he was repeatedly expelled from his see and recalled again, according to the prevailing views of the various emperors. One of his five exiles he spent with the monks in the Egyptian deserts, with whom he entertained friendly relations and whose ascetical and mystical life he greatly admired. This he made known also in the West both personally during some of his exiles spent in Treves and Rome and by his writings, among which are several treatises on virginity which were discovered only in this century.[1]

The life of the virgin, as Athanasius describes it, will easily lead to mystical union with Christ, the Bridegroom. For she is urged to think of nothing earthly but to converse with him in prayer at every moment of her day and to praise him constantly in psalms and hymns. He further enjoins strict fasting; the ascetics of this time normally took only one meal a day, in the evening, consisting of bread, herbs, and oil, rarely of more nourishing food like meat and eggs. He warns the virgins several times not to listen to those who might want to dissuade them from their fast by pointing out that it might damage their health —these are temptations of the devil, whereas fasting is the "life of the angels, and he who practises it belongs to the angelic order." Athanasius insists very strongly, however, on the Christian virtues, especially on obedience, charity, and patience, which

[1] Published in the German *Texte und Untersuchungen* 29.2 (1905) and the French *Muséon* 40 (1927) and 42 (1929).

must accompany the ascetical practices to make them fruitful. For "as through food and disobedience Adam was expelled from paradise," writes Athanasius, "so he who so wishes will enter it again through fasting and obedience." The conception of the mystical life as a regaining of the lost paradise is a characteristically Eastern doctrine. Of course, the paradise the mystic enters once more is not the earthly garden of Eden of the creation story in Genesis, as a few modern scholars have held. It signifies rather the return of man to his primitive state of innocence and familiar converse with God. Such a life of obedience and fasting will also lead to actual mystical experiences, among which Athanasius singles out the "charisma [gift] of tears." Only those receive this gift whose minds are fixed on heavenly things and who have completely mortified their bodies. For they receive the "inner eyes" of which Origen had spoken, with which they will see things hidden from ordinary men, such as the eternal punishments of sinners as well as the crowns and royal garments of the citizens of heaven; indeed, "he who has his mind pure will see God himself with his inner eye," according to the promise of the Beatitude that the pure of heart will see God. Athanasius evidently applies this vision of God even to this life, though he did not, of course, mean that the mystics will see God in the same way as the blessed in heaven see him. It is, nevertheless, remarkable that he promises authentic mystical experiences as the reward of a faithful ascetical life, and that these experiences should concern the last things. The whole thought of the Fathers, and especially that of hermits, monks, and virgins, was directed to the end of this world and the final return of Christ far more intensely than our own, and consequently they did not take this world at all seriously—hence the general decline of natural science with all its implications in the following centuries and in the Middle Ages. The realities the virgins and ascetics in general desired to contemplate were those of heaven and hell, and as these could only be described in symbols—as in the Apocalypse —Athanasius counseled an imaginative approach to the sufferings of the damned and the joys of the blessed.

Athanasius also wrote the first saint's life, which became the model for innumerable others and which was to be a powerful factor in the conversion of St. Augustine about thirty years later. The *Life of Antony* was written about 357, a year after the death of the saint, whom Athanasius had known personally. Antony's is a strange story which may sound incredible to modern, especially Western ears, but in which the great lines of the mystical life and its importance for the Christian community as a whole are nevertheless clearly discernible. Antony (c. 251–356) was the son of a well-to-do farmer. Some time after his parents' death he heard a sermon on Jesus and the rich young man and decided to give away his property, retaining only a minimum to keep himself and his sister. Not long after that he heard another sermon, this time on the words: "Be not solicitous for the morrow," and again he resolved to act on it. He gave away even the little he had kept, sent his sister to a community of women and began to lead a very austere life in his home. Soon, however, this was not solitary enough for him and he locked himself up in an empty tomb outside the town, which was probably the present Qeman el Arous, in the province of Benisouef, south of Cairo. Why a tomb? In his book on the life of St. Antony the French Oratorian Father Bouyer suggests that this idea was inspired by the New Testament story of the Gadarene swine: the man possessed by the demons lived among the tombs, it was there that the devil was particularly powerful. No sooner had Antony installed himself in the graveyard than his temptations began. While still living at home he had frequently been tempted to give up his life of austerity, had dreamt of beautiful women and finally seen a black boy, a vision of the devil. Now, in his retreat among the tombs, the diabolic attacks became more and more frequent and vigorous: once the devil wounded Antony so badly that he fainted, at other times demons appeared to him in the form of reptiles, leopards, and lions; when his fight with them was at its height, however, and Antony felt unable to overcome the powers that attacked him, God sent a light which put the devils to flight. When the saint then asked God why he had waited so long before coming to his rescue God replied: "I was present, but I hesitated in order to see you struggle." He then promises always to be with Antony and to make his name famous.

After this first victory over the powers of evil Antony, then about thirty-five years old, decided to fight them in a place where they were believed to be even more powerful than among the tombs, and where Christ himself had struggled with them: in the desert. He went to a lonely place near Pispir, on the east bank of the Nile, about 50 miles south of the ancient city of Memphis. There he locked himself up in the ruin of a castle and refused to see any of the friends who followed him, living on a kind of hard bread like ship's biscuit that was supplied to him twice a year and on water from a well. Here both his struggles with the devil and his divine visions became even more intense. After twenty years of this life, during which his fame had spread, his friends finally decided to break forcibly into his retreat so that others, too, might be guided by his wisdom. At this point Athanasius inserts a discourse on the spiritual life which probably reflects the teaching Antony himself gave to his disciples, and which contains some important principles that have remained basic to mystical theology ever since. After stating that the devil, however strong and full of deceit, has yet been defeated by Christ once and for all so that Christians need not fear to be overcome by him, Antony is very firm on the subject of extraordinary experiences such as prophetic knowledge, which may often accompany the ascetical life. "It behoves us not," he writes, "to make much of these things, nor to give ourselves to the toil of asceticism for the sake of knowing the future, but that we may please God by living well. And we should pray, not in order to know the future, nor should we ask for this as a reward for the practice of asceticism, but that the Lord may be our fellow-worker in achieving victory of the devil. But if we care some day to know the future, let us be pure in mind. For I feel confident that if the soul is pure through and through and is in its natural state, it becomes clear-sighted and sees more and farther than the demons. It then has the Lord to reveal things to it."

So, first of all, extraordinary experiences and faculties are not to be desired, though they may be given as a reward for a pure life. For then the soul becomes "clear-sighted," a term expressing the same phenomenon as the doctrine of the "senses of the soul," for it is a spiritual sight other than the normal sense-knowledge. This sight develops when the soul is "in its natural state"—an idea which sounds strange to us; but as it is fundamental to the mystical theology of the Eastern Church we must try to explain it. In the view of the Greek Fathers the state in which the first man was created was not, as in the teaching of the later Latin theologians, a "natural" state to which sanctifying grace and "preternatural" gifts such as immortality and absence of concupiscence had been added. The state in which man was created was his "natural" state of sinlessness; therefore man as we know him now, after the Fall, is in a non-natural state; but in the mystical life he is restored to his true "nature" such as it was in paradise. Therefore the object of the ascetical life is to recover his true nature, and in the course of this restoration such gifts as prophetic foreknowledge will also appear. Another important point is Antony's teaching on the discernment of spirits, which he had evolved in his struggles with the devil, and which has remained—with some modifications—the accepted doctrine of the Church ever since. "It is quite possible," he writes, "to tell the difference between the good and bad [spirits] when God grants it. A vision of the holy ones is not turbulent . . . But it comes so quietly and gently that instantly joy and gladness and courage arise in the soul . . . And the thoughts of the soul remain untroubled and unruffled, so that in its own bright transparency it is able to behold those [spirits] who appear. A longing for things divine . . . takes possession of it, and its desire is that it may be wholly united to them." The attacks of the evil spirits, on the other hand, are accompanied by fearful noise, strike terror into the soul, and can lead to a complete disintegration of character. These diverse characteristics of the holy and the evil spirits are also in accordance with St. Paul's description of the works of the flesh—such as quarrels and dissensions on the one hand and those of the Spirit like joy and peace on the other.

After the discourse Athanasius describes the latter part of Antony's life, when he retired even deeper into the desert towards the Red Sea, to the "inner mountain," a small oasis where he grew corn and wove baskets, and where his return to the "paradisal" state was evidenced by his power over the wild animals. Though he still had to fight against the attacks of the demons his life became more and more serene. He had many visions, seeing himself "as it were outside himself" and borne aloft by angels, knowing future events and happenings that occurred far away. At this time his mystical life bore fruit in an increasing apostolate; his fame had spread rapidly throughout Egypt and many visitors, even pagans came to consult him, though sometimes he was unable to speak to them because he was in ecstasy. Besides, he himself traveled regularly to give advice to disciples who formed themselves into groups—the beginnings of the monastic life—and also during the Arian controversy (after 320), when he went to Alexandria to defend the orthodox doctrine of the divinity of Christ. Only is his extreme old age—he lived to a hundred and five—did he abandon his solitary life and allow himself to be looked after by two of the monks he had instructed.

Despite Antony's extraordinary way of life, the great outlines of his spiritual progress form a pattern repeated again and again in Christian mysticism. There is first a complete withdrawal from the world, accompanied by a hard struggle against temptations arising from the revolt of human nature typified by dream visions of beautiful women. This is followed by a period of more violent temptations, attributed to the devil, but also of more intimate converse with God in ecstatic experiences. In the third period, his mystical life overflows on others: the world breaks into his retreat to receive a share in the wisdom which is a gift of the Holy Spirit and the most precious fruit of the mystical life.

The modern reader may perhaps be disconcerted by the lengthy descriptions of Antony's fights with the demons, which became a stock in trade of the later lives of the Desert Fathers. But we must remember that at the time of St. Antony paganism was still very much alive in the only recently Christianized Mediterranean world, and the powers of evil, which the hermit-monk felt all around him, would present themselves to his imagination in the form of black boys, animals, and the like, while his interior struggle against them would express itself outwardly in noises and even self-inflicted wounds; a later example of such experiences is the Curé D'Ars, St. John Vianney, and it is one of the most difficult problems of mystical theology to ascertain in how far these experiences have an objection foundation in a preternatural reality and how much is to be attributed to merely psychological factors. It is not within our competence to give a decisive answer to this question, but it would seem that in such cases as that of St. Antony and the later Fathers of the Desert both natural factors, such as the susceptibility to hallucinations owing to a completely solitary life in the desert, and preternatural ones, namely the demonic aspects of paganism, have combined to produce these strange experiences.

The most famous collection of stories from the lives of the Desert Fathers is the *Lausiac History*[2] by Palladius (d. before 431), a friend of the celebrated preacher St. John Chrysostom (meaning the "golden-mouthed"). Palladius himself had lived for about ten years as a monk in Egypt and Palestine, and his history was written about twenty years later, when he had become a bishop. It is modeled on the life of St. Antony, but shows a much more developed stage of the monastic life, when the flight into the desert had become almost an epidemic and Nitria, a district of Libya to the West of the Nile Delta, was peopled with thousands of ascetics living either in monasteries or as solitaries. Palladius stresses particularly their ascetical exploits, which at times degenerated into competitions as to who

[2] So called because it was written for Lausus, chamberlain at the court of Theodosius II.

could fast most rigorously or do with least sleep. Even contemplation itself became an object of spiritual prowess; for one monk determined to keep his mind for five days undistracted on the contemplation of God, commanding himself not to descend from heaven; however he had to give up on the third day, after the devil had burned everything in his cell. For struggling with demons is the particular object of the solitary life, which may be embraced only after the monk has made considerable progress and has overcome the early temptations of going back to the world. "For the war against impurity is threefold," says one of the Fathers. "At one time the flesh attacks us because it is strong; at another the passions attack us through our imagination; at another the demon himself in his wickedness," and many are never free from temptation throughout their life, so that they may not become proud. For the monks of the desert knew well enough the possibility of illusions, of which the *Lausiac History* offers some very interesting examples. There is for example one Palestinian called Valens, who refused to go to Holy Communion, because he claimed to have seen Christ himself that day and therefore not to need the sacraments, while another, Abramius, a layman, wanted to celebrate the Eucharist because he imagined that he had been ordained priest by Christ the night before. He was cured of his hallucinations by being removed from the desert and compelled to lead a less ascetical life.

Though the *Lausiac History*, like most later saints' lives, delights particularly in the extraordinary ascetical feats and the miracles performed by the Desert Fathers, we are not left without a glimpse of their mystical life. This is firmly grounded in the Scriptures, large sections of which many of the Desert Fathers knew by heart. So we are told that a monk called Isidore had such knowledge "of the holy scriptures and the divine precepts that even at the very meals of the brethren he would have periods of absent-mindedness and remain silent. And being urged to tell the details of his ecstasy he would say: I went away in thought on a journey, seized by contemplation." Of another it is said that he was "in a continual ecstasy," because he spent more time with God than with earthly things. In these mystical states they often received prophetic knowledge and revelations about the next world. But for a more detailed description of the mystical experiences and a theology of the mystical life of the Fathers of the Desert we must turn to the works of Evagrius Ponticus and the Homilies of the Pseudo-Macarius.

V THE MYSTICAL THEOLOGY OF THE DESERT FATHERS

1. THE MYSTICISM OF LIGHT

PSEUDO-MACARIUS

The fifty *Spiritual Homilies* attributed to Macarius of Egypt are, together with the writings of Evagrius Ponticus, the oldest document of the mysticism of the early monks whose ascetical prowess was described in the *Lausiac History*. The *Spiritual Homilies* are of uncertain authorship; they belong for the greater part of the late fourth and early fifth centuries. In modern times they have sometimes been held to have originated with the Messalians, a mystical sect condemned by the Council of Epesus (431), which exaggerated the necessity and power of prayer and despised the sacraments as means of salvation. This view, however, has not been generally accepted; the homilies may have been collected and edited in the circle of the great orthodox mystic Symeon the New Theologian (949–1022), and they have played a very important part in the history of Christian mysticism ever since.

The mysticism Macarius (to use the traditional name) preaches is a mysticism of light. The Homilies open with a mystical interpretation of the four animals of Ezekiel's vision (Ezekiel 1:1ff and 10:2ff), which are symbols of the perfect soul indwelt by the Holy Spirit: "The soul that is accounted worthy to commune with the spirit of his light . . . becomes wholly light, wholly face, and wholly eye, and there is no part in her which is not full of spiritual eyes of light . . . for in her

dwells the ineffable beauty of the glory of light, which is Christ."
This is the goal to which the author of the Homilies wants to
lead his disciple, the vision of which will guide him through all
the vicissitudes of the spiritual life. To reach it he must know
two things: the hideousness of sin and the divine omnipotence,
which alone can free man from it. Even the greatest sinner may
aspire to the mystical life, provided he recognizes his sin and
turns resolutely away from it, trusting in the Lord, "the true
physician." In a charming passage Macarius encourages his
reader to do so: "For even a baby, too weak for anything and
unable to walk to his mother on his own little feet, can yet
roll about and scream and cry because he wants her. Then the
mother is sorry for him, and at the same time pleased that the
little one desires her so much. Therefore, as he cannot come
to her, she, moved by his longings and by her own love of her
child, takes him up and sweetly fondles and feeds him. Thus
also deals the loving God with the soul who comes to him and
longs for him." When the soul of the sinner thus returns to
God like a child to his mother, then, "as he himself is moved
even more by his own love and tenderness, he unites himself
to her spiritually, becoming, as the Apostle says, one spirit with
her. For when the soul clings to the Lord, he has mercy on her
and comes lovingly and joins himself to her, and she abides in
the grace of God . . . Her mind sojourns in the Heavenly
Jerusalem, for she is raised to the third heaven, united to the
Lord and serving him." Such loving union with God presupposes
also strenuous effort on behalf of man. He must completely
deny himself and abhor all worldly joys, material cares, and
idle thoughts. If he does this, God will give him the special
help of his grace, which Macarius stresses more than some
other Greek Fathers. For active asceticism does not suffice to
lead to the mystical union; like St. John of the Cross, twelve
hundred years later, the Homilies, too, teach the necessity of
"passive" purifications brought about by God himself who,
when he wills, "becomes fire, burning away every foul and
foreign affection of the soul," for "the gift of the Holy Spirit,

which the faithful soul is deemed worthy to receive, is obtained only with much struggle and patience, with temptations and trials, for free-will is proved by affliction." On this arduous journey to God man is not, however, left without consolations; for God also "when he wills, becomes ineffable and secret tranquillity, so that the soul may rest in the divine peace; and when he wills, he is joy and rest, cherishing and protecting her."

This tranquil state is the precondition of true mystical prayer, when heart and mind are pacified "so that the soul, in the fullness of her joy, appears as an innocent babe." In such a state nothing troubles her, but she "rejoices over the whole world," which she sees then, as it were, with the eyes of God. If a man who has reached this state is not self-satisfied but presses on in humility and love, he will experience ecstasies, "when the power of God enters into him and holds his limbs and his heart, and takes captive his mind in the love of God" —one of the earliest and most lucid descriptions of ecstasy we possess. It begins in the body, which is rendered motionless, then fills the heart, and finally lays hold of the mind, "in the love of God." Again Macarius presents it in terms of light: "the light that shines in the heart has opened up the more interior, profound and hidden light [i.e. in the depth of the soul], so that the whole man is plunged into that sweetness and contemplation, being no longer master of himself, but is become as a fool and barbarian to this world, because of the exceeding love and sweetness and the hidden mysteries; so that the man during that time is liberated and attains to his perfect measure . . . but after this the grace is withdrawn . . . and he stands on an inferior step of perfection." So light and sweetness are the essence of the mystical experience just described: the mind is illuminated and the emotions are delighted by the intense sweetness of love, while both the activities of the senses and of reason are suspended, and, as far as the outside world is concerned the man has become "a fool and barbarian," quite impervious to what is going on around him.

To reach such a state it is not at all necessary to abandon

all outward activities—we have seen that the Desert Fathers not only worked with their hands but also took part in theological controversies; some even became bishops and had to abandon the hermit life altogether. For "It may happen that a man who has been busy all day gives himself to prayer for an hour, and that the interior man is ravished in prayer into the infinite depths of the other world in much sweetness, so that his whole mind is alienated and caught up, so that during that time the thoughts of his earthly preoccupations are forgotten, because they are filled and taken captive towards heavenly, infinite and incomprehensible things." Ecstasies are generally of short duration so that a man may continue his active work, "the care of the brethren and the administration of the word." An even higher state is what later mystics call the "Spiritual Marriage," and which Macarius describes in the terms of the image theology typical of Patristic mysticism. The soul who has passed through ecstasies and received gifts which go with this state of prayer such as special revelations and the gift of healing, will not be content with these, however desirable they may be. She will press on "until she obtains the perfect union, that is love, which, being unchangeable and unfailing, makes those who desire it detached and stable." Most later mystics, especially the two great Spanish ones, St. Teresa of Avila and St. John of the Cross, stress the stability of the love between God and the soul in the last stage of the mystical life before their final union in heaven. Macarius describes it in magnificent imagery. He presents God as seated on his throne, "in the heavenly city, yet wholly inclined towards the soul in her body. For her image he has placed above in the heavenly city of the saints, Jerusalem, but his own image of the ineffable light of his Godhead he has placed in her body. He ministers to her in the city of the body, and she ministers to him in the heavenly city . . . for the Lord becomes the inheritance of the soul, and the soul the inheritance of the Lord."

This wonderful description of the union of God and the soul

mirrors perfectly both the transcendence and the immanence of God. The one is expressed by the picture of the throne in the heavenly city, the other by God's own image, impressed on the soul even while she is still in her body. This image is all light, and when a man is united to this light, there is a perfect mutual interchange; God and man belong to each other. They belong to each other, they are not identical with each other. It is sometimes asserted by writers on mysticism that all mystics are at heart pantheists of one sort or another, convinced that in their highest experience they are one with God and all differences are abolished. Macarius guards against such a view in the clearest possible terms. In the last but one of the fifty Homilies he writes: "Oh ineffable mercy of God, that he should give himself gratuitously to believers, to inherit God in a short time, to have God dwell in a human body, and to have man as a beautiful house for the Lord. For just as God created heaven and earth for man to inhabit, so also did he create the body and soul of man as his own house, to dwell and repose in it . . . having the beloved soul, made in his image, as his bride . . . He is God, she is not God; he is the Lord; she the slave; He is the Creator, she the creature; he the Maker, she what is made. There is nothing in common between his nature and hers; but because of his infinite, ineffable and incomprehensible love and mercy it has so pleased him to dwell in his rational creature, his honourable and chosen one."

God remains God and man remains man, even in the most intimate union. But because the soul was created in God's own image she may even be called "a sharer in the divine nature," a sharer because of the ineffable love of God who has chosen his rational creature as his dwelling place. This divine indwelling which is fully realized only in the highest stage of the mystical union is a mutual ministering of God to the soul and the soul to God, a bridal union of love between creature and Creator.

EVAGRIUS PONTICUS

Our principal source for the life of Evagrius Ponticus (d. 399) is the *Lausiac History*. He belonged to the circle of the so-called Cappadocians: Basil of Caesarea, who conferred the "lectorate," one of the minor orders, on him, and Basil's friend Gregory of Nazianzus, who made him a deacon after Basil's death. He was in Constantinople at the time of the Second General Council in 381 and during the few months while Gregory was patriarch of the city. After his mentor's departure he stayed in the entourage of the new Patriarch Nectarius and took an active part in the controversy with the Arian heretics. During this time he fell in love with the wife of a high-ranking court official. His passion was returned; he fought against it, being terrified of the effect the scandal would have on the heretics, but seemed unable to overcome his infatuation. Finally he had a vision of angels in the shape of soldiers who bound him with chains, one of whom then transformed himself into a friend who made him swear on the Gospel that he would leave the city at once. Even though he had taken the oath in a trance Evagrius considered himself bound by it and, having packed up his belongings, set out the very next day for Jerusalem. There he made the acquaintance of St. Melania the Elder, a noble Roman lady who had embraced the ascetical life under the influence of St. Jerome and of Rufinus, the Latin translator or Origen. Melania persuaded him to break with the world once and for all and to go to Egypt to join the Fathers of the Desert. There he soon became one of the most prominent members of a learned group—most of the Egyptian monks were quite illiterate—who were followers of Origen and well versed in theological and philosophical speculations. For this reason Evagrius was condemned together with Origen at the Council of Constantinople in 553. Hence the mystical teaching of Evagrius is highly philosophical, indeed esoteric. He divides the spiritual life into two parts, one of which he calls "practical" and which roughly corresponds to what was later called ascetical, the other "gnostic," in the sense of Clement of Alexandria, that is to say contemplative. The contemplative stage is again subdivided into two: the inferior gnosis, the contemplation of created beings in their causes, that is to say the reflection of the divine attributes in creatures, and the higher gnosis, the contemplation of God himself.

Evagrius lays the greatest possible stress on the necessity of a high degree of virtue, without which it is impossible to attain to contemplation. For him wrath is the greatest obstacle to the spiritual life, because it is the special characteristic of the demons. Thoughts of hatred and vengeance will invade the monk especially at prayer time, and unless he overcomes them by gentleness and brotherly love he can never make progress. To soften the soul hardened by sin the monk needs first of all the gift of tears. This gift must on no account be equated with sadness—indeed, sadness, like wrath, is the worst enemy of prayer. No, the tears of contrition are wholesome tears, a sign of beginning spiritual health, not of dejection, and though they are particularly necessary at the beginning, they must to a certain extent accompany the monk throughout his spiritual journey, for Evagrius says: "If it seems to you that in your prayer you no longer need to weep for your sins, consider how far you are from God, whereas you ought to be always with him, and you will weep all the more."[1] These tears should coexist with joy, for prayer is the fruit of joy and gratitude, being built on the solid basis of all the virtues. This is the "practical" life, and the mode of prayer that belongs to it is psalmody, that is to say vocal prayer, which, Evagrius writes, "calms the passions and causes the intemperance of the body to be stilled." In short, through the practice of virtue and vocal prayer man is led to the beginnings of *apatheia*, that is to say freedom from the passions, when anger, covetousness, and all

---

[1] From the treatise *On Prayer*, which after the condemnation of Evagrius circulated under the name of St. Nilus, but has been established as a work of Evagrius by recent research, notably by the French Jesuit scholar, I. Hausherr.

other passions are already largely overcome and the soul is sufficiently at peace to be introduced to the inferior "gnosis" in which God is contemplated as reflected in creation. It is difficult to ascertain what exactly Evagrius means by this sort of contemplation; it seems something like meditation in the modern sense, for he opposes the fatigue and the struggle it involves to the perfect peace and tranquillity of the higher stage. He counsels the hermit, for example, to reflect on the mortality of his body and the vanity of the world, and to remember the state of the souls in hell, its gruesome silence, interrupted only by horrifying groans. Indeed, during this stage the demons will be particularly active, for they hate nothing so much as a man intent on mental prayer. The demonology of Evagrius, which plays a very important part in his mystical doctrine, is based on the experiences of the desert such as they are described in the life of St. Antony and the *Lausiac History*. According to Evagrius the whole struggle between hermits and demons is concerned only with contemplative prayer, which the devil tries to prevent at all costs. This he does by insinuating evil thoughts into the contemplative, especially those of gluttony, fornication, avarice, sadness, wrath, discouragement (or accidie), vainglory, and pride, the basis of the later "seven capital sins." These thoughts prevent the monk from praying as he ought, and as he progresses he will be increasingly able to master them; but when he has reached the higher "gnosis," the stage which we would call mystical prayer proper, the demons have to use other means to be able to attack the monk.

This stage, which Evagrius also calls "pure prayer," belongs particularly to the intellect, in Greek *nous*, according to Evagrius' division of man into body, to which corresponds psalmody, soul, which is active in inferior contemplation, and intellect, which is the highest part of man and the element which truly makes him man. In his philosophical works Origen had indulged in certain speculations about the pre-existence of the soul as a pure spirit, whose "fall" into a human body was due to a sin committed in that former, wholly immaterial life. This was one of the main theories for which he was later condemned, and it is at the root of Evagrius' doctrine of higher contemplation as the only proper activity of the human mind, and thus of man, who is essentially *nous*. Everything, from the practice of the commandments in the "practical" life to the contemplation of spiritual creatures and the acquisition of *apatheia* is but a means to arrive at the true gnosis, the contemplation of God himself, whom Evagrius calls sometimes the "Monad," at other times the Trinity—though in his theology the three divine Persons play no part, and when he says Trinity this is no more than another name for the one God. But how can man contemplate God in this life?

In no other way than by seeing his image in the intellect itself. This becomes possible only by completely denuding it from all images, including that of Christ himself, who, by the way, plays a comparatively very minor part in Evagrius' mystical doctrine. He therefore rejects all visions whatsoever, attributing them to the devil who touches certain parts of the brain and thus produces hallucinations. The true vision of God is a formless light in the "naked intellect" contemplating itself; but like Macarius, Evagrius, too, never loses sight of the fundamental difference between God and man, even in the highest mystical experience, which the Greek Fathers like to call deification. For God alone is God by essence, men become "gods" by grace. Indeed, like Macarius, Evagrius stresses the necessity of grace to reach the true gnosis. God alone can pacify the human intellect sufficiently for this contemplation; for whereas the inferior contemplation of creatures is within the power of the human intellect, "the contemplation of the Trinity does not depend on it but is an eminent gift of grace."

In what does this contemplation consist? It is a converse of the intellect with God, in which the intellect is completely free from any object but is filled with a "formless light," for "blessed is the mind which, at the time of prayer becomes immaterial and without possessions." In the mystical theology of Evagrius there is no question of ecstasy. The mind that is emptied of all content contemplates God in his image in which it was created, and thus returns to its original, purely spiritual state, it becomes equal to the angels. This "angelism" is one of the most important characteristics and also one of the dangers of Evagrian mysticism. The ultimate goal of the contemplative is to free himself both from the body and from the soul—in the Evagrian sense as the seat of imagination—and to become pure intellect, like the angels, for this was his primitive state, from which he fell. This teaching is not for all; novices in the spiritual life ought not to be told anything about these mysteries, but exercise themselves in virtue, psalmody and, later, meditation. God alone can introduce them into the state of pure contemplation, but when this is reached, man must keep his mind completely free and abandon himself to the divine action. This doctrine of the emptying of the intellect in order to contemplate the divine light has had a profound influence on the mysticism of the Orthodox Church and the Hesychasm of the fourteenth century.

2. THE MYSTICISM OF DARKNESS

GREGORY OF NYSSA

Gregory of Nyssa (d. 394) is one of the most original thinkers and mystics of the Eastern Church, whose importance as a mystical theologian has been rediscovered in the West only in recent times. Like Origen, whose disciple he was, Gregory came from a fervent Christian family. His elder brother, Basil, was not only a great bishop who defended the divinity of Christ against the Arians, but also the founder of Eastern monasticism, to which he gave the rule which is still followed in our own day. His grandmother, Macrina the Elder, his mother Emmelia, his sister Macrina the Younger, and his brother, Peter of Sebaste, are all venerated as saints. Strangely enough, though, as a young man Gregory himself showed no signs of spiritual interests. True, at first he wanted to be a priest like Basil, who had undertaken his education, but he soon abandoned this idea and studied for the more brilliant secular profession of rhetor. He also seems to have married. Both his brother Basil and his friend and namesake Gregory of Nazianzus were very disappointed with his worldliness and tried to persuade him to abandon his way of life. Their efforts were finally successful, and in 372 Basil, who had become bishop of Caesarea in Cappadocia, appointed him to the very small and difficult see of Nyssa, which he himself considered "a wilderness." Gregory was no administrator and imprudent in financial matters; as he also was a devoted defender of the divinity of Christ, the Arian emperor, Valens, banished him from his see. After the emperor's death in 378 he returned in triumph, and a year later occurred the death of his brother Basil, whose powerful personality had overshadowed his younger brother. From that time onwards he played an extremely active part in the affairs of the Eastern Church, in addition to writing a series of very important treatises. He traveled extensively; in 381 he was present at the Council of Constantinople, where he had an important share in defending the cause of orthodoxy, and in the same year he went to Arabia to settle a dispute between two bishops over a diocese. As at that time he stood high in the favor of the court at Constantinople, he was selected to pronounce the funeral orations for the Empress Flacilla and her daughter Pulcheria in 385. In his later years he devoted himself especially to mystical theology, which, like Origen, he expounded mostly in the form of scriptural commentaries, especially those on the life of Moses and on the Canticle. In contrast to Macarius and Evagrius, for him the mystical experience is not one of light, but of darkness, a line of thought which was to be developed throughout the ages from Dionysius the Pseudo-Areopagite to St. John of the Cross.

Unlike Evagrius and Macarius, Gregory bases his mystical doctrine firmly on the sacramental life of the Church. Baptism shows forth the death and Resurrection of Christ and restores man to paradise, which thus once more becomes accessible to him. The white tunic in which the baptized were clothed symbolizes the "garment of incorruptibility" which is exchanged for the former garment of fig leaves, and through the sacramental water man is freed from the slavery of the devil. But as baptized man still remains in the body, he needs a food to sustain him, and this is the Eucharist. In his "Great Catechetical Discourse" Gregory explains that, just as a small piece of leaven changes the dough, so Christ's eucharistic Body transforms us into himself. Now this sacramental transformation is possible only because there is in man something that resembles God himself, and this, of course, is the image of God in which man was created, which had played such an essential part already in Origen's mystical theology. "Neither heaven has been made in the image of God," Gregory tells the soul in his sermons on the *Song of Songs*, "nor the moon nor the sun, nor the beauty of the stars, nor anything else that appears in creation. You alone were made the effigy of the Nature that is above every intelligence, the likeness of the imperishable beauty." And because of that man is able to meet God in the mystical experience. But neither the image-relation between God and the soul nor the sacraments are sufficient by themselves to produce such an experience, they are only the necessary conditions for it. The way that leads to it is the way of the moral virtues and of faith. Gregory seems to be the first Christian author to see the spiritual life as an ascent, an image suggested to him by the ascent of Moses to Mount Sinai, described in his *Life of Moses*, which was influenced by the treatise of Philo on the same subject. Moses' ascent suggested something else, namely that the way to God is not simply a way from darkness to light, as it appears in the light mysticism of Macarius and Evagrius, but a way from darkness into light and again into darkness, darkness being a symbol for two quite different things. The first stage means moving away from the darkness of sin and ignorance into the light of Christianity; the second stage is the movement from this light into the deeper understanding of God, which must necessarily be an ever increasing awareness of man's fundamental incapacity of fully grasping the wholly otherness or transcendence of God.

If this should seem odd—and it is perhaps the most difficult part of mystical theology—we might explain it by an analogous case from another sphere. When man knew only very little about the structure of the universe, it all seemed clear and easy to understand; the earth was the center, with sun, moon, and stars revolving round it. But as man penetrated ever more deeply into it, the universe became more and more mysterious: the distances turned out to be such that no human understanding could grasp them, and the number not only of simple stars but of whole constellations defied all imagination. Indeed, the more the scientist comes to know about the universe the more he realizes how little he knows of it and how many more riddles it holds than he can ever hope to solve in his lifetime.

If this happens to the man who investigates the universe, how much more to him who wants to know the Maker of the universe? When a man first sets out on his spiritual journey everything seems, if not completely clear, yet fairly easy to grasp. But the more he enters into prayer, the more he begins to "know" of God, the closer he comes to him, the more he realizes the divine greatness and the divine mystery; "For the knowledge of God," says Gregory, "is indeed a steep mountain difficult to ascend, and the crowds scarcely approach its foot"— as the Israelites had to keep away from Mount Sinai. Indeed, only the Incarnation makes possible the full mystical life, because through it the infinite distance between the divine original and his human image has been bridged without, however, being abolished. But when man progresses in the mystical life even all the mental imagery connected with the Incarnation has to be left behind. For the more closely the mind "approaches to contemplation," writes Gregory, "the more clearly does it see the invisibility of the divine nature. For having left behind all that appears, not only what the senses perceive, but also what the intelligence believes it sees, it penetrates into the invisible and incomprehensible, and there sees God. For in this consists the true knowledge of him . . . that he cannot be seen, because he transcends all knowledge."

This is a very paradoxical way of expression, to see the invisible by not seeing it—but as God infinitely transcends man's intellect, mystical knowledge can be expressed only in paradoxes. Now this realization of God's incomprehensibility is not easy for man to bear, and the more he advances the more he desires to know God, and the more he desires this the greater his feeling of frustration, because he realizes that his most ardent longing can never be fulfilled. This realization is the "wound of love" as interpreted by Gregory of Nyssa in a slightly different way from Origen, who did not stress the incomprehensibility of God as much as Gregory. What happens to man in this predicament? The soul is gradually learning that "the true enjoyment of what she is seeking consists precisely in this, always to progress in seeking and never to cease ascending . . . When the veil of despair has thus been taken away, and she sees the beauty of the beloved defying all hope and all description . . . she is seized with an even more vehement desire, because she has received the chosen arrow of God in herself, and her heart has been wounded by the barb of faith, she has been mortally wounded by the arrow of love."

Gregory of Nyssa, like St. John of the Cross twelve hundred years later, regards faith as the only means of union between God and man, and so the bride-soul in the *Song of Songs* can say: "I will never let him go . . . from the grasp of faith, until he comes within my chamber." The incomprehensible God is apprehended only by faith, and the deepest mystical experience is precisely an experience of dark faith, but of a faith that is very different from the first accepting faith of conversion, which appears as light. For this dark mystical faith is intimately connected with the most ardent love: love is the arrow, faith is its tip—the two produce the wound in the soul that is longing for an ever greater possession and knowledge of God. This wound is—again paradoxically—a healing wound, because the soul is now learning that union with God means a never end-ing journey towards him, each stage of which is but a new beginning. This is so because God is utterly transcendent, "and as God continues to reveal himself, man continues to wonder, and he never exhausts his desire to see more, since what he is waiting for is always more magnificent, more divine, than all that he has already seen." So each encounter of the invisible and incomprehensible God leads to another, and each is more wonderful than the one that went before, and so the soul is never satisfied with her experience of God but presses on to ever new ways of union and mystical knowledge. For this is the great paradox of the mystical life, that "desire is satisfied by the very fact that it remains unsatisfied."

In this state of union with God the soul goes out of itself; it is inebriated with the divine presence; but it is a sober inebriation, which raises the soul above its ordinary state to divine "ecstasy," when the normal sense activity of the body is suspended and the soul becomes a mirror which reflects the divine beauty. Now the spiritual senses are fully developed: the sense of touch comes into contact with the Word, the smell is attracted by the divine perfume of Christ, the sense of hearing contemplates the mysteries. The soul is also given back its wings, which it had lost through the disobedience of the first human pair, "the wings of the dove, by which I [i.e. the soul] have the power of flight, so that I can fly and come to rest again, that is to the rest by which God rested from his works." Thus, in the fullness of the mystical life, man is once more restored to the perfect, immortal nature he had in paradise, made in God's image and likeness.

This wonderful transformation, which had begun in baptism, is worked out entirely within the Church. "The foundation of the Church," writes Gregory, "is a kind of recreation of the world, in which according to the prophet (Isaiah 65:17) a new heaven is created, whose foundation is faith in Christ, as St. Paul says (I Timothy 3:13) and a new earth is fashioned, that drinks up the rain that falls on it, and a new man is formed who through the birth from above is renewed after the image of him who created him." Thus, in Gregory's view, the mystical life is an endless progress to the transcendent God in the darkness of faith and the fervor of love, sustained by the sacraments and the teaching of the Church, and culminating in the full restoration of man to his paradisal state of winged innocence. Even then he will never completely be satisfied, for the fullness of the Godhead will always escape him, but this very absence of satiety, this expectation of something still greater and more beautiful to come, is in itself the most complete satisfaction of the soul wounded by the arrow of divine love.

VI THE LATIN FATHERS

1. CASSIAN

The ascetical life with its mystical aspirations was propagated in the West by a man who had made a thorough study of the Eastern monks and hermits and who, it seems, also had himself mystical experiences. Very little is known about the life of John Cassian (c. 360–435), not even his birthplace, which may have been in the Roman province of Scythia Minor (Dobrudcha), though some scholars believe it to have been in Syria, Palestine, or even Provence. He entered a monastery at Bethlehem at an early age and in 385 traveled to the Nile Delta to gain some first-hand experience of the Egyptian monks and hermits. Apart from one brief journey back to Palestine he seems to have stayed there till about 400, when he is known to have gone to Constantinople, where John Chrysostom was then at the height of his fame as a preacher. Chrysostom ordained Cassian deacon, and, when the former was exiled for his outspoken criticism of the court, Cassian went to Rome to plead his cause. It seems that he was ordained priest in Rome, and some time afterwards he went to Marseilles, where he founded two monasteries, one for men, the other for women. His two principal works, the *Institutions* and the *Conferences* were written in Marseilles. The *Institutions* deal mainly with the monastic rules and customs of the Egyptian and Palestinian monks and with the eight principal vices, following the teaching of Evagrius. The *Conferences* purport to be conversations with the most famous Desert Fathers, many of them no doubt fictitious, but they reflect faithfully their teaching, again especially that of Evagrius. For Cassian had no intention of being original. Indeed, he considered that the only safe way was to follow the traditions of those who had themselves practised the highest virtue and experienced the mystical life.

Cassian bases himself firmly on the Bible, but taking little account of the literal sense. The "spiritual" sense is the most important—as it is for all followers of the Alexandrian school— but to discover it is given only to the contemplative. Cassian severely restricts the possibilities to reach contemplation. Unlike Clement, he considers it absolutely impossible for married people, indeed for anyone not living in the desert or in a monastery, and even in the case of the latter he regards it as very difficult. For to reach it a man must divest himself completely not only from all interest in material things, but also from all his own inclinations and affections; and though the aim of the monk as well as of the hermit is perfect purity of heart, he believes that the hermit reaches a higher stage of it.

The way that leads both monks and hermits to the summit is a spiritual combat. Since, through the Fall, the divine image in man had been corrupted, it can be restored only by an energetic struggle against the vices. But again, the combat of the hermit is more severe than that of the monk, for the monk will struggle especially against the vices that affect his physical nature such as gluttony and avarice, whereas the hermit, who has already overcome these, is attacked by the subtler ones of pride and vainglory. Therefore a life of very high virtue is absolutely necessary if contemplation and, through it, union with God is to be reached. Cassian's conception of the contemplative life is extraordinarily rigorous, nevertheless allowing for a certain amount of relaxation. It needs a tranquillity which nothing can perturb, neither external events nor undesirable thoughts nor even dreams, and this tranquillity Cassian calls "chastity." If a man has obtained this "extinction of the carnal passions" he will enjoy a "vision of God" inasmuch as it is possible in this life.

Cassian describes this mystical prayer in various ways. It is a "prayer of fire," in which all is perceived in a single, simple intuition; but in its highest form the monk himself no longer knows how he prays. Then his prayer will be ecstatic, for Abbot John remembers "that I have often been transported in such ecstasy that I forgot to be burdened with this fragile body, and my mind rejected so suddenly all external senses and left all material things behind that neither my eyes nor my ears fulfilled their proper function." But this prayer is almost impossible even to monks living in community. For Cassian, following the Fathers of the Desert, considers even the facts of charity necessary in the common life as distractions from the highest goal, which is the mystical communion with God. These acts of charity are necessary and an essential preparation for the higher life of the hermit, but when this higher stage is reached they will detract from the fullness of contemplation—a view which, as we shall see, was no longer held by the later mystics of the West, and which is certainly incompatible with the teaching of St. Paul on the pre-eminence of charity.

Thus it is not surprising that Cassian considers even involuntary distractions in contemplative prayer as sins. Not, of course, as mortal or even venial sins, because they are not intentional, but nevertheless as sufficiently serious to require God's forgiveness. According to him the very mobility of the mind, which makes it impossible for a man to celebrate even one Eucharist completely without distraction, is a sin; and any distraction of the mind which is in the least way consented to is even an "exceedingly grave crime." Indeed, Cassian, like his master Evagrius, considers sometimes the human condition itself, which prevents man from being and acting like a disembodied spirit, as sinful. For to him "overcome by the burden of earthly thoughts to fall from the sublime heights of contemplation" means "to be drawn unwillingly, even without knowing it, to the law of sin and death; to be turned away from the vision of God . . . even by good and just, nevertheless earthly, works, is a good reason

why the saints should sigh constantly to God and proclaim themselves sinners."

Side by side with such exaggerated views, however, we find
very sound teaching, for example on the sacrament of the Eucharist. Though the reception of Holy Communion requires a
high degree of purity, the monks should, if possible, receive it
every Sunday and not only once a year under pretext of not being
worthy. For if they are not worthy on other Sundays, neither
will they be so once a year. No man can ever be worthy of
receiving Christ; "it is much more reasonable to receive the
most sacred mysteries every Sunday with a humble heart, as a
remedy for our sicknesses"—words which could just as well have
been written against the Jansenists of the seventeenth century
who held similar views to those of the monks Cassian reproves.

He has an equally balanced view on the matter of hermits
and their visitors. Ever since Antony retired into the desert the
Egyptian solitaries had been unable to remain hidden. The more
intense their spiritual life, the larger the number of ardent young
men who came to ask their advice and of fellow hermits wanting
to exchange experiences. Cassian calls these visits "a very pleasant truce" which affords refreshment for both body and soul.
Besides, without such visits they might get stale, whereas the
interruption of their prayer life will give it all the more impetus
when it is resumed. Like Evagrius, Cassian says nothing about
visionary experiences, nor does he teach a mysticism of darkness,
like Gregory of Nyssa. To the transcendence of God corresponds
the transcendence of the mystical or ecstatical experience, which
is free from all images; because images are of the earth, whereas
God has no connection with anything earthly. Though Cassian
exhorts the monk to unite himself to Christ, the way to do so
is to have "the mind free from all earthly things"; we are far
from the Christ-centered mysticism of Paul and Ignatius of Antioch. Though, of course, the Incarnation is presupposed throughout, it is not at the center of the mystical experience, which is
rather the transcendent God himself.

Through Cassian the teaching of the Desert Fathers was trans-mitted to the West, where it was welcomed and at the same time transformed in accordance with the different mentality and mode of life of the Latin civilization.

2. ST. AUGUSTINE

The story of St. Antony and of the Desert Fathers played a decisive part in the conversion of the greatest of the Latin Fathers, St. Augustine of Hippo (354–430). His personality is much better known than that of any of the Easterns, for he has written the first Christian autobiography, the famous *Confessions*, and later led the life of a busy bishop, involved in much correspondence and controversy. Probably a Berber by race, he was the child of a pagan father, who was baptized only on his deathbed, and a Christian mother, Monica. Both parents desired a brilliant career for the gifted boy, and therefore did not have him baptized, but his mother had him enrolled as a catechumen when he asked for baptism during a dangerous illness. After his recovery, however, there was no more question of his becoming a Christian, and when, at the age of seventeen, he went to study at Carthage, he took a mistress, who soon gave him a son, Adeodatus, and to whom he remained faithful for about thirteen years. Nothing is known of her, not even her name—but she must have been a remarkable woman to have held the love of Augustine for so many years, and we know from his own account how hard he found it finally to leave her, at the insistence of his mother; for he writes that his "heart that had clung to her was broken and wounded and drew blood." At Carthage he studied philosophy and rhetoric, especially Cicero, whose brilliant style he found at that time much more to his taste than the simplicity of the Bible narratives. He also grew interested in philosophy, which he hoped would teach him the meaning of life, and joined the religious-philosophical sect of the Manichaeans. They professed a dualistic religion with the conflict between light and darkness at its center, the object of their ascetical practices being to free the sparks of light that Satan had stolen from the transcendent world of Light and enclosed in the human minds.

When Augustine returned to Tagaste to teach the liberal arts, Monica refused to receive him into her house, no doubt as much for his illicit liaison as for his unorthodox opinions, but she continued to struggle for his soul by her prayers and her tears. In 383, contrary to her will, he went to Rome with his mistress. By that time he had become disappointed with Manichaeism and turned to Greek philosophy, especially to Plato. The next year he was appointed professor of rhetoric at Milan, where St. Ambrose was bishop at the time. Monica had followed her son to Italy, and after getting rid of his mistress tried to interest him in marriage with a very young girl, for whom he would have to wait two years. But this was too long for him and he took another mistress, though with a rather bad conscience. For he had begun to attend the sermons of St. Ambrose and found in them an answer to his problems. He read St. Paul, and Simplicianus, a priest also interested in Neoplatonism, told him of the conversion of a famous rhetor like himself, Marius Victorinus, who had recently thrown up his career to embrace Christianity. Augustine became more and more unsettled, realizing that the only obstacle that still kept him from doing the same was his attachment to women. At the height of his interior struggle a friend told him about the ascetical life of St. Antony and other Desert Fathers and informed him that even in this very city of Milan there were many virgins and widows living in chastity; should he not be able to do what they did? And could they do it without the grace of God? "Cast yourself on him," an interior voice seemed to say to him, "be not afraid, he will not withdraw himself and let you fall: cast yourself on him securely, he will receive and heal you." But still there were other voices murmuring in his ear that, if he gave himself wholly to God, he would never again be allowed to enjoy the pleasures of the senses —and how could he, in the prime of his young manhood (he was thirty-three at the time) do without them? While he thought about this in a garden he suddenly heard the voice of a child

repeating in a kind of sing-song: "Take and read, take and read."
He opened at random the volume of the Pauline epistles which
he had been reading before and his eyes fell on the words: "Not
in rioting and drunkenness, not in lust and wantonness, not in
quarrels and rivalries. But put on the Lord Jesus Christ and make
no more provision for the flesh and its concupiscences" (Romans 13:13f). "I did not want to go on reading," writes Augustine, "nor was it necessary, For immediately, even with the end
of this sentence, as it were a light of certainty was infused in my
heart, and all the darkness of doubt fled away." And so the
greatest theologian of the early Latin Church was born, a theologian who gave much thought also to questions of mystical
theology and who was himself a mystic, as can be gathered from
his writings.

Augustine, together with his son and a close friend, was baptized by St. Ambrose on Holy Saturday 387. A few months later
he started on his journey back to Africa, accompanied by his
mother and his household. They stopped at Ostia, the harbor of
Rome, and there mother and son had a spiritual conversation
which culminated in a shared mystical experience. Both thinking
and speaking of the marvelous works of God, and ascending
from there to their own minds, they arrived at "the region of
never-failing abundance . . . and there life is that wisdom by
which all those other things are made . . . and while we were
speaking and longing for it, we touched it a little with the whole
impact of our heart; and we sighed and we left there the first
fruits of our spirit held captive." The operative words are "we
touched it a little with the whole impact of our heart"—that is
to say the "region of never-failing abundance," the divine Presence. It was evidently a short, fleeting experience of God, after
an intense dialogue on spiritual subjects.

Shortly after this conversation Monica died. In the autumn of
388 her son returned to Tagaste, where he established a religious
community together with some friends. His mystical experiences
continued, and they seem usually to have taken the same form
as that described before, a movement from without, the con-

templation of God in his creatures to within, recollection in his own soul, and from there to the awareness of God. "Ascending through my mind I pass on to You, who dwell above me," as he says in Book X of his *Confessions*. A few chapters later he goes into greater detail, from which it becomes quite clear that these experiences were truly mystical: "And sometimes," he writes, "you introduce me interiorly into a very unusual state, into a strange sweetness which, if it were perfected in me, would seem to be the future life itself."

The presence of God expresses itself as sweetness, but it also makes man aware of his own insufficiency, of his dissimilarity to God, though, strangely, he also realizes the divine likeness in which he was created. So Augustine says that he shudders, because he is so different from the divine Wisdom which shines on him in these experiences, and yet is aflame with love, because he is so much akin to it—a description of man's situation before God, realized to the full in the mystical experience. His comparatively secluded life with his community, so conducive to mysticism, however, did not last long. His reputation grew, and when, in 391, he visited the church of Hippo Regius during a service, both the aged Bishop Valerius and the congregation asked him to let himself be ordained priest. After his initial surprise he consented, and in 395 he became coadjutor to Valerius, who died soon afterwards. From this time to his death he ruled his diocese while continuing to live in community. His literary activity was prodigious. He composed large dogmatic works, among others a long treatise on the Trinity, controversial writings against various contemporary heresies such as Manichaeism, Donatism, and Pelagianism, commentaries on biblical books, as well as many sermons and letters. As in the case of Origen and Gregory of Nyssa, Augustine's mystical doctrine, too, is to be found mostly in his scriptural commentaries, especially in his exposition of Psalm 41 ("As the hart panteth after the fountain of water"). Two characteristics which distinguish St. Augustine from the Fathers of the Desert and from Gregory of Nyssa stand out with great clarity: He lays much more stress on the communal element—which some of the Desert Fathers considered incompatible with true mystical experience—and he is far more optimistic than Gregory of Nyssa about the positive apprehension of God, even though only for a short while, in this experience which, characteristically, is for him an experience of light rather than of darkness.

In his explanation of Psalm 41 he urges his brethren to share his desire for mystical understanding with him: "Together let us love, together let us burn in this thirst, together let us run to the fount of understanding." He has no wish to retire into the desert like St. Antony: for him the mystical experience can also be found in community, for this experience means to reach "the fount of understanding," which is God. He writes that if God "is the fount, he is also light; he is truly also understanding because he also satisfies the soul that desires to know . . . For there is, my brethren, a certain light within, which those who fail to understand do not possess." This "light within" is the very organ of mystical experience, because it corresponds to the divine Light. Not all men possess it, because they fail to understand; they have not yet destroyed the "serpents of iniquity" which prevent this light from shining in the soul. But once a man has destroyed these sinful leanings in himself he will begin to desire the "fount of wisdom" who is God, and created wisdom, the "light within," will gradually begin to shine in him.

For Augustine, too, the beginning of the mystical way is the stage of tears, shed for one's sins and from the ardent desire which seems almost impossible of being fulfilled at this time. "These tears themselves were sweet to me," he writes, "thirsting for this fountain, since I could not yet drink, I fed the more eagerly on my tears." For to reach God a man must go beyond himself, to "the house of my God," where he will be drawn by "some indefinable interior and hidden delight," resembling a sweet music. But these moments of delight when he could "catch a glimpse of this dwelling of God" are brief, soon he must once more occupy himself with the affairs of this world, so that his soul is saddened. It is the mystical experience of the active man—not of the solitary of the desert—who approaches the divine light in his rare moments of complete absorption.

Apart from the visions of the early martyrs and from diabolical appearances in the lives of the Desert Fathers we have so far not met what may be called "the theology of mystical phenomena" except briefly in St. Paul. St. Augustine, with his psychological interest so evident in his *Confessions*, discusses the subject of visions especially in Book 12 of his Genesis commentary (*De Genesi ad litteram*) in connection with Paul's ecstasy. The link between Genesis and the apostle is paradise, in which the first men lived before the fall and into which St. Paul was taken up in his rapture. Augustine does not think very highly of visions seen in the imagination. For Pharaoh, too, had visions in his dreams, but did not understand them; he needed Joseph to interpret them. First of all, visions must have a meaning—if one sees a vision, whether in a dream or in ecstasy, which has no meaning, it is obvious that it is no more than a play of the imagination. If the vision, however, teaches something that the visionary did not know before, Augustine holds that it must have been caused by a spirit different from that of the visionary himself, as against some of his contemporaries who believed that even such visions might be due to a person's own imagination. Today most psychologists would agree with the second opinion against St. Augustine, owing to the discovery of the subconscious activity of the mind. Augustine, however, distinguished only between divine, angelic, or diabolic agencies which might cause such visions, but he taught that it is extremely difficult to distinguish between them and that it needed the special gift of "discernment of spirits." Hence in the saint's view imaginary visions ought not to be relied on, especially as the issue is still further obscured by a man's own conscious activity of trying to interpret them. Therefore he has little patience with those who make much of such visions, which they do only because they are unusual and sensational, "whereas they rarely bother to know about daily occurrences whose origin may be even more obscure." For in his view visions are very much akin to dreams—though no one seems to be very interested in the latter, because they happen to every one.

He writes, however, in a very different tone about other visions —those which are generally called intellectual ones. Imaginary visions are inferior, because they need another agency, the intellect, to judge them, whereas intellectual visions are directly apprehended by the intellect and require no further explanation. In them the human mind "is lifted up as it were into the region of intellectual and intelligible things where, without any image of the body, truth is perceived as evident, unobscured by the mists of false opinions. There the virtues are not irksome for the soul . . . There is seen the brightness of the Lord, not by symbolic visions . . . but by species [i.e. actual appearances, seeing], not by enigmas, as far as the human mind can grasp." These intellectual "visions" in which the mind apprehends God, as far as is possible in this world, directly, without intervening imaginary representations, are the highest mystical illuminations. They generally occur in the state of ecstasy, which Augustine describes thus: "When the attention of the mind is completely averted and withdrawn from the senses of the body, it is more especially called ecstasy. Then, though the eyes may be open, whatever bodily objects may be present, these are not seen, nor are any sounds heard at all: all the mind's attention is directed either to the images of bodies in an imaginary, or without a bodily image to incorporeal things in an intellectual vision." Augustine died in 430, when the Arian Vandals were attacking his city and the fate of Christian North Africa was sealed.

3. GREGORY THE GREAT

The last important writer on the contemplative life in the West before the Middle Ages was the great Pope Gregory I (540–604). He was the son of a senator and became prefect of Rome at the age of thirty-three, but only a year later he decided to give up his worldly career; he sold his vast possessions and gave away the proceeds to the poor; his palace on the Caelian hill, however, he transformed into a monastery which he entered himself as a monk. But he was not destined to continue the contemplative life there, which he loved; only about five years later Pope Pelagius II sent him to Constantinople as his apocrisiarius (*nuntius*); there he wrote his famous *Morals on Job*, which contain most of his spiritual teaching. He returned to Rome about 585 and became abbot of his old monastery; five years later he was elected Pope, much against his will; he accepted only after a painful inner struggle. His pontificate was beset with difficulties; Italy was ruined by invasions which had brought famine and pestilence in their wake, and in 592–93 Rome was threatened by the Lombards. Then Gregory took an action hitherto unheard of: he made peace with them on his own authority, taking no notice of the exarch of Ravenna, the representative of the emperor, to whom such political decisions belonged. He followed this up by nominating governors for the cities of Italy and supplying them with arms; in fact, this contemplative monk became the founder of the temporal power of the Papacy. The conversion of England is also due to him, for he sent out the future St. Augustine of Canterbury with about forty monks to Christianize the Anglo-Saxons.

Gregory divides the contemplative life into three sections. The first step is recollection, when a man withdraws into himself; the second is introversion, when the soul considers its own nature, and the third is contemplation proper, in which the mind rises above itself and is occupied only with its creator. To reach this stage the soul must first divest itself completely of bodily images, for itself is spirit, not body. This is very difficult and requires great effort, but it is essential, if the soul would come to the knowledge of its Maker. For Gregory the mystical experience is not darkness, as for his namesake of Nyssa, but light; it is, however, clouded by human imperfection; however much we may strain the eye of our mind to see the light of eternity, "When we raise the glance of our mind to the ray of the supernal light it is clouded by the darkness of our weakness." So God is not seen as darkness, as in Gregory of Nyssa and Pseudo-Dionysius, but as light, however as a clouded light, the cloud not being produced by the excess of his light but by human weakness. In the end, of course, this comes to the same thing; nevertheless, the attitude of mind is different: the Eastern view being more paradoxical, describing the excess of light as darkness, the Western view being more commonsensical, and therefore more easily understandable. Gregory says that the human mind "blinks" before the divine light, which it sees as through a chink or, another image, through a darkness or fog. These glimpses of the divine light in mystical contemplation are always brief. "When the mind is suspended in contemplation," he writes, "when it exceeds the constraint of the flesh and strains with all its might to find some freedom of inner security, it cannot long remain above itself, for though the spirit carries it above itself, yet the flesh drags it down."

Like St. Augustine, Gregory frequently describes these short moments of divine union as sweetness, experienced by the spiritual sense of taste. "Sometimes," he writes, "the soul is admitted to some unaccustomed sweetness of the interior taste, and is suddenly somehow renewed when breathed upon by an ardent spirit, and it is the more desirous, the more it tastes what it loves. And it wishes to have within itself what it feels to taste so sweet . . . It tries to cling to it [this sweetness] but is kept back from its strength by its own remaining weakness, and because it cannot contemplate its purity it considers it sweet to weep." This taste of sweetness recurs again and again in Gregory's descriptions of the mystical union; the soul is rapt to the sweetness of supernal contemplation, which is a foretaste of eternal delight, and when the mind tastes this interior sweetness it is fired with love. In other passages Gregory calls it interior quiet, which is an earnest of the eternal rest.

The divine light is not always clouded over; there are moments in the mystic's life when it is seen more clearly, even though never in the same way as in the beatific vision. This experience takes place in the *acies mentis*, the eye of the mind, the highest point of the spirit. In the mystical union this is "illuminated by the resplendent flame of the uncircumscribed light. When this is in anyway seen, the mind is as it were absorbed in secure joy and rapt above itself as if the present life had ceased, and is somehow recreated in a certain newness. There the mind is sprinkled with heavenly dew from an immense fountain; there it realizes that it is not great enough for that to which it is rapt, and because it feels the truth it is aware that it does not see how great is this truth itself."

In Gregory's view of the mystical experience, therefore, the realization of the divine transcendence is the focal point. This awareness is the cause of rapture and joy as well as of a transformation of the man who experiences it. It is not vision but rather a "feeling," because God is too great to be experienced in this life other than through the spiritual sense of touch. The knowledge is like dew from a fountain, the fountain itself remains hidden. For, as Gregory says in another passage, in contemplation the divine wisdom is touched, since "its very immensity, which raises man to itself, refuses the human mind perfect knowledge, so that it might love this wisdom by touching, not penetrate it by grasping it."

Mystical contemplation, however, is not an end in itself. Like most Western theologians, Gregory holds that it must be abandoned for the duties of the active life—which he, like St. Augustine, compares with the bleary-eyed Leah as opposed to the beautiful Rachel. Indeed, Gregory himself had to do this, when he was called out of his monastery, first to go to Constantinople, then to take on the duties of the Papacy. In his *Homilies on Ezekiel* he regretfully remembers how, as a monk, he was able to keep his mind almost uninterruptedly intent on prayer, and in his later *Dialogues* he mourns the loss of contemplative peace and joy: "Troubled by its many engagements, my sorrowful mind remembers how it was with me formerly in the monastery, how all transitory things were below it, how it rose above all that was perishable and, though still in the body, went out in contemplation beyond the barriers of the flesh."

After Gregory's death Italy continued to be constantly harried by the barbarian invasions, and both theology and mysticism went into a decline. In the East, however, the mystical tradition was not only continued but produced a mystical theologian whose influence in both East and West was to be phenomenal.

VII THE LATER MYSTICS AND MYSTICAL THEOLOGIANS OF THE EASTERN CHURCH

The immense influence of the works of the Eastern author known as "Pseudo-Dionysius" was due in large measure to his assumed name. He pretended to be Dionysius, the Athenian disciple of St. Paul (cf. Acts 17:34), naming as his friends various personages, such as Timothy, who are mentioned in the Pauline epistles. This authorship was generally accepted throughout the Middle Ages and gave the writings circulating under his name an authority which many modern scholars consider quite out of proportion to their contents. The first doubts of the Dionysian authorship of these works were voiced in the time of the Renaissance. Today scholars are unanimous in dating them at the end of the fifth century, as there is no evidence whatever before this; but they are divided on the author's identity. A discussion of the many names that have been put forward is quite outside the scope of this book; it is even impossible to say with any degree of certainty whether he was an orthodox theologian or whether he belonged, as is frequently asserted, to the sect of the Monophysites. Suffice it so say that he was an original thinker who wrote in a very heavy, frequently obscure style, being fond of extraordinary compounds such as "superessential," "supercelestial," "principle-of-all-sacraments" and others, which make his writings difficult to understand and even more difficult to translate.

Apart from the author's obvious liking for mystification, this strange style is at least partly caused by his doctrine of the utter transcendence and unknowability of God. Because of his complete transcendence, human language is totally inadequate to express him, hence he can only be described in negatives. He is not intelligence, not essence, not even being—because these human words always denote something limited. God is none of these things—precisely because he is all this in a way totally beyond the reach of human language or understanding. The theology of Pseudo-Dionysius is as far removed as possible from any anthropomorphic conceptions so vigorously castigated by the Anglican bishop, Robinson, and other modern theologians. For him, as for Karl Barth, God is, indeed, the "altogether Other."

How is man then to be brought into contact with this ineffable Being who is so far beyond his understanding? To effect this contact Dionysius uses the idea of hierarchy, which is closely related to the concept of symbol. Among the works mentioned by Pseudo-Dionysius as his own is a *Symbolic Theology*; whether this is lost or has never been actually written cannot now be ascertained. It seems to have discussed—or been meant to discuss—the use of symbols in Scripture. For in his extant works, for example the *Celestial Hierarchies*, the author strongly defends the use of symbols for God and divine things, and especially of seemingly inappropriate ones such as bear or leopard, used by Hosea (13:7f), because they lead the human mind from the inadequate image to the realization that God is immeasurably above anything our human intellect or imagination could conceive. For man cannot go directly to God, the Incomprehensible. Therefore God himself has provided means of a gradual ascent in the hierarchies and the sacraments. There are, in the view of Pseudo-Dionysius, two kinds of hierarchy, the heavenly one of the angelic powers and the earthly one of the Church's ministry. The angelic powers transmit the gifts they have received from God in strictly hierarchical order, the lower ranks receiving them from the higher ones, and the former finally transmitting them to men. For the hierarchical order of heaven is reproduced in the Church in the three main orders of bishops, priests, and laity.

Dionysius lays as much stress as the other Fathers on the necessity of the sacraments, dispensed by bishops and priests, for the development of the mystical life. For through baptism man is introduced to the "divine existence" and made ready for "the holy combats which he will henceforth undertake in the service of Christ," because in this first great sacrament he has mystically died with Christ to sin. But this death does not mean that man's sinful tendencies have been destroyed; the victory over evil won in baptism has to be renewed in the Christian's daily struggle against the powers of darkness; he is now well set on the so-called purgative way. His greatest help in this will be the second great sacrament, the Eucharist. This is the sacrament of union and aids man to become more unified in himself. For to Dionysius God is primarily the One; like Evagrius, he takes very little notice of the three divine Persons. For man to become united to God, the first great requisite is to be harmoniously one in himself. The Eucharist is the most efficacious means to this end, for in the theology of Pseudo-Dionysius this sacrament is intimately connected with contemplation. It leads to an intuitive insight into the mysteries of the Christian faith, for he writes in the *Ecclesiastical Hierarchies* that the faithful "are led by the ministrations of the priests to the stable possession of the contemplative faculty." This corresponds to the second stage of the spiritual life, the so-called illuminative way.

Only after traversing these two stages with the indispensable assistance of the sacramental discipline of the Church, is it possible for the Christian to enter the mystical life of union with God. Pseudo-Dionysius symbolizes it by the circular movement; this he contrasts with the straight movement, by which a man meditates on created things which darkly reflect the Divinity, and the spiral movement, when he grasps the divine truths through the mediation of priests and sacraments in the quick movement of thought. In the circular movement, however, the soul, "leaving the things outside, enters into itself and gathers together in a unifying action its spiritual faculties which give it, as it were in a circle, freedom from distraction . . . recollects itself first within itself and then, when it has become as it were unified, unites itself to the powers that are perfectly unified [i.e. the angels], and thus reaches the Beautiful and Good [i.e. God], which is above all beings and one and the same, without beginning and end" (*Divine Names* 4.9).

Even within the unitive (or mystical) stage of the spiritual life Dionysius thus preserves a threefold hierarchical order, leading from union of the soul within itself to union with the angelic powers and finally to union with God.

This highest stage of the mystical life is described in Dionysius' famous but extremely short treatise on *Mystical Theology.* This is obviously influenced by Gregory of Nyssa, for, like the Cappadocian, Dionysius uses Moses' entry into the darkness of Mount Sinai as the symbol of the mystic way. Darkness, silence, obscurity—these are the terms in which he presents the genuine mystical experience. For because of his infinite transcendence God is essentially unknowable to the human mind, therefore he can—paradoxically—be known only through "unknowing." In order to arrive at the mystical experience of God, Pseudo-Dionysius therefore advises his fictitious disciple, Timothy,[1] to whom the treatise is addressed, to leave behind not only the world of the senses but also all intellectual activity, indeed all things and activities whatsoever, "and raise yourself as far as you can to union, in ignorance, with him who is above all being and knowledge." That is to say, though the hierarchies of the Church and of the angelic powers are indispensable for leading man to God, once his spiritual life, assisted by the practice of virtue, prayer, and fasting, has developed sufficiently, he may aspire to a direct intuition of God. This, however, can only be achieved if all a man has learned so far is abandoned and he

---

[1] He uses this name, of course, because St. Paul addressed two letters to Timothy, thus reinforcing his claim to be Dionysius the Areopagite.

enters on a way that leads him ever more deeply into darkness and ignorance.

This mystical way of unknowing ought not to be taught to those who are not yet ready for it. Dionysius is very firm on this. The entrance into the mystical darkness comes at the very end of the Christian life. But those who are called and prepared for it, it will be raised "in a pure ecstasy that is free from self and from all things to the super-essential ray of the divine darkness."

The ecstasy Pseudo-Dionysius has in mind is not an extraordinary psychosomatic state in which the body becomes impervious to all external impressions and receptive to supernatural experiences. What he means is rather an outgoing from all, including supernatural, experience into the divine sphere of darkness. It is not an ecstasy of love, but one of the intellect, which leaves itself and all its activities behind and surrenders itself entirely to the "ray of the divine darkness." "Ray of darkness" is, of course, a paradox. It is meant to express the fact that the divine darkness is not a real darkness, but that the light which is God is so far removed from anything we understand by light and so overpowering to the eye of the human mind that it appears as darkness to it; it is, indeed, a "ray," but a ray of darkness.

Again paradoxically, what is revealed in this darkness is none other than the divine Beauty itself. For this process of revelation Dionysius uses the simile of a statue hewn from the shapeless stone from which the sculptor "first must remove all the superfluous matter that hinders the pure vision of the hidden form and thus reveal the hidden beauty merely by this removal." What this beauty is neither Dionysius nor any other mystic can express in words. This is why this treatise is so extremely short.

It has sometimes been questioned whether the mystical experience at which Dionysius hints—for he does not really describe it, as it is indescribable—is an authentic Christian experience or whether it is not rather a kind of natural mysticism, as neither Christ nor the three Persons of the Trinity seem to play a part in it. True, the author of the treatise was profoundly influenced by Greek philosophy, especially by Platonism. Yet he never for a moment suggests that the highest mystical experience can be had without a strenuous preparation through Christian faith and discipline. But whether in the presentation of Dionysius, this experience itself is not too thoroughly emptied of all definitely Christian content is a question which many theologians have answered in the affirmative.

MAXIMUS THE CONFESSOR

Maximus the Confessor (580–662) combined the light mysticism of Evagrius with the mystical theology of darkness and unknowing represented by Gregory of Nyssa and the Pseudo-Dionysius. Like many monks and bishops of the Hellenistic age, he did not feel called to the religious life in his youth. He received the usual philosophical education, studying Plato and Aristotle as well as the Neoplatonists, and then embarked on a political career which soon led him to the influential position of first secretary to the Emperor Heraclius. He was in his middle thirties when he decided to give up all worldly ambitions and become a monk at Chrysopolis, the present Scutari, near Constantinople. There he soon found a disciple, Anastasius, who stayed with him throughout his life. About 624 he went to another monastery, at Cyzicus, and there began to write theological works. Two years later the Persians advanced on Constantinople and the monastery at Cyzicus was dissolved, so Maximus went to Africa, probably via Cyprus and Crete, and settled in a monastery near Carthage. The following years were filled with controversies, for he defended orthodoxy against the Eastern Christological heresies of Monophysitism and Monothelitism, which would admit in Christ only one (divine) nature and one will respectively. Maximus wrote several works against them, but these activities did not prevent him from living a very authentic contemplative and mystical life. Nevertheless, they caused him once more to change his residence, and he went to Rome to be able to defend orthodoxy more effectively. There he was arrested in 753, together with the Pope, Martin I, because the Emperor Constans II favored the Monothelite heresy. He was tried in 655, and, just as happens today, was accused of political crimes. This accusation, however, could not be proved, and so he was exiled to Thrace. In 662 he was recalled to Constantinople for a further trial before a Monothelite court, and despite his great age, cruelly sentenced to have his tongue and his right hand cut off. He died shortly afterwards as a result of his sufferings.

Unlike Pseudo-Dionysius, Maximus has not written a treatise on mysticism. His teaching on the subject is scattered throughout his writings, especially his early work on charity, the *Questions to Thalassius*, the *Theological Chapters* (*Capita Theologiae et Oeconomiae*), the *Opuscula Theologica* and various letters, especially that to Marinus the Priest.

There are certain indications in his work that he himself has had mystical experiences, for he writes that he who has not himself received the mystical knowledge by grace cannot really know its force. In fact, Maximus, like Evagrius, lays very great stress on the necessity of grace for the mystical life. For in Christ God dwelt bodily, but in us the fullness of the Divinity (a very strong expression) dwells by grace. For even though we must prepare for the mystical life by strenuous ascetical effort, God alone can introduce us to the direct contact with him that is its essence, after all our sinful leanings have died in baptism. Like Gregory of Nyssa and Pseudo-Dionysius, Maximus insists on the divine transcendence which calls for faith. This faith will lead man from the first beginnings of the spiritual ascent to the mystical union, because it is a power that effects a union between the believer and the God in whom he believes. In his exposition of the Our Father, Maximus expresses this union as a mystical birth of Christ in the soul, who thus becomes a "virgin mother" and realizes the divine likeness. The prayer that belongs to this mystical state is very different from that of the active state, though each is the highest in its own order. The prayer of the active ones—the division is that of Evagrius—is undistracted through man's own effort, that of the contemplatives (here equated with mystics) is a rapture in which man is raised to God without any activity of his own. Maximus insists again and again on the passive nature of mystical prayer. It is suddenly given, without any human effort, to those worthy of the Spirit, for God himself teaches the pure mind.

In his interpretation of St. John's saying that God is light (I John 1:5) Maximus says that he is this also in those that live virtuously. "For," he writes in his *Questions to Thalassius*, "if we, by virtue and knowledge, are in God as in light, he is in us as in light. For God, who is light by nature, is in the light that is imitation [that is in the mystic], as the archetype is in the image." As in most of the Fathers the image and the likeness in which man was created play a fundamental role in his spiritual teaching, for the mystical life consists in the growing likeness of man to his Creator; and as according to St. Paul (II Corinthians 4:4 and elsewhere) Christ is the most perfect image of the Father, so the mystical life is the birth of Christ in the soul who thus becomes a "virgin mother."

But though, following St. John and also Evagrius, Maximus uses the image of light, he also follows Gregory of Nyssa and Pseudo-Dionysius in their presentation of the mystical life as an entry into the divine darkness, especially in his later works. Like Gregory he compares this life with the entrance of Moses into the darkness of Mount Sinai, and like Evagrius he insists on the "nakedness" of the intellect needed for mystical contemplation. For he asserts again and again that mystical prayer is formless. Because God is above all (human) knowledge, the mind that would reach him must also divest itself of all knowledge, all forms of thought, and, a fortiori, of all passions; for Maximus emphasizes as much as his predecessors the necessity of *apatheia*, the perfect tranquillity and detachment from creatures. This detachment will finally lead to "deification," a stable state in which we are most closely related to God "and become gods, receiving from God that we should be gods," a possibility given to our fallen nature through the Incarnation, which plays a far more central part in the mystical theology of Maximus than in Evagrius and Dionysius.

This deification is a *pathos*, which in this context does not mean passion but something that is suffered; it is an authentic mystical state in which human activity has no part, but which is wholly given by grace, of course only to those who have made themselves worthy of it by leading as perfect a life as is possible here on earth. The knowledge that belongs to this state is an unknowing, for the mind that is wholly intent on the Cause of all things reposes in divine ignorance; it rises ecstatically to God, leaving behind both bodies and spirits. It is clear from this that in the mystical theology of Maximus there is no place for visions and other phenomena; indeed he says explicitly that the mind united to God must be free from all visions "or, better, fancies."

Thus Maximus synthesizes the mystical theology of his predecessors; himself a mystic who both worked and suffered in the service of the true faith, he did not place mysticism in a separate department but integrated it into the whole of his theology.

JOHN CLIMACUS

John Climacus (d.c. 649) is famous for his work *The Ladder* (Greek *klimax*, hence his name) *of Paradise*, but little is known of his life. According to his earliest biography written by a monk of Raithu in Palestine he entered the religious life at the age of sixteen and lived for forty years as a hermit; but some modern authors think he became a monk considerably later in life, because his work reveals more knowledge of the world than could have been acquired in a monastery or hermitage. Be that as it may, *The Ladder* certainly continues the tradition of the desert life of a St. Antony. John Climacus is violently opposed to the speculations of Origen and Evagrius. His is an almost completely unintellectual spirituality; it is rooted in the thorough-

going asceticism of the desert and culminates in the achieve-
ment of *apatheia,* freedom from the passions, and *hesychia,* a
notion combining the idea of solitude with that of perfect repose.

Like many of the Greek mystics, Climacus, too, favors a certain angelism. That is to say he despises the body, which he
considers the enemy of the spiritual life, and aims at an angelic
life beyond the human condition. In the very First Step of his
mystical Ladder he defines the monk as one who aims at the
state of the incorporeal beings, and in one of the last Steps he
calls the hermit the earthly image of an angel. This resemblance
to the angels is brought about by purity, which, according to
him, means that "we put on the angelic nature." For purity is
"supernatural denial of nature, which means that a mortal and
corruptible body rivals the heavenly spirits." But to do this, the
body must be completely subjected; it must not simply be
"buffeted" as St. Paul buffeted it in the service of Christ, it
must be reduced, by fasting and vigils, to a state in which it is
no longer subject to the natural reactions but has acquired perfect insensibility to other bodies and their beauty. Though
Climacus admits a state of purity in which a man may look on
earthly beauty without harm, he considers such an attitude quite
extraordinary. Purity is absolutely essential for the monk and
solitary, and this includes indifference to all human ties; it is
a sign of the highest purity achieved by the mystic to look on
all human beings in the same way as if they were inanimate
objects—an attitude which is hardly compatible with the second
great commandment of loving one's neighbor. Indeed, for Climacus, as for some other mystics of the Eastern Church, prayer
comes before charity. To welcome visitors is for him to become estranged from God—an attitude very different from the
Benedictine ideal of hospitality. Further, he considers it great
cruelty if a person is interrupted in his prayer, because he may
not have another such opportunity for having his sins forgiven.

The prayer of which Climacus speaks here is, of course, the
highest form of it, that is to say mystical prayer. Prayer, he says,
is the test of the spiritual life, and in particular of the life of

the solitary, the "hesychast." It unites man to God and thus is the source of all graces and the food of the soul. Mystical prayer is absolutely simple, it should be without distractions which are to be banished by ejaculations, especially by the name of Jesus which should be remembered with every breath; this was later developed into the so-called Jesus prayer of Hesychasm. John Climacus describes three stages of prayer: after the ejaculations, which free from distractions, comes the concentration of the mind on the subject of prayer, and after that the perfect prayer, which is rapture in the Lord. Again in contrast with the later Western mystics, Climacus considers that even involuntary distractions spoil prayer, which should be totally uninterrupted, for it is essentially "estrangement from the world, both visible and invisible." This definition rules out such phenomena as visions, which, as we have seen before, play very little part in the mystical theology of the Greek Fathers. The rapture of which Climacus speaks transports the mind ineffably and unexpectedly into the spiritual light of Christ; there is no mention in *The Ladder* of the mystical darkness of Gregory of Nyssa and Pseudo-Dionysius. In this spiritual light a man receives mystical knowledge, that is to say "a sense of the Divine" in which the senses, the ordinary media of human knowledge, have no part; for the objects of this knowledge are the doctrines of the faith, especially the Trinity, and only the mystic can speak adequately of these mysteries.

The mystical union can also have effects on the body of the mystic, which will often reflect the splendor of the soul in a supernatural radiance. Its foundation is faith, which Climacus calls the "wing of prayer," and it is nourished by the Eucharist, which perfects the change worked in the mystic by his prayer; it delivers him from all defilement and everything pertaining to matter.

The life that leads to the mystical union as Climacus conceives it is wholly contemplative. Even such occupations as basket weaving, the means by which most Desert Fathers earned their meager living, are supposed to detract from contemplation; Climacus will only allow them as a means of overcoming sleep; for extensive vigils are essential to the life of the hermit as he sees it. This "angelic" life is wholly opposed to the needs of nature. Climacus advises the aspirant to the mystical life of complete solitude to remember that he will become the food of worms so as to encourage his abstinence from food, and to think of the flames of hell when wanting to drink: "And you will certainly refuse your nature all it wants." This struggle against even the most legitimate needs of human nature was common to the Eastern mystics of the time, but what is particularly interesting is that Climacus must have had some misgivings about it. For he has noticed that the austerities of the solitaries often have undesirable consequences. In Step 15 he admits that "those inclined to sensuality often seem sympathetic, merciful and given to compunction; while those who practise chastity do not seem to have these qualities in the same measure." In Step 26 he is even more explicit. He asks why it is that man's heart becomes hard when practicing silence, why the solitaries are overcome by sleep when fasting and not when they eat their fill, why they are tempted by dreams when hungry. "At least we can say," he writes, "that such a change does not always come from the demons. And this sometimes happens to me, I know not how, by reason of the constitution I have been given."

Climacus was very discerning in not attributing these failures invariably to demons, as was usually done at the time. His frank admission shows what is generally realized today, that human nature, when driven too hard, will take its own back; that even praiseworthy austerities have to be practiced in moderation if they are not to defeat their own end. Many of the extraordinary experiences such as are recorded in the lives of the solitaries from St. Antony onwards were undoubtedly due to a nervous condition brought about by their unnatural way of life; and this in its turn was caused by a hostility towards the body which is not part of authentic Christianity, but is due to the dualistic belief in the opposition between soul and body, between good spirit and evil matter that is of Gnostic origin and penetrated into Hellenistic Christianity at a very early time. It is certainly quite unbiblical.

SYMEON THE NEW THEOLOGIAN

The centuries following Maximus the Confessor and John Climacus show little evidence of a vigorous mystical life in the Byzantine Church, though monasticism was flourishing, especially in the famous monastery of Studios near Constantinople. Then, in the second half of the tenth century Symeon, later called "the new theologian" (949–1022) rose to great fame as an outstanding mystic, but also aroused considerable controversy. Symeon has remained almost unknown in the West (Pourrat gave him no more than a footnote in his four-volume *History of Spirituality*) because his writings had never been published here; they have begun to be edited only quite recently in the French collection *Sources Chrétiennes*, to which the present brief summary of his teaching is indebted.

Like many other Eastern mystics, Symeon, whose baptismal name seems to have been George, had first embraced a lay career and led the worldly life of a "young man about town," as he was very well connected; his uncle held an important position at the imperial court, and in Symeon's later mystical writings illustrations from court life are frequently given. Nevertheless, he also read some spiritual works, notably the lives of the saints, and these made him dissatisfied with the superficiality of his present life. He kept looking for a holy man who would show him the way to God, and even though his friends assured him that such persons no longer existed, he did not give up hope, and his trust was finally rewarded. In the monastery of Studios he met an old monk, Symeon, who instructed him in the spiritual life. Though the young Symeon continued to live in the world, he began to pray with great fervor, especially at night, tears streaming from his eyes, and after some time he had his first mystical vision, which he described as a divine light shining all around him: "And when this happened, the young man [i.e. himself] could distinguish nothing more . . . because he only saw light on every side, and did not even know whether he was walking on the earth . . . Being completely surrendered to the immaterial light, and having apparently become light himself and having forgotten all the world, he was wholly filled with tears and inexpressible joy and exultation. Then his mind ascended to heaven and he saw another light, even brighter than the first." And near this light there appeared suddenly his spiritual father.

Though this vision made a deep impression on him, the young Symeon nevertheless soon returned to his former life, even though he never quite severed his relation to his spiritual father. He says himself that he fell into all his old sins and quite forgot his supernatural experience. In this state he remained for about six or seven years, when he received another grace, feeling himself violently dragged up out of the mud, by whose hand he did not know, and handed over to his former teacher. This time his conversion was decisive and resulted in his becoming a monk at Studios, he being then about twenty-seven. He placed himself entirely under the direction of his old master, Symeon, an act which was not approved by the abbot and caused so much friction that he finally left Studios and joined a smaller monastery in the neighborhood, St. Mamas, while continuing under the direction of his spiritual father. At St. Mamas he was ordained priest and after three years, at the very early age of thirty-one, he was elected abbot.

Symeon soon became famous and a much sought-after director; but not all his monks took kindly to his efforts to lead them into the ways of the mystical life. About 996 thirty monks revolted against him and were sent into exile by the patriarch Sisinnius. A few years later, in 1003, there were more serious difficulties over the cult of his spiritual father, who had died in 987, and which Symeon had established in his monastery on his own authority. The reason for this attack was most probably Symeon's contention that the teaching authority in the

Church belonged to those who had themselves experienced mystical revelations rather than to the ecclesiastical authorities, an erroneous view which he claimed to have learned from his teacher. The controversy dragged on till 1009, when Symeon was finally condemned by the Patriarch and the Holy Synod, and exiled from Constantinople. He went to a sanctuary near Chrysopolis, where he gathered a group of disciples round him and remained also after he had later been rehabilitated.

Symeon differs from all the Byzantine mystics we have so far discussed in that he describes his personal experiences in his works and thus allows us an extremely interesting insight into his own mystical life. In his first mystical experience he only saw a light, but later the Person in and behind this light revealed himself as Christ. For Symeon's mysticism is Christ-centered. In his first catechesis he entreats Christ to dwell in us, so that we may see him in all his beauty. For though he is the Christ who has suffered, he is even more the risen Christ, as he now is in the glory of heaven, the King of kings and Lord of lords, a view that has always been at the center of Eastern devotion. In catechesis two Symeon urges his monks to make every effort to see and contemplate him, "for if we are accounted worthy to see him sensibly (or with our senses) here below, we shall not die."

This will sound strange to Western ears. What does it mean to see Christ with our senses, and even more, how can we achieve such a contemplation by our own efforts? Symeon here continues the line of the Macarian homilies. The first difficulty is explained by the stress the Greek Fathers laid on the development of the spiritual senses in the mystical life; Symeon himself writes in his *Theological Chapters* that the Lord gives us (that is to say the mystics) "another sensibility above [our ordinary] sensibility so that we may perceive clearly and purely his gifts and favours which surpass [ordinary] perception in a supernatural way." Thus, when Symeon speaks about contemplating Christ with our senses, he means these spiritual senses which enable the mystic to be aware of his presence. But how can we achieve this by our own efforts?

Symeon does not consider the mystical life to be an extraordinary gift, but sees it as the necessary flowering of the contemplative life lived in its fullness. For he advises those who have not yet received what he calls "the pledge of the Spirit" to make every effort to obtain it by good works and fervent penance.

In this striving for the mystical life and in this life itself tears play an extremely important part. To understand what Symeon says about them we have to remember that in other civilizations weeping is not considered unmanly. For Symeon tears are a sign of true compunction, their absence reflects a hardening of heart and conscience. "Ineffable marvel," he exclaims, "that what flows from the physical eyes should wash the soul spiritually from the filth of transgressions." And not only that, for, he continues, "where there is an abundance of tears, with true knowledge, there is also an effulgence of the divine light." The tears of compunction will be transformed into the mystical tears which refresh the soul that is burning with divine fire. "But without tears," he insists, "nothing like that has ever happened or ever will happen, neither in ourselves nor in anyone else." For tears, Symeon is convinced, are "a second baptism," and a more efficacious one than the first baptism of water and oil; because this sacramental baptism is but a figure of the truth, while the mystical baptism by tears is the truth itself—a view which could never be accepted by the Church, but which is quite in keeping with Symeon's opinion that what matters is not the objective action of the sacraments, but subjective experience.

Therefore he insists that not only a spiritual director but every superior must himself have mystical experience, else he is not fit to lead the flock of Christ. On the other hand, a superior or spiritual guide who fulfills this condition must be regarded as God himself and never contradicted. Unquestioning obedience to him will lead the monk to the mystical goal.

Symeon lays extraordinary stress on the conscious possession of grace. "He who knows that signs and wonders happen within him is truly a Godbearer," he writes. The Christian must know that he has received the pledge of the Spirit; for the Son of God has come on earth to "unite us to himself consciously through his Holy Spirit." Symeon believes that even in this life a vision of God can be obtained that at least approaches extremely close to the beatific vision, if it is not all but identical with it. He sees God principally in terms of light; applying the Beatitude on the pure of heart who shall see God to the present life, he says that they are introduced to the vision of God and see him purely, and a little later, in the same catechesis (two), he describes what is evidently his own experience: "The intellect sees strange spectacles, it is altogether enlightened and becomes itself luminous . . . for the intellect itself is light and sees all things as light, and this light is living and gives life to him who sees . . . He grasps the light in his soul and is taken out of himself, and being thus in ecstasy he sees the light from afar, but turning again he finds himself in the midst of it." And in this light Symeon believes to have seen the Father and the Son themselves, for in a later catechesis he affirms against some of his monks who doubted his teaching that a great contemplative would "receive the Holy Spirit and through him perceive the Son with the Father." This vision is, of course, not imaginary, but an intellectual awareness of the three divine Persons in the soul which is taught, for example, also by St. John of the Cross.

Symeon also clearly describes, and in the first person, the psychological accompaniments of these experiences. "I had hardly," he writes, "remembered the beauty of unsullied charity when suddenly the light was found in my heart and I was ravished by its sweetness. I lost the perception of all outward things and was so completely estranged from this life that I forgot what I had on hand." The effects of such an ecstasy are ineffable joy and contempt for all earthly things; the mystic receives through them a knowledge of God far above anything he could acquire by his own studies. This knowledge Symeon expresses not only in terms of light but also in terms of darkness, thus joining the "negative" theology of Gregory of Nyssa and Pseudo-Dionysius, and his explanation makes it clear that in this context light and darkness are not opposites but refer to the same thing. "The development of the knowledge of God," he writes, "becomes the cause and source of our ignorance of all other things and even of God himself. His tremendous effulgence is complete blindness and the perception surpassing perception no longer perceives anything that is outside it. For how can a knowledge that does not know the nature, origin, place, identity and quality of its object be a perception?"

Here we are in the midst of the mystical paradoxes that arise from the total transcendence of God whom the human mind simply cannot grasp. Indeed, the more profoundly the mystic becomes aware of the otherness of God the more will his knowledge appear to him as ignorance and the divine light as darkness. Thus the light that Symeon has seen in his ecstasy is also darkness, because God is incomprehensible in his essence, inaccessible in his glory, eternal because he is outside time, invisible because he cannot be grasped by our intelligence. Nevertheless, we can see the divine light even here on earth, because it has become accessible to us in Christ, and so Symeon perfects the twofold tradition of light and darkness in Byzantine mysticism through his Christ-centered spirituality, which he himself had most deeply lived before he taught it to others.

VIII THE EARLY MIDDLE AGES

a. The Monks

ST. BERNARD

In the West the period between St. Augustine and the age of St. Bernard is generally called the Dark Ages, and though there were some theologians of mark like St. Bede and Paschasius Radbert, and the Benedictine monks kept the spiritual life going, there were no great mystics in the troubled centuries of the emergence of the Germanic tribes. But early in the twelfth century, when the Christianization of Europe had been completed, a Cistercian monk gave Christian mysticism a new direction. Hitherto both Eastern and Western mysticism had been highly intellectual; and even the Christ-centered spirituality of Symeon the New Theologian had visualized principally the risen Christ, the glorified Lord of heaven and earth.

The young Christians of the medieval West, however, were not yet mature enough for mystical speculation on light and darkness, nor for the full realization of the divine transcendence. More, the mysticism of the Early Church had taken little account of the suffering humanity of Christ, and so something was missing from the fullness of the Gospel image of the Son of Man. It was this image that now moved into the center of Western mysticism, and its first outstanding exponent was Bernard, abbot of Clairvaux (1090–1153). Bernard was born at Fontaines near Dijon, of noble parentage. His family were good Christians, but wars and feuds were very much more in their line than prayer and sacrifice. Bernard, however, was drawn to religion from early childhood. When still a small boy, he fell asleep one Christmas night while waiting for the night office to begin. He had a dream vision, in which he saw Mary and the Holy Child, and he understood that this was the very moment of his birth. Though this can hardly be called an authentic mystical experience, it had a great influence on his later life, in which devotion to the humanity of Christ and to his Mother continued to play a central part. Bernard grew up into a very sensitive youth who found the educational methods of the contemporary schools irksome, though he was an excellent scholar. His mother died when he was sixteen, and as he had been very devoted to her, her death produced a severe emotional shock. Under its impact he turned to worldly distractions and felt for the first time the power of woman. As he was good-looking and very attractive he was soon surrounded by a crowd of companions bent on enjoying their youth. Bernard felt the pull of the senses and of worldly pleasures as keenly as any young man, perhaps even more so, for he soon realized that for him there was only one alternative: either to become completely submerged in the pursuit of pleasures and ambitions or to give himself wholly to God. It did not take him long to make his choice: he would become a monk, but not in a rich monastery like Cluny, but in the poorest he could find, which was Cîteaux, near Dijon, a recent foundation which had not prospered at all and whose abbot, St. Stephen Harding, was almost on the point of dissolving it.

But Bernard was not content to enter Cîteaux alone. He was determined to take most of his family and his friends with him. He set to work on his father and his brothers, on his cousins and his friends, with such extraordinary success that he gathered about thirty men, most of them young, formed them into a community and then, at the age of twenty-two, presented himself with them at Cîteaux. There he continued the austerities he had already begun in the world: he deprived himself of sleep and food to such an extent that his health was ruined for life. He closed his senses to his surroundings and became completely absorbed in God; solitude and contemplation were his only desires.

But this time of retirement did not last long. After three years at Cîteaux, Stephen Harding sent Bernard to make a new foundation at Clairvaux, and the young man of twenty-five became the abbot of a community many of whom were much older than he, both in years and in the religious life; he had not even been ordained priest. But miracles began already to be reported: when food and drink failed, the young abbot prayed and the necessaries arrived. Probably in the summer of 1115 Bernard went to Châlons to be ordained by its bishop, the learned William of Champeaux, who became his close friend. After his return to Clairvaux, Bernard became gravely ill, and when William came to visit him he ordered him to relinquish his monastic duties for the time being, to retire to a cottage near the abbey and there to be nursed by a kind of doctor, who, however, was unfortunately extremely ignorant and made matters worse rather than better. Bernard submitted to this regime, which nevertheless left him free to continue his life of contemplation which was to prepare him for the tremendous activities which were in store for him. To detail them all would almost require a volume by itself. Suffice it to say that, apart from his extremely effective preaching to his monks, he soon was called out of his monastery again and again: he made sixty-three new foundations, he settled many political feuds, attended various synods and diets, carried on a tremendous correspondence, preached the Second Crusade, reformed many religious houses belonging to other orders and acted as adviser to popes, kings, and princes. It seems almost incredible that this frail man, whose health was broken, should have traveled so much and got through such a gigantic amount of work while all the time continuing his intense mystical life; but just this life was probably the source from which flowed his superhuman strength. Wherever he went the people gathered round him, venerating him as a saint and miracle worker, and he was not afraid to oppose even the Emperor Lothar himself when it was a question of defending the rights of the Church. It is a new type of mystic that he represents; no longer a Desert Father or even the bishop of a small Eastern diocese like Gregory of Nyssa, but a man of action and exceptional drive, whose voice made itself heard throughout Europe.

Besides this tremendous activity Bernard has fortunately left a volume of religious writing that allows us a profound insight into his mystical life and teaching. For Bernard, too, the possibility of the mystical life is based on the divine image and likeness, in which man was made. This image consists in free will, which man retained even after the Fall, while the likeness, which he distinguishes from the image, rests on two other freedoms, freedom from sin and freedom from suffering; these latter two were lost through original sin, so that man was exiled into the region of "unlikeness." Since he could not find his way back from his exile by his own power, Christ opened up this way for him and is at the same time the example we must follow if we would leave the region of unlikeness for the likeness which is the kingdom of God. Now the Christ St. Bernard tells us to follow is no longer the exalted Christ of the Fathers, but the helpless Child and the Man of Sorrows. In his sermons in praise of the Virgin he urges his hearers to strive to become like the little One in the manger, "that the great God may not have become a little man without cause." The very smallness of the Christ Child should teach men humility, and his obedience to his Mother should be the pattern of their obedience.

In his sermons on the Canticle, which contains his most exalted mystical teaching, Bernard makes the physical sufferings and the wounds of Christ a center of devotion in a way unknown in the age of the Fathers and in the Eastern Church. For him both the Church and the individual soul dwell "with perfect devotion in the wounds of Christ, remaining in them in permanent meditation." There only does man find security and rest: "The nail calls, the wound calls that truly God has reconciled the world to himself in Christ. The iron has penetrated his soul and approached his heart, that he may thoroughly know to have compassion on my infirmities. The secret of the heart is revealed through the openings of the body; there is made manifest the great mystery of his mercy." Here we are at the beginnings of the devotion to the Sacred Heart which springs from the mystical contemplation of the wounds of Christ crucified, which became the center of medieval mysticism. The manhood of Christ is expressed also in the name Jesus, which for Bernard is both the light and the food of his soul. For nothing can so restore the tired senses and invigorate the virtues as the name of Jesus: "Every food of the soul is dry unless it is soaked in this oil . . . Whenever I mention the Man Jesus, I see him meek and humble of heart . . . merciful and full of all goodness and holiness, who is also himself almighty God who heals me by his example and strengthens me by his help. All this I hear together when I hear the name of Jesus."

Nevertheless, this devotion to the humanity of Jesus is only a station on the mystical way, it is not its ultimate goal. For medieval mysticism goes through Christ the man to Christ the God. The childhood and the sufferings of Christ are the means by which the senses of "carnal man" are drawn away from the attractions of this earth, to the love of Jesus: but this love must become rational and finally spiritual, following the threefold division of the mystical way. Bernard expresses this also in another way under the image of three kisses. The first is the kiss of the feet, which is that of the penitents, the second is the kiss of the hands, which belongs to those who have already brought forth worthy fruits of repentance, and the third is the kiss of the mouth. This kiss signifies the most intimate union between Christ and the soul: "It is nothing other than to receive the infusion of the Holy Spirit," an infusion which is not simply the sacramental infusion in baptism and confirmation, but a special revelation of the Spirit which "not only enlightens unto knowledge, but inflames unto love," producing the full flowering of the mystical life. The mystical union this "kiss" produces is not a unity of substance—Bernard carefully guards against any danger of a pantheistic interpretation; it is a "communion of wills and an agreement in charity."

In one of his later homilies on the Canticle, Bernard describes his own mystical experiences very lucidly: "I confess that to me, too, the Word has come . . . and that several times. But though he entered frequently into me, I did not feel it when he entered. I felt he was there, I remember that he has been there, sometimes I also felt it before he entered, but his actual entry I have never felt, nor his withdrawal . . . Perhaps he did not enter at all, because he did not come from outside . . . Therefore you ask . . . whence I knew him to be there? He is living and effective: as soon as he came into me he roused my sleeping soul; he moved and softened and wounded my heart . . . When therefore the Word-Spouse sometimes thus entered into me, he never made his entry known by any signs, neither by a sound nor by a form nor by a perceptive entry . . . I knew his presence solely by the movement of my heart, and by the flight of the vices; from the renewal and reformation of my mind, that is of my inner man, I did somehow perceive his beauty."

In this description of the mystical union there is no question of ecstasy or of any extraordinary phenomena such as visions, though St. Bernard had also had these. At time of the experience just described he was obviously accustomed to the divine visits, this is why they were so gentle and without imaginative accessories. At other times he calls such divine visitations visions, though not in the ordinary sense. For imaginary visions, which he also had in the earlier stages of his mystical life and calls "Certain imaginery likenesses of inferior things (that is not of God himself) divinely infused and conveniently adapted to the senses" he believes to be caused by angelic activity, not by God himself; he therefore rejects them, saying that he does not accept "visions and dreams, I do not want figures and dark riddles; I reject also angelic forms." The mystical experience he desires is of a far higher order, it is the visit of the divine Bridegroom himself, "but O, how rare is the hour and how brief its stay." The vision that is given in such sublime moments "terrifies not, it soothes; it excites no restless curiosity but it calms, nor does it fatigue the senses but tranquillizes them. The tranquil God tranquillizes all things, and to behold him is to rest."

To behold God does not, of course, mean to see the divine Essence, which is impossible; it means this imperceptible entry of God into the soul described before, which is peace and tranquillity itself and brings with it a power of moral and spiritual renewal transcending all human and angelic agencies. This mystical union which St. Bernard describes and has himself experienced is without sensational phenomena, a perfect rest and repose in God that gently invades the soul and gives it new vigor. It is comparatively brief and rare, as it necessarily must be in an active life such as Bernard had to lead. But it is all the more profound and authentic, devoid of all those accretions which are popularly supposed to be of the very essence of the mystical life, but which are only the by-products of its lower stages. The way to this sublime union is through the humanity of Christ, through his humiliations and sufferings, the goal is the peaceful union with the God who transcends all thought and imagination.

WILLIAM OF SAINT-THIERRY

William of Saint-Thierry (c. 1085–1148) was an intimate friend of St. Bernard. He was a native of Liège, of noble parentage, but left his home at an early age to study, probably at Laon. He later entered a monastery in Rheims, and in 1119 he was elected abbot of Saint-Thierry, near the same city. In contrast to St. Bernard, William was a philosopher and a scholar who was well acquainted with some of the Greek Fathers, especially Origen, whom he read in the ninth-century Latin translation of Scotus Erigena. But he was also a contemplative who desired above all tranquillity in order to draw nearer to God, as is already clear from his treatise *On Contemplation*, written about 1119, a tendency which increased under the influence of his friend of Clairvaux, whom William wished to join. Finally in 1135, he resigned his office and entered the Cistercian monastery of Signy where he remained until his death. There he wrote an

exposition of the *Songs of Songs*, which had been suggested by
St. Bernard, but which is very different from the latter's work
on the same subject, and also the so-called *Golden Letter* to the
Brothers of the Mount of God on the eremitical life.

Like St. Bernard and the Fathers before him, William centers
the mystical life in the image of God in which man was made,
but in his view this image does not consist in man's free will, but
in his rational nature, through which he can know God. William
follows the threefold way of perfection. Its first stage is what
modern spiritual writers call sensible devotion, in which the humanity of Christ plays a central part. But William lays much less
stress on it than St. Bernard, he is much more Patristic, much
less medieval in his lack of emphasis on the wounds and the
blood of Christ. He only touches on devotion to the man Jesus
and immediately quotes John 16:7, "It is expedient for you that
I go. For if I go not the Paraclete will not come to you." The
humanity of Jesus is no more than a stepping-stone that is meant
to lead to the second stage of the spiritual life, which he describes as the prayer of the "rational" man. This means that the
imagery on which prayer had so far been nourished is abandoned, and the Holy Spirit comes to the aid of man to renew
in him the divine image and to lead him to a higher knowledge
of God. At this stage man desires to know God as far as is permitted to him, and this is possible because God can at times
impress a similitude of himself in the soul, which nevertheless
is without any imaginative representation. It goes without saying that this similitude is still very far from the divine reality;
it is not God as he is in himself, but it is God within the
creature; but this mystically experienced presence produces a
great sweetness which enriches and illuminates the soul.

The third and final stage is the prayer of the spiritual man. In
its fullness it is reserved for eternity, but it has its beginnings in
the mystical life on earth. This life is not constant, and often
the contemplative will have to revert to the former stage; on the
other hand, there will often be moments when he will suddenly
be lovingly drawn to God, and even "if imaginations occur, they

will serve and help rather than hinder." They are a help for the body in which the mystic still lives, and will draw him through imaginary representation towards divine truth itself.

William himself had evidently experienced the mystical union, for he not only described it in a very personal way but also composed an impassioned prayer for the mystical coming of the Holy Spirit into his soul. "Come, O come," he prays, "in the abundance of your blessings into me, your servant, into my heart which is your dwelling place . . . now, as your science testifies in my conscience, I love only you with a unique love . . . And when you have come into your poor servant in the riches of your fullness and the delights of your goodness, and when you have begun to show him by a certain experience in his consciousness how truly you are a God of love and how God and his love are one . . . then your son's sacrifice of praise in your Canticle will honour you."

This shows clearly that William meant to express in his interpretation of the Canticle his own mystical experience, which was fundamentally trinitarian and in which the Holy Spirit played a decisive part. He writes that sometimes, when grace abounds, he arrives at a certain and manifest experience of something of God; then "suddenly, in quite a new way, becomes tangible to the senses of enlightened love what surpasses all hope of the body's senses and can never be thought by reason or understood by the intellect except by the intellect of enlightened love." For William the mystical experience has a twofold aspect: it is intellectual, but it is also an experience of love. Indeed, it can be genuinely mystical only if intellectual illumination and love are both present. But this intellectual illumination is of a higher order than ordinary human understanding. This is how William interprets the "Voice of my Beloved" (Canticle 2:8): "Voice is better than word, because there is no distinction of syllables nor is it formed by the tongue, but it comes into being by a pure affect in the enlightened intellect, while all the senses of the body and the reason are inactive or asleep; and this whole work

is accomplished by the Holy Spirit operating in the sense of love
. . . This voice can be heard only in the secret of silence, it
operates only in a pure heart." When this voice sounds in the
Bride-soul, "The Word of God utters himself and his Father
in the Spirit of his mouth so that the conscience of the loving
soul, completely penetrated by the fullness of illuminating grace,
can hardly express the flame of her heart in these few words:
The Voice of my beloved." The trinitarian life itself has entered
the mystic and overwhelmed him; his senses and understanding
are at rest, God alone works in him and enlightens him in love
in a way that surpasses all understanding. The mystical knowledge that a man receives in such an ecstasy is called wisdom
and nourishes love, it is not acquired by effort, but by enjoyment and is open even to the simple children of God who seek
him in the simplicity of their heart. These moments of mystical
enjoyment and illumination are brief, but they are so rich in
effects that the man who experiences them seems to himself to
be separated from the beatific vision of heaven only by the impediment of his mortality.

b. The Victorines

The mystical life flowered not only among the sons of St. Ben-
edict but also among the Augustinian Canons, notably those of
the monastery of St. Victor near Paris, which had been founded
by Bernard's friend William of Champeaux. Hugh of St. Victor
(d. 1142) was its foremost theologian, whose influence was very
great and who combined profound theological learning with authentic mystical experience. Practically nothing is known of his
life, even the country of his birth is disputed, being variously
given as Saxony, Lorraine, and the Low Countries. All that can
be definitely said of him is that he was a famous teacher, copies
of whose writings were in great demand throughout Europe. For
his mystical doctrine his great work on the sacraments is important as a foundation, while *The Moral and Mystical Ark of Noah,
On the Vanity of the World, The Soul's Betrothal Gift*, the

treatise on contemplation and others contain more specialized
discussions of the ascetical and mystical life.

The image of God in man, so Hugh teaches in his work on the
sacraments, enables the rational creature to know his creator; and
this image is trinitarian. Hugh finds it in the created trinity of
mind, wisdom, and love, corresponding to the three stages of
the mystical way. Further, the rational soul is furnished with a
twofold sense; the one grasps what is visible through the flesh,
the other through reason. For the age of the Schoolmen is just
beginning, and reason is being given an essential part in the
spiritual life. Nevertheless, reason is not the highest faculty of
man. Beyond the eye of the body and the eye of reason there is a
third eye—corresponding to the "spiritual sense" first taught by
Origen—which sees God within the soul, and this is the "eye of
contemplation." Both the eye of reason and the eye of contemplation were clouded over through the Fall, but were restored
through the Redemption of Christ, so that now there is faith,
through which those things that are not seen may be believed.

Faith, too, may be threefold. In the first category are those
who simply believe by piety without understanding what they
believe; then there are those who approve by reason what they
believe by faith; and finally there are the pure of heart who already begin to experience what they believe by faith—in other
words the contemplatives. Though perfect contemplation is reserved for the next life—and Hugh is very firm on this—yet
through faith man begins to see God in some dark manner already here on earth, and this faith will increase through an increase of knowledge, while knowledge again inflames love. And
so, as Hugh says in *Noah's Ark*, we seek God by desire, we find
him by knowledge, and we touch him by taste—touching and
tasting being the most mystical of the spiritual senses. For God
dwells in the human heart in two ways, by knowledge and by
love. This knowledge is the knowledge of faith, and it is essential
to love, for we cannot love what we do not know; on the other
hand, no one can know God without loving him. In the mystic
this love becomes so deep that it makes a wound, as Hugh says

in his *Praise of Charity*, which he who has received it desires to go ever deeper. The power of this love is so great that it often makes the mystic forget all else; it fills the heart to overflowing with interior sweetness, so that it scorns all external sufferings. For when the soul is "raised to a certain peak of contemplation, it sees as from a distance a new country of light, which it cannot remember having ever seen before"; this country exercises such attraction that the man who has once caught a glimpse of it no longer desires earthly things, but becomes more and more spiritual until he almost escapes all human sight and understanding, "glorying interiorly in the hidden face of the Lord." This face is hidden, because Hugh follows the mystic tradition that describes the divine experience as surpassing all understanding. We cannot know God directly, but we taste him by charity and thus know him by taste. For he dwells in our heart, and therefore Hugh calls on his disciples to enlarge their heart, "for the Lord is great; he cannot dwell in a narrow space. Enlarge your heart, therefore, so that you may contain him whom even the whole universe cannot contain. Enlarge your heart, so that you may be worthy to receive God as your guest, not for one night only, but to have him dwell in it for ever." Because God is present in the depths of the human being, a man must enter deeply into himself; for by penetrating into his depths he will transcend his own self and ascend to God—another form of the mystical paradox. The mystical union with the transcendent God takes place in the depths of the soul, that mysterious region which the Greek Fathers called the *Hegemonikon*, and which Hugh, following St. Augustine and Gregory, calls the *acies mentis*, the edge or the eye of the spirit.

Hugh writes only of the union of the human spirit with his Maker; he takes no notice of visions and other phenomena. It was left to his disciple Richard to treat the mystical life in greater detail.

We know hardly more of Richard's life (d. 1173) than of Hugh's. He was a Scot, who joined St. Victor, by then famous for its intellectual and spiritual standards, probably while still quite young, either shortly before or immediately after Hugh's death. He was subprior in 1159 and became prior in 1162, retaining this office till his death. He first studied philosophy and later devoted himself particularly to the spiritual life and the study of mysticism. His main works dealing with this subject are *Benjamin Minor*, treating of the first stages of the spiritual life, and *Benjamin Major*, expounding the mystical life proper. The titles refer to the Vulgate translation of Psalm 67:28 (68:27): "There is Benjamin a youth, in ecstasy of mind," a mistranslation of the Hebrew "in command of them," or "leading them." Further, Benjamin was the child of Rachel, who from Patristic times had symbolized the contemplative life as opposed to Leah, representing the active life, a symbolism Richard uses throughout both works.

Richard distinguishes three activities of the mind: Thinking (*cogitatio*), meditation, and contemplation. Of these thinking is the lowest, indeed, Richard actually seems to despise it, for he characterizes it as undisciplined, wandering about aimlessly regardless of where it may lead. Meditation, on the other hand, is disciplined, requires sustained mental effort and keeps to its object. Contemplation is the highest of the three, soaring up and capable of hovering in sublime spheres. Thinking, in Victor's terminology, belongs to the imagination, meditation to reason, and contemplation to the intelligence. Of these contemplation is closely allied to the mystical life. The spiritual life proper starts when man has done penance for his sins and begins to be visited by God, who softens the heart by his presence and gives it great joy, a state which today is called the "prayer of affection." In this state the imagination still has a part, helping reason to represent to itself the subjects on which it wishes to meditate. So Richard advises a man at this stage to imagine what he cannot yet perceive by reasoning, for Scripture itself uses this method, describing invisible things by visible imagery, promising a land flowing with milk and honey or expressing heavenly joys by earthly song. When a man has ascended to contemplation, however, the imagination no longer has a part in his spiritual life. Following Hugh, Richard, too, sees contemplation as an entering into one's heart, where a man will taste a hidden manna. For taste, he says, is better than sight; through it we assimilate that which is tasted and are made one with it. For God, Richard says, "is seen in one way by faith, in another he is seen by reason, and in a third, different way he is discerned by contemplation," the first way being below, the third above reason. The first and second ways are accessible to man's own powers, the third is God's free gift, though no one receives it without making a tremendous effort. For contemplation will lead directly to ecstasy, which, if it occurs frequently, gives a foretaste of eternal life.

Richard's teaching on ecstasy is very rich and detailed. According to him it has three causes: intense devotion, wonder, and excess of joy, through all of which the human mind is raised above itself into a state where all its powers are, as it were, asleep, because it is completely engrossed in the divine things which it is shown. Richard, too, compares this with Moses entering into the divine cloud, but unlike Gregory of Nyssa (whose life of Moses he most probably did not know), he does not speak of divine darkness, but of the divine light, the cloud representing not God, but the human concerns which are concealed from man through the abundance of the divine light. The first mode of ecstasy may be caused either by burning devotion alone or by devotion accompanied by a divine vision, which, Richard says, strengthens the ecstatic contemplation. Visions play an even greater part in the second mode of ecstasy, because this is often caused by them. The newness and unexpectedness of a vision causes the mind to wonder and thus to be raised above itself into an ecstasy which increases its knowledge. This vision need not be imaginary, that is dealing with physically perceptible objects, but may often be purely intellectual and formless; indeed, Richard seems to hold—against St. Paul, St. Augustine and the whole Byzantine tradition—that contemplation means "seeing the truth in its purity, without any hindrance or veils." For in this ecstatic wonder the human intelligence ceases to be human, and he applies to mystical contemplation here on earth St. Paul's description of the Christian's heavenly state, when "beholding the glory of the Lord we are changed into the same image from glory to glory" (II Corinthians 3:18), with the sole difference that here on earth this state is transitory.

Whereas in the forms of ecstasy produced by devotion and wonder the intelligence plays its part, the third, caused by the intensity of joy, is brought about rather by an abundance of feeling. The divine visit causes the soul to overflow with delight, and the intensity of this supernatural happiness takes it out of itself into the divine sphere. Though it would gladly experience this joy over and over again, it completely depends on the will of God, and a man is often left for long periods without it. Then, Richard advises, he should go back to meditation, he should recall former graces, praise God with great devotion and thus, as far as in him lies, open the way for another divine visitation.

Though Richard greatly encourages his readers to desire mystical experiences, he advises them also not to receive them uncritically. Referring to the mountain of the Transfiguration he tells them not to believe that they have seen Christ there unless Moses and Elijah, that is to say the authority of Scripture, are present too. "I suspect all truth," he writes, "that is not confirmed by the authority of Scripture, nor do I accept the glorified Christ unless Moses and Elijah stand near him." He is quite prepared to accept Christ in the valley or halfway up the mountain, that means in the earlier stages of the spiritual life, which is concerned with external matters of one's own inner life; but when it comes to ecstatic experiences and what is now called "private revelations," they must be confirmed by Moses and Elijah, representing the authority of Scripture and the Church.

Richard is well aware that the heights of the mystical life cannot be reached without trials and temptations, though he lays less stress on them than the Desert Fathers before and St. John of the Cross after him. God allows them, so that a man may not become too sure of himself and thus attribute to his own merit what is wholly due to divine grace.

The mystical life, however, does not end with ecstasy. Richard divides the life of divine love into four degrees. Beyond the three degrees of recollection, contemplation and ecstasy there is a fourth, when the soul, having reached God, descends from the heights through compassion for its neighbor and gives itself to the apostolate and works of mercy. The Desert Fathers regarded such activities as a temptation; Richard, and with him all the later mystics of the West considered this the fourth and highest stage of the mystical life, when the soul in conformed to the humility of Christ, imitating his self-emptying in the Incarnation. "In the third degree," Richard writes, "the soul is so to speak put to death, in the fourth it is raised in Christ." Here its great pattern is St. Paul, who, though longing to die in order to be with Christ, nevertheless willingly continued to live because his presence was still needed by the churches he had founded (cf. Philippians 1:21–25). In this fourth and most sublime degree man is rendered in some way immortal and impassible, because he is already inseparably united to Christ and no longer cast down by sufferings, but rather rejoices in them. This is the mystical love described by St. Paul in I Corinthians 13, a superhuman charity that flows out to all men because it is wholly anchored in God. Later mystics have called this the mystical marriage or the transforming union. Hugh likens it to the Transfiguration and the Resurrection.

c. The Nuns

Since the martyr mystics of the Early Church, women have not been mentioned in this book. This does not mean that there necessarily cannot have been any, but simply that we have no records of them. The Desert Fathers generally regarded women as temptresses and would have nothing to do with them; the great theologians such as Gregory of Nyssa and Augustine were interested in mystical theology but much less in mystical phenomena, and women have at all times supplied the phenomena rather than their interpretation. Thus there are no accounts of women mystics until we come to the Middle Ages, when such phenomena came to be greatly appreciated and nuns who had such experiences were encouraged by their confessors to write them down or dictate them.

HILDEGARD OF BINGEN

Such was the case of Hildegard of Bingen (1098–1179). She belonged to a noble family of the Rhineland and, having had strange visionary experiences from the age of three, was sent to be brought up by a famous anchoress, Jutta, who had gathered a community around her which followed the Benedictine Rule. About 1116 Hildegard was clothed as a nun and in 1136 she succeeded Jutta as abbess. Her visions continued all the time, and about 1141 she wrote to St. Bernard to consult him on the subject. The saint replied in very guarded terms; chiefly inculcating the practice of the Christian virtues which is the solid foundation of the spiritual life for everyone, whether favored with visions and other extraordinary phenomena or not. Soon afterwards she dictated an account of her experiences under the title *Scivias* (*Know the Ways*). Between 1147 and 1152 she transferred her growing community to a large new convent at Rupertsberg near Bingen, from where she traveled throughout the Rhineland and also founded another Benedictine house near Rüdesheim.

Despite the cautious attitude of St. Bernard, Hildegard's fame as a visionary and prophetess had quickly spread throughout Christendom and she counted among her correspondents not only many prelates and princes, but even the German emperor, Frederick Barbarossa himself, whom she vigorously admonished to do penance and to mend his life. Her revelations were approved by three popes, Eugenius III, Anastasius IV, and Hadrian IV, as well as by the Council of Treves. Hildegard was never formally canonized, but the Roman Martyrology has listed her as a saint from the fifteenth century.

Hildegard's *Scivias* is a very odd work, a peculiar mixture of the scientific ideas of her own age with profound spiritual insights, which raises a difficulty also present in the teachings of many other later mystics such as Catherine of Siena and Margaret Mary. This problem is the mixture of divine and human elements in mystical experiences, which has little importance where it is only a question of the mystic's personal union with God, but which comes to the fore when he or she claims to have received particular revelations during these experiences, which he believes ought to be made public. For many of these revelations, especially in Hildegard's case, simply reflect the erroneous ideas of her time, which she nevertheless attributes to direct divine revelation. On the other hand, her mystical teaching is full of wisdom and a deep understanding of divine things. How is such a discrepancy to be explained? In his widely read work on *The Graces of Interior Prayer*, Père Poulain tries to solve the problem by the hypothesis that God might in some way supernaturally instruct a person in the knowledge of the day, even if this is erroneous, "whilst giving in some way a general warning that he does not guarantee the contents of the whole and that it is, therefore, to be accepted only at the receiver's risk." But this explanation is rather over-subtle, apart from trying to absolve Hildegard from error at the expense of the veracity of God himself. Hence Poulain's hypothesis is no longer widely accepted. A much simpler explanation is this, that a mystic is as subject to error as any other human being and can therefore never distinguish with certainty what is direct divine inspiration and what is his own—conscious, or more often subconscious—contribution to it. Moreover, even if the revelation itself is of divine origin, there is still the possibility of an erroneous interpretation by the mystic himself. For this reason those great mystics who were at the same time also great theologians and experienced psychologists like St. Augustine, St. Bernard, and St. John of the Cross never paid much attention to all these phenomena which are really only on the periphery of the mystical life, whose center is the intimate union between God and man. But those mystics less well versed in theology and the psychological possibilities of error—and most of the women mystics of the Church, though by no means only the women, belong to this category—would be unable to distinguish between the divine elements of their experiences and their human accompaniments; hence the caution with which their accounts should be approached, however great their subjective veracity and their sanctity. For this reason we will give a brief account only of Hildegard's very impressive spiritual teaching, disregarding her sometimes quite fantastic descriptions of her visions.

One of the most striking features in Hildegard's work is the almost complete absence of emotion, so prominent in the writings of most later women mystics like St. Gertrude and St. Teresa. There are no descriptions of loving conversations between Christ and the mystic; instead, Hildegard's mind is dominated by the knowledge that man is a "rational animal," that the intellect is God's highest gift to him. In the midst of her visionary world of allegorical beings and strange ideas about the cosmos she rings the changes on the importance of the rational element: "But you, O man, say, I cannot do good. But I say you can. You ask: how? I answer: By intellect and reason." Of course she does not mean that he can do so without divine assistance; but she explains that God has constituted man in such a way that he can know what is good and evil through his divinely given reason.

Thus a man cannot only resist evil but also practice asceticism, mortifying his desires for comfort and an easy life. She calls asceticism the "mother of virtue" and places it at the beginning of the mystical way, which she describes very beautifully in the fourth vision of the *Scivias*. The soul, seeking her lost home, asks: "Where am I, a wanderer?" and receives the answer: "In the shadow of death." The dialogue continues: "In what way do I walk? In the way of error. What consolation do I have? The comfort of a wanderer." Then she hears from far away the voice of Sion her mother, the call to a life of prayer. She follows the voice, but the way to where it comes from is so hard that she nearly gives up the venture. Then the mother tells her that God has given her wings to fly—the ancient metaphor describing the ease of contemplation as opposed to the early stages of laborious meditation. So the soul takes courage and receives new strength through contemplation, which leads her to a "tabernacle," where she is protected from the arrows of her enemies. By this is meant a deeper region of the soul, opened up by contemplation. Here outward temptations cannot follow her; but the devil now uses subtler weapons, firing her thirst for knowledge and her ambition. When the soul has overcome these attacks she enters on a still higher way, which begins with very painful purifications which resemble the "Night of the Spirit" later described in such detail by St. John of the Cross. The soul now wishes to ascend beyond her own intellect into the divine sphere "and to begin what I cannot accomplish. But when I attempt this a great sorrow comes over me, so that I perform no work in high sanctity nor in the fulness of good will, but feel nothing within myself but the unrest of doubt and despair. Wherefore also this iniquity attacks me that all happiness, all good both in man and God becomes wearisome and distasteful to me." It is a condition well known to the mystics, which the Greek Fathers used to call *akedia* (accidie) —the listlessness of the contemplative who is becoming hateful to himself and who feels himself abandoned by God so that he cannot find consolation anywhere. Hildegard realizes that this intense purification is necessary to men so that they may learn true humility and thus bring forth much fruit. For humility, she says, is to charity what the body is to the soul, they can never be separated in this life.

This humility, produced by the purifications of the dark night, was particularly necessary to her, because she lived in a world of visions. According to her own description these took two forms. One she calls "the shadow of the living light," far brighter than a cloud through which the sun is shining, which, she says, was always present in her soul. This, she writes, "has neither height nor length nor breadth . . . And just as sun, moon and stars appear in the water, so I see scriptures and sermons, virtues, and certain deeds of men reflected in it. And whatever I see or learn in that vision I remember for a long time . . . but what I do not see in this way, that I know not, for I am, as it were, illiterate." This is very difficult to interpret, for on the face of it it would seem that Hildegard thought all her knowledge came to her in vision, for she affirms that whatever she does not see in it she does not know—an affirmation which flatly contradicts her stress on the human intellect. But perhaps just this offers an explanation. That she calls herself illiterate probably means no more than that she did not know Latin well enough to read and write it easily (she dictated her works to an amanuensis who either translated them from the vernacular or improved the Latin in which she tried to express herself). It is hardly possible to believe that her mind was a complete blank unless divinely illuminated, and she herself constantly asserts that God has given reason to man to make decisions. So I would suggest that what she means by this permanent vision is really the light of reason, but that she describes it in the rather abstruse language that was natural to her. We shall find something similar in St. Catherine of Siena, and perhaps this attitude of these women mystics to their own minds was no more than a kind of humility that would not attribute anything to their own intellectual efforts, especially in view of St. Paul's injunction that women ought not to teach in the Church. If a woman wanted a hearing in those days, she had to attribute whatever she had to say to private revelations, which she probably did in complete good faith, as it is not easy for a mystic to distinguish between her own thoughts and infused mystical knowledge.

For Hildegard also tells us that she had a different kind of vision, which she described as the "living light." This light, she tells us, she sees "in the ordinary light," and while she sees it, "all sadness and sorrow leave my memory, so that I feel like a young girl and not like an eldery woman." This is obviously the state in which she received genuine mystical experiences, one of which she described as "a mystic and wondrous vision, so that all my inner parts were shaken, and the sensibility of my body was extinguished; my consciousness was turned into another mode as if I knew not myself." This is a description of mystical ecstasy, in which she received visions which were strongly influenced by the prophetic visions of the Old Testament and by those of the Apocalypse. In these she saw angels and rivers, anti-Christ and the Woman, and in her interpretation of them is enshrined pure Christian doctrine on a great variety of subjects.

MECHTHILD OF MAGDEBURG

A whole century lies between Hildegard of Bingen and Mechthild of Magdeburg; a century which saw the foundation of the Mendicant Orders and, in the secular sphere, the development of courtly love and *Minnesang*, the poetry expressing this love. The mystic and visionary of Magdeburg (1210–97) lived throughout this extraordinary century, but very little is known about her long life, of which we just catch a glimpse here and there from her own writings. She was a native of the archdiocese of Magdeburg and had her first spiritual experience at the age of twelve. She was then more and more drawn to a dedicated life, and in 1233 she left her family and entered a *béguinage* at Magdeburg. The Béguines had been founded in the twelfth century by a priest of Liège, Lambert le Bégue (i.e. the Stammerer); they lived in community, devoting themselves to the care of the poor and the sick, but taking no vows and being allowed private property. The Béguines of Magdeburg had close spiritual relations with the Dominicans. Mechthild later entered a Cistercian convent in the same city and seems even to have become its abbess. She was, however, very critical of anyone who did not come up to her ideals of perfection; besides, her teaching, which, like Hildegard, she claimed to have received directly from God, contained some unorthodox ideas. She was therefore at one time excommunicated and even forbidden to take part in the monastic offices. Since she also had difficulties with her own nuns she finally left Magdeburg and entered the Cistercian convent of Helfta in Thuringia, then governed by the famous abbess Gertrude (the subject of the following section), where she remained till her death.

The collection of Mechthild's teaching and experiences, called *The Flowing Light of the Godhead*, is really a compendium of medieval mystical piety with all its glories and all its short-comings. Few books reflect so faithfully the highly charged spiritual atmosphere in which these nuns were living, deeply influenced by paintings and sermons on hell, purgatory and heaven, as well as by the ideas of courtly love, *minne*, translated into religious terms. Nevertheless, in her teaching there is a deep cleavage between the world and the spiritual life, between body and soul. Mechthild sees the body as the enemy of the soul in much the same way as the Desert Fathers; she calls it a pack horse whose bridle is unworthiness and which feeds on scorn and contempt. Hence the joys of marriage are for her something that detracts from the joys of heaven—married couples will have less of the latter because they had the former. On the other hand, Christ is a noble youth, "of ineffable beauty," followed by maidens in great state, like an earthly prince, but walking with them "in heavenly places." Her love for him is expressed in terms of the minnesingers: she can never turn from love, but must be imprisoned by it and dwell wherever love dwells. The frequent dialogues between Christ and her soul are not always without an erotic flavor; she speaks of him taking her into his divine arms, and "Oh, how she was then kissed!" She complains of his absence like a young girl of the absence of her lover—she would rather go down to hell than endure his absence for another week. God, the Father, or Christ (it is not always quite clear of whom she means to speak), in his turn, does not fail to compliment her very frequently—a feature of the mystical life of many women. The "all-glorious God" calls her his dove and tells her that her voice sounds like music in his ears, she is his queen and she alone is a greater delight to him than all else. He comforts her when she is excommunicated and complains that she cannot even hear Mass. Then God tells her that she is his desire, that she is a cooling presence to his breast and a caress to his mouth—accents which we have not met before and which show the powerful influence of the love poetry of the time as well as the way a woman may compensate psychologically for the spiritual deprivations which her excommunication inflicted on her.

For Mechthild's was a much more emotional nature than Hildegard's, and the stress the contemporary preaching of the Mendicant Orders laid on Christ's humanity and its sufferings also expressed itself in her mystical experiences. When advising an acquaintance how to turn away from the world, she suggests that he should look on the blood-stained body of the crucified Lord, describing how the nails had been hammered through his hands and feet and how the thorns had pierced his head. In another passage she affirms that his wounds will remain open till the Last Judgment, and she speaks about kissing his wounds and the rose-colored scars on his feet. Thus the mystical experience now becomes much more sensuous, and though Mechthild's mysticism is, as we shall see, also trinitarian, the humanity of Christ plays a much more essential part in it than in the Fathers or even St. Bernard. Hence it is not surprising that in Mechthild we find also a fairly developed mysticism of the Sacred Heart. Describing the union between her and God (or Christ) she writes that he places her soul into his burning heart so that both become one as water is lost in wine. In another passage Jesus asks her to place her heart's desire in his own divine heart, and we are nearest to the modern devotion when she addresses St. John the Evangelist and tells him that she has reposed with him on the heart of Jesus, where she has seen such wonderful things that she has been thrown into ecstasy.

For in ecstasy the highest mysteries are experienced. Mechthild describes this state as a sweet sleep, in which the soul is almost separated from the body. It loses contact with the world and forgets everything in its flight. Nevertheless when this state is at its most sublime the soul must leave it and descend once more into the body to carry on her earthly tasks. Elsewhere Mechthild speaks of an effortless rapture by which she finds herself in the Holy Trinity like a child under its mother's mantle. She often speaks of this union with the Holy Trinity, in which she feels herself to be "engulfed" or "immersed like a fish in the sea." She also feels the power of the Holy Trinity flow through her soul and body, giving her true wisdom, and again she sees a prayer "written in the Holy Trinity" and one night she saw it "in the heights" together with the soul of Christ.

Mechthild does not say in what way she "saw" the Holy Trinity. Taken at their face value these "visions" of the Trinity itself would have to be intellectual visions, the very highest mystical experiences there are which only come to the mystic at the summit of his mystical life. What makes one somewhat doubtful about Mechthild's visions is that she claims to have seen a prayer written in the Trinity and also that the Trinity speaks to her and that elsewhere she sees four rays of light going forth from it. All this seems to point rather to an imaginary vision in which she visualizes the Trinity under some symbols.

This would be in keeping with Mechthild's other visions, which are invariably highly imaginative and in perfect accord with the teaching and the artistic expressions of her time. She sees souls in purgatory blackened, burned, and evil-smelling, and her visions of hell almost defy description, being filled with horrible torments, sinners within the belly of the devil, gluttons eating red-hot stones and drinking sulphur, thieves hanging by their heels, and usurers being constantly gnawed by demons. Heaven, on the other hand, is conceived as the brilliant court of an emperor where God himself meets the blessed and crowns them with various crowns according to their status. The life of Mary and the Child Jesus, too, she sees in terms of medieval art and legend: the birth of the Child happened without Mary being actually aware of it; he simply passed through her and she suddenly found him on her lap; when the visionary asks her where Joseph is Mary tells her that he has gone into the town to buy fish and bread, while Satan sits in hell gnashing his teeth.

Some of Mechthild's visions were censured by the Church authorities, especially a very elaborate one in which she saw John the Baptist saying Mass, which was criticized because the saint had not been a priest and therefore could not say Mass. Mechthild replied, not without reason, that these things could not be taken literally; the mystical reality she had experienced was as different from her description of it as candlelight from sunlight, but if it had to be described this could only be done in human words and imagery. Then she in her turn attacks her critics, calling them blind teachers and telling them that they would have to suffer for their lies and hatred.

For Mechthild, though she often humbly calls herself a "poor maiden," had a fairly violent temper and reacted strongly against criticism. At one time she was told that her book ought to be burned, but God assured her that this could not be, because the book was his, the words had come into her soul from his own divine mouth. She ends with a prayer to preserve it from the eyes of the deceivers who come from the underworld, not from heaven, and who are full of hatred and spiritual pride. She reiterates her conviction of the divine origin of her book in another section, again affirming that it was written "from God's heart and mouth" and did not have a human origin.

That the book was attacked is not surprising, for apart from some strange theological opinions, such as that through the Incarnation the divine nature had flesh and bone and that Christ shed the blood of the heavenly Father, it rebuked impartially lukewarm spiritual people, cathedral clergy, "unholy Church," princes and women living in castles "steeped in impurity." Nevertheless, beside these wholesale condemnations, not at all uncommon in the works and preachings of the saints, and her not always acceptable visions, Mechthild's book reflects the intense love of God of the true mystic, often in language of great poetic beauty. The mystical union, which is essentially a union of wills, comes in "a blessed stillness," in which God and the soul give themselves to each other. The soul will often suffer from the wound of love produced by her intense longing for her divine lover, then she experiences a loneliness that is more bitter than death; she calls upon God and waits for him with a heavy heart, she is restless and suffers torments, feeling utterly forsaken, and neither angels nor our Lady herself can comfort her. For because the soul is created in the image of God, God alone can satisfy her longing. But when he has come, "when the blessed hour has passed, in which God has granted the loving soul his sublime consolation, then is the soul so full of delight that everything seems to it good."

ST. GERTRUDE

St. Gertrude (1256–c. 1302) was the abbess of the Cistercian or Benedictine convent at Helfta where Mechthild found refuge in her old age and developed the mysticism of the Sacred Heart. Of Gertrude's life, too, very little is known. She was received at the convent as a girl of five and stayed there throughout her life. At first her main interests were intellectual; she was a good Latin scholar and well versed in the so-called liberal arts, philosophy, rhetoric, and the rest. But during one Advent, probably in 1280, her hitherto peaceful life became troubled by a strange restlessness and a feeling of interior emptiness. This continued until shortly before the Feast of the Purification (February 2). Then one night, while she was in the dormitory after compline, Christ appeared to her and placed his hand into hers saying: "I will save and deliver you, fear nothing . . . I will accept and inebriate you with the streams of my divine joy." From that time she gave up her former interests and devoted herself to prayer and the study of Scripture and the Fathers, especially St. Augustine, Gregory the Great, St. Bernard, and Hugh of St. Victor.

Being a Benedictine, her quickly developing mystical life centered in the liturgy. Many of her ecstasies occurred during Mass; they were usually occasioned by some words which called

forth her raptures. Thus at the Mass "Gaudete" of the Third
Sunday in Advent she felt her heart pierced by an arrow of love,
and during one Second Sunday of Lent, which has the Gospel
of the Transfiguration, it seemed to her that her face was pressed
to another face. "In this vision," she writes, "your eyes, bright
as the rays of the sun, appeared before mine, and when you
showed me your most adorable face, a light of ineffable sweetness passed from your divine eyes into my mind and thence
into my innermost being." Sometimes during Mass in the convent chapel Gertrude would also see Christ offering Mass in
heaven, experiencing this "mystical" liturgy with the spiritual
senses, sight, hearing, taste, smell, and touch all playing their
part in it.

Hence it is not surprising that her great vision of the Heart
of Christ should also have been intimately linked to the liturgy.
It occurred on the Feast of St. John the Evangelist during the
recitation of matins in choir. There the apostle suddenly appeared to her, inviting her to come with him so that they might
rest together on the breast of the Lord. Then, taking her "up"
with him, he presents her to Jesus and places her on his right
side, reposing himself on the left. This he does, as he explains,
so that she may drink more easily the consolations flowing from
his divine heart, since this was pierced on the right side by the
lance. Then, as the beating of the divine heart fills her with
immense joy she asks the apostle why he had written nothing
about it in his Gospel, and he tells her that the knowledge of
the divine heartbeats was reserved to a later age, so that the
love of Christians which had grown cold should be rekindled
by the knowledge of these mysteries.

In contrast to the modern devotion, there is no question of
suffering and reparation in Gertrude's mystical experience. To
her the heart of Jesus shows itself radiant in glory, loving and
beloved, and the mystic responds joyfully, singing "a canticle
on the instrument of your divine heart by the virtue of the
Spirit of consolation." The whole mystical life of St. Gertrude,
dominated by her close union with the divine heart, breathes an

extraordinary happiness. This heart is a treasure house in which are enclosed all riches, it is a lyre moved by the Holy Spirit, a golden censer from which ascends sweet-smelling perfumes, a lamp suspended between heaven and earth. It is also her home, to which she is called by the voice of her heavenly lover: "Come, my love, to me, enter, my love, into me." She believes that during her contemplative prayer she is frequently drawn into this heart, where she asks Christ many questions about his actions and is answered by him. This idea of being instructed during a mystical experience is very common in the mystics; as the gift of wisdom is particularly closely associated with the mystical life this is only to be expected. Nevertheless, there is a great difference between the words which it is not lawful to utter, which St. Paul heard in his ecstasy, and the detailed dialogue of (frequently very naïve) question and answer which St. Gertrude and other visionaries claim to have had with Christ, which like Hildegard's strange revelations would seem to owe more to human imagination than to divine inspiration. This is not to say that Gertrude's great liturgical visions do not contain a divine element. But some of their accompaniments, and especially long conversations with Our Lord and the saints, must certainly be ascribed to human factors. As had been said before, this often quite inextricable mixture of divine and human elements occurs very frequently in the visions of the saints and has to be borne in mind when assessing their value.

One essential characteristic of genuine supernatural experiences is that they do not foster conceit, but rather humility. "When she humbled herself at the remembrance of her faults," Gertrude writes, "Our Lord poured forth on her from his sacred heart all the virtue and beauty of the divine perfections," and she places on the lips of Christ the words: "My graces usually serve to humble you, because you think yourself unworthy of them." He also teaches her a safe rule for the discernment of spirits: "Whoever knows in his heart that his will is so united to mine as never to dissent from it, whether in prosperity or adversity, and who acts and suffers in all these things only for my glory, may surely believe that what he learns interiorly is from me, if it is useful to others and not opposed to the Scriptures."

She herself had to learn this total acceptance of God's will; for once, when she was ill, Christ showed himself displeased when she asked him to restore her to health so that she might once more be able to follow her Rule; he told her that in this case she would do what pleased herself, whereas, if she continued to be ill she would do what pleased him, for "I am better pleased with your good intentions in a state of suffering than with the sweetness of your devotion that gives pleasure to yourself." But apart from such comparatively minor struggles St. Gertrude's mystical life seems to have been extraordinarily tranquil. There is no tension in her between the heavenly world and her earthly surroundings; on the contrary, they seem to penetrate each other, and the rich brocades and precious stones in which her visions and allegories abound are as perfectly suited to this monastic mysticism as to the tender virgins and saints of contemporary paintings. Nature and supernature are blended into an harmonious whole in this nun, who wrote that "no one should esteem spiritual things less because they are hidden under corporeal images."

IX THE MYSTICAL EXPERIENCE
AND THEOLOGY OF THE
MENDICANT ORDERS

The most important religious event in the thirteenth century was the foundation of the Mendicant Orders of Dominicans and Franciscans, both of which had a tremendous influence on mystical doctrine and experience, the Dominicans being by and large responsible for the development of so-called speculative mysticism, the Franciscans for a more affective spirituality. Both St. Dominic and St. Francis were mystics in their own right, though very little is known about their inner life. St. Dominic's greatest son, St. Thomas Aquinas, laid down the principles of the mystical life in the context of scholastic theology.

ST. THOMAS AQUINAS

St. Thomas (d. 1274), the "Angelic Doctor" as he is often called, was the descendant of a noble family, the counts of Aquino. He was educated at the Benedictine abbey of Monte Cassino whose abbot his parents expected him to become one day. In 1240 he went to Naples to complete his education; here he came into contact with the new Dominican Order and was immediately attracted by its ideals of poverty, learning, and the apostolic life. His family was violently opposed to his joining the Dominicans, who seemed much less socially acceptable to them than the more aristocratic Benedictines of Monte Cassino;

but he persevered, and in 1244 he took the black and white habit of the Preaching Friars. In the following year he was sent to Paris where he studied under Albert the Great; later he followed him to Cologne to the General House of Studies of the Order. St. Thomas subsequently taught in various Dominican centers including Paris, Rome, and Naples, taking part in the philosophical and theological controversies of the time and writing his great works, especially the *Summa Theologiae*, which became the most authoritative theological work in the Catholic Church and has remained so until our own day. Thomas was above all a philosopher and theologian; but the evidence points strongly to the fact that he also had mystical experiences. There is the well-known story of the angels who, after a violent temptation, gave the young Thomas a mystical belt which protected him against sensuality for the rest of his life. Later in life he prayed in ecstasy before the image of Christ on the Cross and heard the words: "Thomas, you have written well about me [he was just then engaged on writing the Third Part of the *Summa*, dealing with the death and Resurrection of Christ], what reward do you want?" To which Thomas replied: "None other than yourself, Lord." Finally, a few months before his death, his mystical contemplation became so overpowering that he gave up writing. When his close friend Reginald urged him to continue his work he replied that he could not do it, because everything he had written seemed like straw to him if compared with what he had seen.

Despite his strictly objective scholastic method St. Thomas' writings, too, show evidence that his descriptions of the spiritual life were no mere intellectual exercise but rested on personal experience; to "adhere to God" is a favorite term of his. He sees the whole spiritual life as a wonderful organism, based on the virtues and the gifts of the Holy Spirit, especially the gift of wisdom. In a beautiful passage of the "Secunda Secundae" of the *Summa Theologiae* he explains how in the perfectly purified man even the so-called cardinal virtues, which were known already to the pagan philosophers, unite to God: for such a man's prudence considers only divine things, his temperance disregards earthly desires, his fortitude despises sufferings and his justice is always concerned to imitate the divine mind.

Both the root and the consummation of all virtues is, of course, charity, and one of its principal effects is spiritual joy. For to think about God causes joy, a joy which in itself admits of no sorrow, though it can never be perfect on earth, because the desire for God cannot be satisfied this side of eternity. Even meditation on the Passion of Christ, so prominent in medieval mysticism, causes joy, because it shows the love of God for men, though it is accompanied by sorrow because of sin, which caused Christ to suffer. True, God in himself is the first object of devotion; but because of his weakness, man needs other guides to the knowledge of divine things better suited to his sensibility, the first of which is the humanity of Christ. For, writes St. Thomas in his commentary on Colossians, "If anyone considers piously and diligently the mysteries of the Incarnation he will find there such a tremendous depth of wisdom as surpasses all human knowledge." For in the sense in which St. Thomas uses the term in this context wisdom is a gift of the Holy Spirit, not simply a product of human experience. This wisdom produces a certain "connaturality" with the divine things to which it is directed, and this natural affinity is brought about by charity, which unites a man to God. The man who possesses this gift of wisdom to a high degree will be guided by it both in his contemplation and in his action. For though contemplation in itself is higher than action, yet here on earth the combination of the two lives of Martha (action) and Mary (contemplation), by which a man gives to others what he has learned in contemplation (*contemplata aliis tradere*), is to be preferred to the purely contemplative life. For, St. Thomas reasons in his treatise on the *Perfection of the Spiritual Life*, "The greater and the more exalted the contemplative life is as compared with the active life, the more seems to be done for God by a man who suffers detriment to his beloved contemplation in order to devote himself to the salvation of his neighbour for the sake of God. This . . . seems to belong to a higher perfection of love than if a man were so attached to the sweetness of contemplation that he would not give it up in any circumstances, even when the salvation of others is at stake."

St. Thomas' views on the phenomena of the mystical life are laid down in his questions of the "Secunda Secundae" that deal with prophecy and rapture. In prophecy—and this applies also to other forms of mystical knowledge—there is a light in the soul which exceeds the normal light of natural reason. This light is not permanently in the soul but is transitory,[1] it produces the utmost certainty. Much prophetical or mystical knowledge, however, cannot be considered supernatural with such certainty; for often a man cannot distinguish between divine inspiration and his own thoughts. Frequently also the divine teaching is given in imaginary visions; but Thomas does not consider him a "prophet" whose mind is not enlightened to judge these visions. For the spirit of the prophet—and the spirit of the authentic mystic—is subject to the prophet, that is to say, he must be able to know and judge his own experience, his mind must not be confused so that he can neither properly remember nor interpret his visions, as happened, St. Thomas says, with the prophetesses of the second-century Montanist sect. These visions occur always in a state of ecstasy, when the senses are closed to all external impressions so as to be open only to the images by which the divine teaching is conveyed. There is, however, another and much superior manifestation of divine truth which is not conveyed by images but "by naked contemplation," that is to say it is directly impressed on the intellect; this is what later mystics have described as "intellectual visions," though these are not visions properly so called, because nothing is actually "seen" in them.

St. Thomas distinguishes the phenomenon of ecstasy from

[1] Compare with this teaching St. Hildegard's description of the two lights in her soul; the first is obviously the light of human reason, even though she mistakenly believed it to be supernaturally infused.

rapture. Ecstasy, he says, means simply an outgoing from one-self, whereas rapture adds a certain violence. There are three causes of rapture. He gives as the first a pathological one: when a man suffers this sudden alienation from his senses through some natural infirmity. The second cause is diabolic, as happens in the possessed. The third cause is divine; such were the raptures of Ezekiel and St. Paul. In this last kind of rapture a man is raised suddenly above the natural to the divine sphere and receives supernatural revelations.

It is typical of St. Thomas that he discusses the theology of the mystical life including its phenomena in the context of the Christian virtues and the gifts of the Holy Spirit. For him it is not a series of extraordinary happenings but the highest flowering of the Christian life.

ST. BONAVENTURE

Bonaventure (1221–74), the friend and contemporary of St. Thomas, was a son of St. Francis, and deeply imbued with the spirit of the founder of his order whose life he wrote. St. Francis (1181/2–1266) was, of course, himself a mystic of the first water, who instilled into his followers his own profound love of the Child Jesus, the crucified Christ and the Blessed Sacrament, and who praised God through all his creatures in his famous Canticle of Brother Sun. Francis was the troubadour of Lady Poverty, and his devotion to the Passion was finally sealed by the ecstasy on Mount Alvernia, when, two years before his death, he had a vision of a crucified seraph and received the wounds of Christ into his own body. This event, made known after Francis had died, made a tremendous impression throughout Western Christendom and greatly contributed to the growing devotion to the man Jesus and his sufferings. It also influenced very deeply the mystical teaching of the great Franciscan doctor, Bona-venture. A native of Bagnorea in Italy, he was educated in Paris and entered the Franciscan Order about 1243, continuing his studies under the famous Schoolman Alexander of Hales. In

1248 he received the degree of baccalaureus and taught Scripture at the university, being made a master five years later. As such he became involved in the controversy between the Mendicant Orders and secular theologians who resented the "intrusion" of the newly founded Dominicans and Franciscans into the universities. In 1257 he was elected minister general of his Order, and in this capacity he had not only to undertake extensive journeys but also to intervene in the quarrels that had arisen within the order on the subject of poverty. Nevertheless, just during this period of intensive activity Bonaventure wrote his spiritual *opuscula* which contain most of his mystical teaching. He was created cardinal in 1273 and accompanied Pope Gregory X to the Council of Lyons, where he died.

His principal spiritual works are entitled *On the Threefold Way, The Mind's Journey to God,* the *Soliloquy,* and *The Mystical Vine. The Threefold Way* describes the traditional stages of the soul from the purgative through the illuminative to the unitive way, culminating in the state of ecstasy. In the purgative way man is goaded by the "prick of conscience," which produces in its turn a threefold activity; namely the remembrance of sin, knowledge of self, and consideration of what is good. In accordance with the Franciscan ideal Bonaventure makes severe demands on the man who would attain to union with God: not only must all natural desires be curbed, but even their first motions should be suppressed. To be able to do this Bonaventure counsels three points to meditate on: the day of death should be considered as imminent, the blood of the Cross as recently shed and the face of the Judge as present. The later medieval dances of death, the realistic crucifixes and the paintings of the Last Judgment which adorn so many medieval churches bear witness to the effect of this Franciscan teaching, which was designed to bring about a thorough moral reformation in sensual man. For who, asks Bonaventure, "would be so devoid of feeling that he would allow . . . wickedness to rule in him, while he considers that the most precious blood has been poured out on him?"

Once man has been sufficiently purified he will enter on the illuminative way, which is dominated by the "ray of intelligence." Man need now no longer reflect on his own sins, on death and judgment, but will be enlightened about the great mysteries of Christianity and the mercy of God, who has given us his Son for our brother and friend and the Holy Spirit for the sign of our acceptance and adoption. This is the time when man recovers his spiritual senses, so central in the teaching of the Greek Fathers. By his spiritual hearing he understands the words of Christ, by his renewed sight he considers the splendors of this Light; when he sighs to receive the in-breathed Word he recovers his spiritual sense of smell. With the last two senses, taste and touch, he is already leaving the illuminative way and approaches the mystical life; for when the soul "lovingly embraces the incarnate Word as receiving delight from it and passing over into it by ecstatic love, it recovers taste and touch . . . hence in this grade, having its interior senses restored . . . the soul is disposed for spiritual ecstasy."

This love for the incarnate Word is at the center of Bonaventure's beautiful treatise on *The Mystical Vine*, which contains the Franciscan Doctor's teaching on the Sacred Heart. "For this has your side been pierced," he addresses the crucified Lord, "that an entrance might be open to us; for this has your heart been wounded, that in this vine we might dwell protected from external disturbances. Nevertheless, it had also been wounded for this, that we should see through the visible wound the invisible wound of love . . . For the fleshly wound shows the spiritual wound." The contemplation of the wounded side and heart of Jesus intensifies the love of the mystic, so that he himself begins to feel with the heart of Christ: "Behold, I have one heart with Jesus." Thus this contemplation, too, leads to the unitive way, for, Bonaventure exclaims, "how happy you will be if, after you have entered into . . . the flowers of blood, I mean the wounds of Christ, you will be freed from the clamour of this world . . . and being occupied only with him, to whom you have gone in, you can taste and understand how good and sweet is Jesus"—a passage which shows very clearly the importance of the suffering humanity of Christ for the Franciscan mystic, because the contemplation of "the flowers of blood" leads him to union with the heart of Jesus, which becomes one with that of the contemplative.

The emblem of the unitive way is the "spark of wisdom"; for here God and the soul are united to each other, and from this union springs "true wisdom," which is the experimental knowledge of God. In *The Mind's Journey to God* Bonaventure describes this unitive way under the image of the seventh day, the day of rest, for he defines ecstasy, which to him is the highest stage of the spiritual life, as a repose of the mind. In it the mind does not only transcend the world of the senses but even itself, and the way to this transcending is Christ. The Franciscan Doctor presents it as a kind of death, in which man lies in the tomb with Christ, dead to all external stimuli, as St. Francis was on Mount Alvernia, "where he passed over into God by the excess of contemplation." When this passing over is perfect, all intellectual activity will be left behind, and what Bonaventure calls the "apex of the affection" must be completely transformed into God. This apex is the seat of the mystical life, which has been mentioned before, and which the medieval mystics call by many names. It is this apex, this spark or ground of the soul, which is transformed into God or, as the Fathers said, "deified."

Bonaventure refuses to explain how this happens, because it cannot be explained rationally; if we would know about it, we should ask grace, not doctrine, desire, not the intellect, prayer, not books, God, not man, darkness, not light. "Therefore," Bonaventure ends this passage from *The Threefold Way*, "let us die and enter into darkness; let us impose silence on all solicitudes, desires and imaginings; let us pass with Christ crucified from this world to the Father." So for Bonaventure, too, the mystical way is a way of darkness, of silence; when God is experienced in the highest part of the soul all human activity, all understanding and imaginings must cease. But one feature of this description is characteristic of the thirteenth-century Franciscan, which never enters into the negative way of Gregory of Nyssa or Pseudo-Dionysius: even in the darkness of mystical contemplation Christ crucified is present to man, he accompanies him into the supernal sphere of the Father.

The way to this ultimate union is not without suffering. In another description of the spiritual life, Bonaventure divides it into "six steps of the love of God." The first of these is "sweetness," when a man first learns "to taste how sweet is the Lord," thus losing his attachment to creatures. The second step is already painful; man realizes how far God really still is from him and longs for him with unfulfilled yearning. The next stage is called "satiety"; it means that the soul is so vehemently carried towards God, whom it yet cannot reach, that everything else becomes loathsome for it. It is a period of trial, during which man hovers between the natural and the supernatural spheres, yet belonging to neither; for there is still an impediment arising from his lower nature that prevents him from soaring into the heights. In order to break away completely man must resolutely embrace the cross and ascend the fourth step, which Bonaventure calls *ebrietas*, inebriation. Here torment will become his consolation, and for the sake of God he will delight in pain and affliction. This corresponds to what St. John of the Cross will later call the "Night of the Spirit," this painful process of passive purifications, without which a man cannot reach the heights of the mystical life. Nevertheless, this period is not without spiritual joy, which is caused by the love of Christ for whose sake all these trials are endured. It is succeeded by the much happier state of "security," when the mystic is so filled with trust in the divine assistance that he believes it impossible ever to be separated from God. This "security" is followed by the last and highest stage possible in this life, the state of "tranquillity," "in which there is such peace and rest that the soul is in some way in silence and slumber," dead to the outside world. It is the state of ecstasy, the pattern of which is the life of heaven. Bonaventure stresses neither the rigidity of limbs nor the intellectual visions so often associated with ecstasy, but only the profound peace that invades the ecstatic soul, causing it to exclaim "It is good for us to be here." This peace is a reflection of the eternal peace in heaven, won by the crucifying sufferings of "satiety" and "inebriation," a peace that surpasses all understanding.

RAYMOND LULL

Raymond Lull (1235–1316) was one of the most colorful personalities of the Middle Ages. He was a native of Mallorca, one of the Balearic Islands off Spain, now one of the playgrounds of Europe, but then a kingdom that had for a long time been in the possession of the Mohammedans and had only recently been reconquered by the Christians. Thus large numbers of Moors were still living there as well as many Jews, so that the impressionable young Raymond came into touch with various cultures and religions. His father had taken part in the conquest of the island, and Raymond himself became a close friend of its young king. He led the life of a courtier, took mistresses, and even his marriage with a noble lady failed to improve his moral conduct. At this time he composed many love lyrics in the manner of the troubadours, none of which, however, have survived. When he was thirty years old a vision of Christ on the Cross, five times repeated, converted him, and from that time his only desire was to serve God and to bring others to him.

On the Feast of St. Francis he heard a bishop preach about the saint, and he felt at once attracted to his ideals, sold his possessions, made provision for his wife and family and became a Franciscan tertiary. He made a pilgrimage to the Spanish shrines of Santiago and Montserrat, and then spent nine years in Mallorca in prayer and the study of Oriental languages. When he was forty years old he retired to Mount Randa, near Palma, to meditate in complete solitude. There he believed to have received by divine inspiration a new system, which he called "the great art" (*Ars Magna*), by which he thought that all truth could be known and all error banished. This teaching, which seemed to lay too much stress on reason to the detriment of faith, was later (1376) condemned and prevented his canonization. About the same time he wrote the *Book of Contemplation* which soon made him famous, so that King James of Mallorca called him to his court at Montpellier, where the book was declared orthodox by two Franciscans. His great wish was to convert the Mohammedans, and for this purpose he founded a missionary school for Oriental languages at Miramar (Mallorca), the first students being thirteen Franciscans. Though the school was approved by Pope John XXI (1276) it did not prosper, for twenty years later Raymond complained about its decline. At Miramar, Lull probably wrote his mystical *Book of the Lover and the Beloved.* In the service of Christ, the "Beloved," he now, in middle age, began an extraordinary apostolic activity, embracing a life of almost incessant travel and hardship until his death at eighty-one. He probably visited Turkey and Palestine, Egypt and Abyssinia before returning to Montpellier in 1284, where he wrote his novel *Blanquerna,* the description of a Utopian "City of God." He went repeatedly to Rome to seek support for his missionary plans and new missionary schools, but without success. Hence he decided to visit the Saracens himself, though only after grave interior struggles and misgivings. In Tunis he disputed with learned Mohammedans, but was exiled and narrowly escaped death by stoning. Back in Rome he had more disappointments; Boniface VIII was too much involved in European politics to be interested in the plans of this strange layman in penitential garb with his long white beard, who was not afraid to castigate the worldliness of the clergy. From Rome he went to Genoa and from there to Montpellier, finally to Paris, where he tried to win Philip the Fair to his ideas, but again without success. He returned to Mallorca in 1299, but far from spending his old age in well-deserved rest, he now began to be more active than ever. A false rumor that there was a possibility for Palestine to be conquered once more by the Christians caused him to go to Cyprus, where he barely escaped murder by poison. In 1305 he was once more in Montpellier, where he wrote a famous treatise, addressed to the Pope and the Christian princes, outlining a plan for the conquest of Palestine and the colonization of North Africa. In 1307 he went again to Africa where he preached in public and was put in prison. But the Kadi was so impressed by his wisdom that he was allowed to receive visitors and hold discussions with them. He was finally sent back to Europe, being shipwrecked on the way and losing all the possessions he had taken with him. In 1311 he attended the Council of Vienne, where he pleaded successfully for the introduction of Oriental studies at various universities. After a short stay in Mallorca, where he wrote several books, he went to Sicily, where he worked for the conversion of Jews and Mohammedans, and finally, at the age of seventy-nine, he went to Africa for the last time. In Tunis he was at first left unmolested, preaching and writing, but as his attacks on the Prophet became more violent, his Mohammedan audience stoned him and he was put on a Christian merchant ship, where he is believed to have died of his sufferings when his native island came into view.

Lull's almost incredible apostolic and literary activities and constant travels were the outcome of a profound mystical life which made him a true knight errant of Christ. This life is expressed in love lyrics which recall the glowing language of the minnesingers. When men ask him why he mortifies his body and gives his possessions away he replies: "To seek the honour of my beloved, who is more dishonoured and scorned than honoured and loved by men." He calls himself "a loving fool" or a "fool of love," because men cannot understand his way of life, which seems to be so contrary to what they call reason. As the troubadour is inebriated with love of his lady, so Lull is drunk with the love of Christ, and his poems speak of singing birds and trees, of solitude and the tears of love just as the worldly poets of the time. But the love he describes is the mystical love of God that consumes the lover and throws him into ecstasy. Yet at the same time this love is based on reason and has its seat in the will, not in the passions, for Lull is also a Schoolman; indeed reason is given a highly important place in his system. Following the teaching on the three powers of the soul Lull writes that "memory and will joined together and ascended the mountain of the Beloved, so that reason, too, should rise and love should be doubled in the love of the Beloved." For in the mystical life the Beloved shows his glories to reason and memory and gives himself to the will as its goal. Lull differs from many other mystics in his teaching that God can be sufficiently known even in this life; darkness and the night have scarcely any place in his mystical experience except as expressing the momentary absence of the Beloved. True, the lover knows that his Beloved is "beyond all boundaries, for he is where man cannot reach him," yet, paradoxically, he also knows "that the Beloved is in his memory." When the Beloved raises up the understanding of his lover, the lover can comprehend the greatness of the Beloved, and when the lover is asked whether the Beloved could take love away from him he answers, "No, because the memory can remember and the understanding can grasp the greatness of the Beloved." Again, the will of the lover wanted to rise up high so as to love his Beloved yet more, and therefore it ordered the understanding to rise up with all its might; then the understanding ordered the memory to do the same, "and all three rose up to contemplate the glory of the Beloved." Here we see quite clearly the scholastic influence as well as the absence of the "negative way" in Lull.

This, however, does not mean that his mysticism is predominantly intellectual; for it has also a wonderful Franciscan tenderness. The Beloved is not only the disincarnate Divinity, he is also the suffering Christ on the Cross; for he showed himself to his lover "in red and new clothing, and his arms extended to embrace him, and he inclined his head to kiss him, and he stood up high, so that the lover could find him." There-

fore the mystical love is as full of suffering as it is of joy.
Lull's poetry abounds in both. For the heart of the lover rose
to the heights of the Beloved so that the baseness of this world
should not hinder its love. And when it had reached the Beloved it was filled with delights, but then the Beloved led it
back to this world, so that it should also contemplate him in
sorrow and longing. Once the "fool" was asked who knew more
of love, the one who had joy in it or the one to whom it caused
sorrow? And he answered that "love does not know the one
without the other," for both are really the same in the will of
the lover.

The external phenomena of the mystical life, ecstasy and
visions, play hardly any part in Lull's mysticism, but he describes
the mystical union in very beautiful language. Love, he writes,
illuminated the veil of clouds that had come between the lover
and the Beloved, "and it rendered it so bright as the moon is
in the night, the evening star at dusk, the sun at noon and the
intellect in the will. And through this luminous cloud the loved
and the Beloved spoke to each other." For love is the bond
that unites God and man and finally leads them to what later
mystics call the "transforming union," when lover and Beloved
are so much one "that they are only one reality in their essence;
lover and Beloved are different things, but which are in harmony
without any opposition and difference of essence." This is one
of the paradoxes without which it is almost impossible to
describe the intensity of the highest union. Lull safeguards very
carefully the objective difference between the human lover and
his divine Beloved, yet their union is so intimate that there is
no opposition or essential difference in their perfect harmony.

We have seen that Lull's mystical experience led him to a
most intense apostolate and finally to martyrdom; he himself
expressed the essence of his life in his "testament" in which
he "left guilt and wrong to contrition and penitence and worldly
joys to contempt; to his eyes he left tears, to his heart sighs
and love; to his understanding he left the essential image of his

Beloved and to his memory the sufferings the Beloved had endured for his love; to his activity he left the care of the infidels who unknowingly go to perdition."

ANGELA OF FOLIGNO

Angela of Foligno (c. 1248–1309) was like Lull a Franciscan tertiary. She spent her whole life at Foligno in Umbria with very little outward activity. She was the mother of a family, and according to her own account had led a very worldly and even sinful life till she was about forty years old. Then she was suddenly converted, she does not tell how, and became a Franciscan tertiary. She soon received mystical graces, descriptions of which she dictated to her Franciscan confessor who took down in Latin what she told him in Italian. Like many visionaries she also suffered frequently from "mysterious" illnesses; during a pilgrimage to Assisi there seems to have been a crisis with screams and strange behavior that frightened her companions. Today such phenomena are generally attributed to nervous disorders, due to mental strain and exaggerated penances; but they in no way detract from the value of her mystical experience and teaching.

Angela describes the beginnings of her spiritual life as "twenty steps of penitence," being led from still imperfect knowledge and confession of sin to true self-knowledge and the beginnings of the knowledge of God. Then she was told to "seek the way of the Cross and to give my heart to Christ, and to go by a thorny road, that is by tribulation." But she could not follow this call while she was still living with her husband, her mother, and children, who had claims on her. Therefore she began to pray for their death, and her prayer was answered: one after the other they all died. "And because I had started on the way I spoke of before," she writes, "and had asked God that they should die, I received great consolation from their death." It must be admitted that to pray for the death of a person who seems to be an obstacle to one's spiritual life is wrong under all circumstances except in response to an irresistible divine in-spiration, but it may safely be said that this exception is so rare as to be unique. After her conversion Angela was evidently in a state of almost unbearable nervous tension, which might account for this terrible prayer; whether the subsequent deaths of all her family were really an answer to this prayer or merely a strange coincidence is impossible to decide. In any case, it should not be assumed that she was really glad at these deaths, for she writes later, when describing some intense suffering: "And to live was even more painful to me than the death of my mother and my sons."

After the initial period of penitential self-knowledge follows the illumination of the mind, when Angela began to under-stand the Our Father in a new way, "and the individual words were explained to me in my heart . . . and I began to taste something of the divine goodness," and she felt that even her faith was changed into something far more living than she had known before. She was also given a new understanding of the Gospels, which filled her with light and love, "and I began to have constantly, whether waking or sleeping, a divine sweetness in my soul." She had now arrived at the threshold of the mystical life, and her Franciscan advisers, who had until then prevented her from giving away all her property, allowed her to do so. With this act of perfect imitation of St. Francis she had reached the twentieth step of penitence and was ready to enter on the life of mystical union, which she described as a sequence of seven steps. It begins with the revelation of the Trinity and of Christ in the Blessed Sacrament, which are made intelligible to the "taste of the mind"—again we have here the ancient doctrine of the spiritual senses. Later she sees "the whole world and all things as something very small, and God filling and exceeding all" and then, "in a rapture," "the power of God and the will of God, by which she was satisfied on every question," especially as to those who were saved, those who were damned and the demons, that is to say the last things which were so much in the mind of medieval men.

After Angela had been enlightened on these mysteries she received what she calls "the revelation of the divine union and love," by which she was mystically instructed on the Passion, on the intercession of the Blessed Virgin for all mankind and on the Eucharist. These mysteries of God's love flooded her with light and consolation; they were followed by a martyrdom of soul and body caused by the remembrance of her sins and by an intense awareness of the Cross by which, she writes, "my soul was liquefied in the love of God." About this time she was also inundated with consolations which caused her to lie motionless for eight days, during which time she could neither speak nor get up. This was evidently something resembling a cataleptic state; and it must be admitted that it is not always easy to distinguish authentic mystical ecstasy from pathological phenomena, and the kernel of supernatural experience from its accompanying psychological elements. The ascetical practices of most mystics were bound to weaken their physical health and thus could easily lead to trance states and even to hallucinations; on the other hand, God could use just these states to infuse supernatural knowledge, though, again, this knowledge might be presented in imagery coming from the mystic's own experience.

Angela herself was aware of the ambiguity of such states, for one day, when she believed to have heard a voice saying to her, "You are full of God," and her whole body seemed to feel divine delight, she asked God to give her a sign, for example a precious stone, to convince her that it was really he who spoke to her. It was a naïve request—she had probably read in some saints' lives about such marvels—to which she received the answer that even a precious stone would not rid her of her doubts. But God would give her a surer sign: "This sign shall be always with you . . . You shall be burning with the love of God . . . and this love will be so fervent that, if someone says something evil to you, you will hold it to be a favour . . . For thus have I borne ignominy with great humility and patience."

The best proof of the reality of a mystical experience is the increase of virtue in its recipient—though even this does not guarantee the divine origin of all the concomitants of the experience such as images and words, which may well come from the unconscious of the mystic himself, but only its essence. Angela's life continued to be a succession of mystical illuminations and purifying sufferings. For a time she was raised so high above all earthly things that she could think of nothing but God, whatever she might be doing, but this happiness was followed by weeks of desolation when she felt as if she were totally forsaken by him. After this period of darkness she experienced even higher consolations: she felt herself embraced by Christ and entered into his side, and was given a vision of the transcendent power and will of God.

In the "fifth step" Angela described other ecstatic experiences. She now could recognize the divine presence by "a certain unction which suddenly renews the soul and softens the limbs of the body" so that they participate in the delight of the soul; Angela's confessor gives an interesting description of her appearance when in this state: "She became white and red, radiant and joyful, and her eyes so bright that she seemed no longer herself," though she was at this time about fifty years old, and weakened by her penances.

This state is again followed by great suffering, in which Angela finds herself tormented by devils, while all her vices seem to have revived and she appears to herself quite powerless to resist the evil that is constantly attacking her—a state well known to the mystics before they reach the final peace of the transforming union. In this dark night, Angela says, "God is completely shut out and hidden from me, so that I cannot even remember him." Seeing her sins, she tries to fight against them with all her strength, but being unable to prevail she is filled with anger and bitterness, which makes these sufferings even worse, because she feels that such reactions must be very displeasing to God. They are, however, nothing but purifying temptations to prepare her for the ultimate union. This last stage of the mystical life is described in the "seventh step." It begins with another vision of God in which she joins the negative way of Dionysius, for there she sees God in darkness, which is darkness only "because he is a greater good than can be thought or understood . . . and she sees nothing, and she sees all"—the well-known paradox of the mystical experience. In this dark vision she receives so deep a knowledge that it cannot be expressed, and at the same time she is introduced to that strange region of the soul which is the seat of the mystical life, where, she writes, "there is neither joy nor sadness nor delectation . . . but where there is all good and all truth." She sees herself no longer in herself, but in God; there is an exultant note of triumph in the words of the sinner who has become a saint when she writes: "And I see myself with God wholly pure, wholly sanctified, wholly true, wholly upright" and when she hears the words: "In you rests all the Trinity, all truth, so that you hold me and I hold you."

X THE "MYSTICAL"
FOURTEENTH CENTURY

The fourteenth century may well be called the mystical century par excellence. In the West it abounds in such great names as Master Eckhart, St. Catherine of Siena, Julian of Norwich, and Ruysbroeck, whereas in the East Gregory Palamas was the outstanding figure of the Hesychast movement. Many of the mystics of this century played a role similar to that of the Old Testament prophets: they were voices calling a decadent generation to repentance; others were a leaven of spiritual energy in an age suffering from many calamities. Under the influence of French politics the Popes had moved from Rome to Avignon (1309), where they lived in external splendor; and when, in 1377, they returned to Rome the consequence was the election of anti-Popes by the French cardinals, so that the Church had two, at times even three heads, until the schism was finally resolved by the election of Martin V at the Council of Constance (1417). In 1339 began the Hundred Years' War between England and France which exhausted both countries, in Italy there was constant internal strife between her city states. In Germany the ideals of knights and minnesingers had been replaced by the outrages of the robber knights; and in England, Wycliffe and the Lollards preached church reform as well as rebellion; insecurity and epidemics prevailed almost everywhere. In the face of all these evils both in the Church and in the secular sphere, religious men and women everywhere sought God in their own hearts and withdrew from the world, often gathering a circle of disciples around them and later returning to this world to preach to it.

A. The Western Church

1. *THREE GERMAN DOMINICANS*

Whereas in the thirteenth century the representatives of mysticism came largely from the Franciscan Order, in the fourteenth some of the most influential mystics were Dominicans. Above them all towers the great and controversial figure of Master Eckhart (c. 1260–1327). The descendant of a family of German knights, he was born at Hochheim in Thuringia and entered the Dominican monastery of Erfurt at an early age. He studied in the Dominican house at Cologne, where Albert the Great had died in 1280. Later Eckhart was appointed prior of the Erfurt monastery and vicar-general of Thuringia. About the turn of the century he was sent to Paris to complete his studies, receiving the title of Master in Sacred Theology. He left Paris in 1302, was elected provincial of Saxony, and in 1307 he was appointed vicar-general of Bohemia, an office which demanded constant traveling. Four years later he was once more sent to Paris, and after a short stay there moved to Strasbourg as prior, preacher, and professor of theology. Later he taught at Cologne. The last years of Master Eckhart's life were darkened by his trial for heresy. In 1326 forty-nine propositions were extracted from his writings as unorthodox by delegates of the archbishop of Cologne. He replied that his accusers did not understand him and that, in any case, he was not a heretic because "only obstinate addiction to error constitutes both heresy and the heretic." But his opponents were not satisfied with that and drew up another list of fifty-nine propositions. He admitted that they might sound unorthodox if taken literally, but not if properly explained. In February 1327 he declared solemnly in the Dominican church at Cologne that if he should have written or preached any false doctrine at any time he now publicly revoked it.

Nevertheless, this did not silence his opponents. The case was referred to the Pope at Avignon, where it was heard later in the year in the Dominican's presence. Eckhart died soon after his return from Avignon; the bull condemning some of his propositions, though emphasizing his own good faith, was published only two years after his death, in 1329.

Owing to his often obscure language Eckhart's mystical doctrine is not easy to explain. Its principal theme, which he never tired of emphasizing, is the necessity of the birth of the divine Word in the soul; this is the very essence of the mystical union. To achieve this a strict ascetical discipline is indispensable. For all created things contain the shadow of nothingness; hence the man who would attain to the uncreated Godhead must be completely stripped from all attachment to them; his life must be directed to God alone. Eckhart's God, however, has more affinity with the One of the Neoplatonists than with the Christian Trinity, because in his view the latter introduces number into the Godhead, whereas number is completely foreign to it. On the other hand, all things, including man, are in God, hence "man in God is God." This strange pronouncement requires a good deal of explanation to prevent it from being taken as pantheistic; it may simply mean that as the ideas that are in God cannot be different from God, so man as a divine idea must be identical with him; but in his actual mystical doctrine Eckhart would seem to go farther than that. For there he teaches that, when Christ says "I and the Father are one," this word applies in the very same sense also to Christ and the Christian. For, he writes, "It would be too little for me that the Word should be made flesh for man in Christ, that person distinct from me, if it were not also made flesh in me personally, so that I, too, should be the son of God." "For," he continues, "it should not be falsely imagined that Christ is the Son of God, as it were another son and another image different from the way in which the just and Godlike man is the son of God." So for him the mystic is the son of God in the very same sense as Christ—which would mean that he, the perfect Christian, is God himself. Indeed, he does not fear to write: "The nearer we are to the One, the more truly are we God's sons and Son, and God the Holy Spirit also flows out from us"—again identifying the mystic with the divine Son himself. Eckhart can make this identification because he believes that there is a power in the human soul, which he calls the spark or the ground of the soul, or the "castle" which, being an image of the divine nature, is the sphere where the Son is born. He writes: "The Father gives birth to his Son in eternity, equal to himself . . . Now I say, moreover, he has born him from my soul. Not only is it [the soul] with him and he with it as equal, but he is in it; and the Father gives birth to his Son in the soul in the same way as he gives birth to him in eternity and not otherwise . . . he gives birth to me as his son and as the same son. I say even more: he gives birth to me not only as his son; he gives birth to me as himself and himself as me and me as his being and his nature."

It is not surprising that Eckhart was accused of heresy, making this total identification between creature and Creator. He did even more: he dared place the spark or castle of the soul above the very Trinity. For he considers that this "castle" is so absolutely one and simple that even God himself, inasfar as he is "in the mode and property of his Persons," "will never look into it even for a moment." So when God is to enter into the deepest sanctuary of the soul he must divest himself of all his properties and even of his Persons and enter there only as the One. But here Eckhart modifies his identification of God and the soul somewhat, for he writes "With this part the soul is equal to God and not otherwise." But even this is questionable, for it would make the soul partly equal with God or divine and partly not. In any case, he insists time and again in all his works that the eternal birth of the Son is identical with the (mystical) birth of Christ in the soul, and this was one of the propositions condemned in the bull of John XXII.

It is strange, indeed, that a revered Dominican, whose ascetical teaching and spiritual direction were admirable and in complete harmony with the teaching of the Church, should have
made such extraordinary statements when it came to the description of the mystical life, and should, moreover, have held
such un-Christian views on the Trinity. The decline of Scholasticism, the influence of Mohammedanism and especially of the
Jewish Kabbalah certainly had something to do with this. But,
above all, there was in Eckhart a craving for the Absolute, for
total oneness, a titanic desire for transcending all human limitations that is characteristic of a certain side of the German
nature, and it is therefore not surprising that he should have
played a considerable role not only in German mysticism but
also in German philosophy. His immediate disciples, however,
were well aware that they had to tone down his exaggerations
if they were to make his teaching acceptable to the Church and
intelligible to a wider public.

JOHN TAULER

John Tauler (c. 1300–61) entered the Dominican Order as a
young man between fifteen and twenty years of age and became
acquainted with Eckhart's teaching when he studied in Cologne.
After he had completed his education he became a famous
preacher who traveled throughout the Rhineland. Between
1340 and 1343 he was in Basle, where he came into contact
with a mystical group, the *Gottesfreunde* (Friends of God).
During the fearful epidemic of the Black Death in 1348 he
devoted himself completely to the care of the sick.

While Eckhart had soared into the realms of the most daring
speculations about the unity of God and the soul, Tauler was
above all a preacher of penance, of return to the inner life in an
unhappy age of strife between Pope (John XXII) and Emperor
(Louis of Bavaria), when many German cities were placed
under the interdict, deprived of the sacraments, because they
remained faithful to the allegiance to their prince. Where

Eckhart speaks about the ground or castle of the soul, Tauler speaks about the "inner man," that is the highest faculties in man by which "he is exalted above himself and above all things and dwells in God," whereas his lower faculties are "subjected under all things, into the very ground of humility." The inner man must guide these faculties which constitute the "outer man," by the light of his superior knowledge, while nevertheless remaining unruffled by all earthly change, "sunk and united" in communion with God. But even the "outer man" should be drawn as far as possible "into the other man of inwardness," so that he will live according to the orders of the inward man and not according to his own animal desires. To do so a man must humble himself; indeed, humility plays a central part in Tauler's teaching, "for God seeks and wants a humble man."

When a man has become humble there are, however, still five "prisons" from which he must escape if he would reach union with God. They are love of creatures, love of self, undue reliance on the power of reason, which bars the entrance of faith, further, attachment to devotional feelings and visionary experiences and finally, the roots of self-will, by which a man will desire the grace of God for his own selfish interests rather than for the sake of God himself. This surrender of the will ought to be carried so far that a man becomes indifferent even to his own salvation, if God should withhold it—a teaching given by several other later mystics, but which is really no more than an exaggerated expression of submission to the divine will, for it is self-contradictory that God should condemn to eternal punishment a man who only desires God's will.

In common with most medieval mystics Tauler teaches that the way to union with God leads through the passion of Christ. "The wounds of our Lord," he tells his hearers, "are all salvation; let the holy five wounds remain open until the Last Day . . . these five doors shall be our inheritance here, through which we shall enter into the eternal inheritance of our Father's Kingdom"; for they will teach us how to abandon ourselves and to suffer, how to despise the world and how to deny ourselves.

When a man has learned this he will enter on the mystical way, the first stage of which is great joy, which Tauler calls jubilation, for now a man so drinks in God that he becomes truly inebriated with him and completely forgets himself. But this joy does not last; just when it seems to have reached its climax, the mystic is cast down from the heights and into the state of Job when "the spirit went from him." He is tossed about like a ball between knowledge and ignorance, tranquillity and restlessness, confidence and fear. For though he has left the human sphere, he has not yet entered fully into the divine life, for which these painful purgings are meant to prepare him. The sufferer must pass through these trials in hope, faith, and humility and never give way to despair, for "those who must suffer in this dark misery will become the most lovable and noble of men. But nature must die many a death."

All these disturbances, however, take place only in the lower part of the soul, where God does not actually dwell, because this place is too narrow for him. But when the mystic has endured manfully, his "spirit is drawn above all its powers into a wild desert of which no one can speak, into the hidden darkness of the modeless God. There the spirit is led so closely into unity with the simple, modeless Unity, that it loses all distinction, being without either object or feeling, for in the Unity all multiplicity is lost, and Unity unifies all multiplicity." Here Tauler uses the language of Eckhart, speaking of unity rather than of union, but he guards very carefully against the Master's exaggerations by continuing that, when these persons return to themselves they have a far better discernment of things than others: "they discern clearly and truly all the articles of the pure faith, how the Father and the Son and the Holy Spirit are one God, and so of all other truths." For, he says, no one understands true distinction better than those who have reached Unity.

He then explains why the divine light is so often described as darkness: "This is how we must understand this darkness: it is a light which no created intelligence can either attain or understand naturally; it is wild because it is inaccessible; there the spirit is lead above itself, and above all its concepts and understanding." This is an ecstatic experience, for Tauler further describes it as "a mist, a darkness, in which your spirit is stolen away for about half an Ave Maria so that you are beside your senses and your natural reason. And in this darkness God speaks to you in truth." It is extremely short—half an Ave Maria —he evidently did not have longer ecstasies himself and also perhaps did not want to encourage those long states of unconsciousness most frequent among women mystics. But in these brief moments God speaks to the soul "in truth," and they will suffice to produce rich fruits. For once the actual union is past, "man shall do much more than he did before; he shall love more, thank more, praise more, and live more deeply than before." The mystical experience is not given for the personal enjoyment of its recipient, but for his spiritual advancement, this is the doctrine of the preacher and spiritual guide, who had to warn his hearers against the dangers of mistaking the means for the end.

HENRY SUSO

Henry Suso (c. 1296–1366) was a native of either Constance or Überlingen on Lake Constance. His mother was very gentle and pious, his father a rather stern man. Henry was a very religious boy who entered the Dominican monastery at Constance with a special dispensation before he was fifteen years of age. It seems that this dispensation had been bought, a fact that caused him many scruples until Master Eckhart himself calmed him. When he was eighteen years old he had an ecstatic experience which changed his life from one of ordinary piety to the complete self-giving of mystical fervor. He described it in the language of St. Paul, not knowing whether he was in or out of the body and hearing what no tongue could express. "It was without form or mode and yet contained the delights of all forms and modes." It completely satisfied him, all his desires were stilled. This ecstasy lasted for about an hour and a half; when he came to himself again he felt as if he returned from a different world. From now on the divine Wisdom became his chosen bride, and for love of her he resolved to lead a life of great austerity and accept unresistingly whatever trials God would send him. The autobiography of Suso describes the most fearful penances which cannot but strike the modern reader as pathological; but recent research has shown that this autobiography has been worked over by several nuns who inserted a certain amount of hagiographical material to enhance the spiritual stature of their hero. Hence these passages cannot be taken as authentic, though there is no doubt that henceforth Suso led a very penitential life, making constant use of such instruments as discipline and hair shirt and keeping long fasts and vigils.

About 1320 Suso was sent to Cologne to complete his studies under Master Eckhart, but when the trouble about the Master's teaching started he probably returned to Constance. About this time he wrote the *Book of Divine Truth*, in which he attempted to present Eckhart's teaching as completely orthodox. It is his only speculative work, since he himself was far more a poet than a thinker. Nevertheless, he was accused of teaching suspect doctrine and had to defend himself before a general chapter of his order; it seems that he was censured, because he was forbidden to lecture and henceforth he devoted himself to preaching, traveling all through the Rhine valley, Alsace, and Switzerland. In 1336 he became prior of a Dominican community which had fled from the Rhineland to a place near Constance, because they remained faithful to the Pope during his quarrel with the Emperor. Here he had to endure many trials: some knights, whose daughters and mistresses he had induced to become nuns sought to murder him; his sister, who was a nun, escaped from her convent and fell into sin, and, worst of all, one of his penitents, a woman of "easy virtue," who had feigned a conversion so as to receive material help from the Church, accused him of being the father of her child when he discovered her deception. This tale was widely believed, and finally he was sent to Ulm to put a stop to these slanders. Very little is known about his last years, except that he continued his preaching and the direction of the nuns of his order. His most famous spiritual daughter was Elsbeth Stagel, who collected his letters and wrote down her conversations with him; she and some other nun also worked over the story of his life and are responsible for the hagiographical additions already mentioned.

After Suso's first ecstasy his mystical experiences became continuous. He tells us himself that during ten years he received twice daily, in the morning and the evening, an infused grace during which "he was so absorbed in God, the eternal Wisdom, that he was unable to speak. It often seemed to him that he was floating in the air, hovering between time and eternity on the deep tide of the unfathomable marvels of God." He was also sometimes for weeks so absorbed in God that he was unable to use his senses, "so much that only the One answered him everywhere and in all things, and all things in the One, without the multiplicity which is in this or that." Here Eckhart's influence becomes evident, though Suso is careful not to identify himself with the One. Though he has an intense devotion to the suffering Christ, he aims at union with the mode-less One. "Where, then," he asks, "is the Where of the Son in his naked Godhead? It is in the imageless light of the divine unity, it is according to its nameless names a nothingness . . . according to his uncreated causality a being that gives all things their cause." The mystic will live in this supernatural Where together with the eternal Son, and this Where may also be called, "the being, nameless nothingness" where the spirit enters into the "nothing of unity. And the unity is called a nothing for this reason, that the spirit cannot find a temporal mode; but the spirit realizes that it is held by another than itself, therefore that which holds it is actually rather a something than a nothing, but to the spirit it is a nothing. When now the spirit dwells in this transfigured, bright darkness in ignorance of itself it loses all that hinders it . . . In this absorption the spirit is lost, but not completely; true, it gains some quality of the Deity, yet it does not become God by nature; what happens to it happens by grace, for it [the spirit] is a something created from nothing which remains always."

Suso here follows the teaching of Eckhart but with the necessary safeguards. Though in the experience of the mystical union the human spirit seems to be completely absorbed by the Divinity this is not in fact the case; it is, indeed, in some way deified—the traditional terminology of the Fathers—but it does not itself become divine. What happens to it is a divinization by grace, not by nature, because the nothing from which it was created will always remain with it, however intense the union with God.

Eckhart stressed almost exclusively the actual union—or even unity—with God, he did not say much about the way towards it. Suso, on the other hand, emphasizes also the growing conformity of the mystic to the suffering Christ and desires to be the spiritual knight of the Eternal Wisdom, for whose sake he wishes to endure all torments. More, like St. Thomas he realizes that the soul cannot always cling to God without any images, therefore "it should have something in the nature of an image to lead it into the pure Good. And as far as I understand it, the best way towards it is the lovable image of Christ, for there we have God and man . . . And when a man is formed into this image he will then be transformed by God's Spirit into the divine glory of the Lord of heaven from splendour to splendour, from the splendour of his tender humanity to the splendour of his Godhead." So Suso, too, teaches the traditional way summed up in the words: "Through Christ the Man to Christ the God," combining it with the speculations of Master Eckhart on the mystical union, but without his exaggerations.

2. RUYSBROECK

Jan van Ruysbroeck (1293–1381), though not himself a Dominican, was also influenced by Eckhart's teaching. He was a native of the village from which he derived his name; when he was eleven years old he went to Brussels to be educated by his uncle Jan Hinckaert, who was a priest at the church of St. Gudule. His mother followed him there, though she did not live with him but entered a *béguinage* in the neighborhood; she died before he was ordained to the priesthood. While devoting himself to his priestly duties, Ruysbroeck also gave much time to contemplation. He vigorously opposed the pseudo-mystical teaching of the Brethren of the Free Spirit, a sect—or a variety of sects—which Tauler and Suso also had to combat, but which were particularly widespread and influential in the Netherlands. These Brethren were opposed to all ecclesiastical authority and taught a more or less pantheistic doctrine without sacraments and dogma. In 1343 Ruysbroeck retired to the hermitage of Groenendael near Brussels, accompanied by his uncle and several friends. There they gave themselves up completely to a life of prayer and contemplation; in 1350 the community adopted the Rule of the Canons Regular of St. Augustine and Ruysbroeck became their prior. By this time the fame of his sanctity and wisdom had spread throughout Europe and attracted many disciples who sought his guidance.

Ruysbroeck taught the traditional threefold way to the mystical union; he described its stages as "The life of beginners, which is called the active life, and which is necessary for all men who wish to be saved . . . the interior, exalted and God-desiring life, at which men may arrive by their virtues and by the grace of God . . . and thirdly the super-essential, God-seeing life, which few men can attain or taste, by reason of its sublimity." Because the errors of the Brethren of the Free Spirit were so prevalent in his own country he laid particular stress on the preconditions of the life of mystical union, which are divine grace, a free turning of the will to God and a conscience free from mortal sins. All of these were either denied or at least greatly neglected by the Brethren, who, Ruysbroeck says, "would be free without the commandments of God, and without virtues, and empty and united with God, without love and charity." He emphasizes the necessity of humility and meekness, which

will reverence the Church and the sacraments. Ruysbroeck had
an intense devotion to the Eucharist; he held that in receiving
Holy Communion a man "should melt and flow forth in desire,
in joy, and in delight; for he embraces and is united with him
who is . . . the most gracious and lovable of all the children
of men." He realizes, however, that such feelings may not always be present, in which case, one should also go to Holy
Communion "if he intend the praise of God and his glory and
. . . if his conscience be clean from mortal sin."

When a man has overcome his sinful leanings and detached
himself from creatures he will enter on the second stage, the
"God-desiring life," in which the understanding will be illuminated and the will enkindled by love. Ruysbroeck assigns to this
stage ecstasies as well as very painful longings, which he calls
"the wound of love." For when the innermost heart has been
so wounded, "the stirring of the divine rays will cause a perpetual pain." On the one hand the mystic desires God with all
his heart, on the other he realizes that he cannot reach him,
and this causes him great restlessness. "In this state there are
sometimes spoken from within sublime and salutary words, and
special teachings and wisdom are given," when the spirit is
caught above itself into ecstasy—a state most other mystics
assign to the unitive way. Though admitting that these experiences can be very useful, Ruysbroeck nevertheless warns his
disciples of their dangers. Frequent long ecstasies, especially,
may damage a man's health; he therefore counsels his disciples
to resist them as much as possible, for "those who can govern
themselves will not die." Contrary to the popular idea, the
Flemish mystic is well aware that ecstasy in its physical aspect,
that is to say the fainting away of the body whose senses are
then completely closed to its surroundings, is but a weakness,
because the body is not yet accustomed to the impact of the
divine union. The mystic ought not to seek these dangerous delights; moreover, God will soon enough wean him from them.
Ecstasy will be followed by great dryness and many sufferings
both in the spiritual and the material spheres; not only will a

man feel himself forsaken by God, he may also lose his friends, his reputation, and other earthly good things. Instead of complaining, he should then be glad to be able to suffer for the glory of God, for ecstasies are dangerous, but aridity and self-abandonment are not.

Ruysbroeck, who was a great lover of nature, likened these painful periods in the mystical life to the autumn season, when the fruits ripen quickly. For they are meant to lead to the perfection of the mystical union, when visions and ecstasies are no longer needed, because then "a spiritual light will shine in the understanding. These men have no need of revelations, nor of being caught up above the senses, for their life and dwelling-place . . . are in the spirit." Their whole life, whether working or sleeping, is wholly lived in God, for the image of the Holy Trinity is perfectly restored in them.

When describing this highest state of the trinitarian transformation of man Ruysbroeck uses a terminology that is reminiscent of Eckhart. He says that "all those who are raised above their created being into a God-seeing life are one with this divine brightness [that is, the revealing Son]. And they are this brightness itself, and they see, feel and find, even by means of this divine light that, as regards their uncreated essence, they are that same onefold ground." He guards, however, against taking this language too literally when he continues: "And this is why inward and God-seeing men will go forth in the way of contemplation, above reason and above distinction, and above their created being through an eternal intuitive glance. By means of this inborn light they are transfigured and made one with that same light through which they see and which they see." Ruysbroeck does not deny that man's being is created, nor that it is essentially other than God. What he is trying to express is that at the moment of intense union man is raised above his created self into the divine sphere; he is not—as Eckhart frequently asserted—identical with the divine light but "made one" with it; there is union, not identity. It seems that these explanations are meant to tone down the "uncreated essence" of which he had just spoken and which can be explained as being no more than a very strong affirmation of the image-doctrine, the divine image being the essence of man, hence a reflection of the uncreated Godhead. That Ruysbroeck did not mean to identify God and man is clear from other passages. One comes from *The Sparkling Stone*, where he says that the human spirit, when observing itself, "finds a distinction and an otherness between itself and God; but where it is burnt up it is undifferentiated and without distinction, and therefore it feels nothing but unity; for the flame of the love of God consumes all that it can enfold in its self." So what he means to say is that, objectively speaking, the human self even in the highest union remains other than God; but as regards the subjective impression it feels only unity, as if it were wholly consumed by God. Again, in the *Book of Supreme Truth*, he writes that man and God are one "not as Christ is one with the Father, one single divine substance, for this is impossible to us; but so one, and in such a unity, as he is one fruition and one beatitude with the Father without distinction in essential love."

Though Ruysbroeck's language, therefore, sometimes resembles that of Eckhart, he always guards against it being understood as a union of nature, a metaphysical union; what he emphasizes is a union of love, a union of grace, which transforms the mystic into God, which "deifies" him.

3. ST. CATHERINE OF SIENA

Though St. Catherine (c. 1347–80) belonged to the same order as Master Eckhart—she was a Dominican tertiary—her mystical life and teaching were very different from those of the German Dominicans. Like many other women mystics, she was an ecstatic who had had visions from early childhood and whose ecstasies were almost daily occurrences. Her father was a wealthy Siennese dyer, Jacopo Benincasa, her mother, Monna Lapa, was a busy mother of a family; Catherine was her twenty-fifth child. When Catherine was six years old she had her first vision on her way home from a visit to her married sister, Bonaventura. To the surprise of her slightly older brother, Stephen, who accompanied her, she stopped suddenly in the middle of the road, for she saw a magnificent balcony, slightly above the ground, on which Christ was seated on a throne. He was robed in pontifical vestments and held a crozier in his hand; St. Peter, St. Paul, and St. John the Evangelist were with him; the earliest account added: "as she had seen them in the pictures in church." When her brother saw that she no longer followed him he shouted to her to come along; but she told him angrily to go away: "Can't you see that I do not want to come." But while she had taken her eyes off the vision it had disappeared.

Catherine was an exceptionally pious girl; she is reported to have practiced many penances and been rapt in contemplative prayer for hours; but it is not quite clear whether these reports accord with the facts or are rather the usual hagiographical embellishments to be found in all the saints' lives of the period. It does seem correct, however, that she made a vow of virginity at the tender age of seven. When she was twelve she went through a critical period of "worldliness"; for her sister Bonaventura persuaded her to take an interest in dresses and to go to the popular dances. But this time of relaxation came to a sudden end when Bonaventura died in childbirth, an event which made Catherine realize with overwhelming clarity the vanity of all earthly joys. To show that she meant henceforth to live only for God she cut off her beautiful hair, and, about 1364, after considerable opposition from her family, she joined the Third Order of the Dominicans, then called *Mantellate*. She could thus wear a religious habit while yet not tied to convent life, which did not suit her independent cast of mind.

The Third Order of St. Dominic is a penitential order, and consequently she now embraced an even more austere life than she had led before. She lived in an extremely small attic in her parents' house, keeping the shutters of the window almost always closed, so that the only light in the room came from the flames burning before the holy pictures on the walls. Catherine scarcely ever went out except to go to church, and she hardly ever spoke except to her confessor. Her food consisted of herbs and water, occasionally supplemented by dry bread, and she slept on a hard board for no more than an hour every other day. She also scourged herself and wore a chain studded with nails, which she never took off so that it grew into her skin.

It is hardly surprising that such an abnormal way of life should have produced psychological states in which the supernatural cannot always easily be separated from the natural. When she had received Holy Communion, for example, she used to fall to the ground and remain unconscious for hours, so that often her Dominican sisters had to carry her out of the church when it was locked up at noon. Her visions multiplied, and she was in trance also at other times, not only after Holy Communion. It seems quite possible that, apart from her genuine supernatural experiences, these states were also frequently caused by the physical exhaustion due to her abnormal life, which she continued to lead for three years. It ended with a vision called her "spiritual espousals." This took place on the last day of the carnival, which was universally kept with orgies of eating and drinking, dancing, and love-making, before the Lenten Fast put an end to all revelry. While the crowds of Siena shouted and made merry under her shuttered window, Catherine suddenly saw a very different pageant in her tiny room, which was invaded by Christ and his Mother, St. John the Evangelist, St. Paul, St. Dominic, David with his harp, and a host of angels. The Blessed Virgin took Catherine's right hand and asked her Son to accept her as his spouse. Then Jesus placed a ring on her finger and told her that "he espoused her to himself in faith." When the vision faded, Catherine remained in ecstasy. A few days afterwards the full meaning of her espousals —which were very similar to those told in the legend of her patron saint, Catherine of Alexandria—became clear to her: her period of retirement was at an end and she was henceforth to devote her life to the spread of Christ's kingdom.

From this time onwards Catherine's life became one long

series of striking charitable and apostolic activities. She joined her fellow tertiaries in their hospital work, nursing the sick day and night in the large infirmary of Santa Maria della Scala, the smaller Mercy Hospital and the lazar house reserved for hopeless cases. She also began to interest herself in the politics of the Italian cities constantly at war with each other and in the reform of the Church, so badly needed in the age of the Avignon Popes. A group of fervent disciples gathered round her, and soon her fame began to spread; she wrote to princes and prominent churchmen, upbraiding them when she thought it necessary and giving them advice. All these activities together with her extraordinary way of life and her constant ecstasies, roused not only admiration but also criticism, and in 1374 she was summoned before a chapter of the Dominican Order in Florence to give an account herself. She was vindicated, and after this begins the period of her ceaseless travels, always accompanied by a group of her followers, in the service of the Church. The most famous of these travels was her journey to Avignon as a kind of unofficial envoy of the city of Florence, then under a papal interdict, to make peace with the Pope. At Avignon she set out to induce Gregory XI to return to Rome, to reform the Church, and to start a Crusade, which she saw as a means to restore peace among the warring Christian nations by uniting them against a common enemy. Having received the Pope's promise to return to Italy, she herself went back to her homeland at the end of 1376, causing great popular excitement and preaching and performing miracles on her way. Her remaining years, during which she wrote her famous mystical work, the *Dialogue*, were full of disappointments, as the Pope's return to Rome had not the desired effect but rather was responsible for the ensuing Great Schism, when there were two Popes, one in Rome, the other in Avignon. Towards the end of 1378 she went to Rome herself, living on alms with her disciples and furthering as much as she could the cause of the Roman Pope Urban VI. She died on April 30, 1380, after weeks of intense sufferings.

Catherine's mystical teaching is contained in her letters and her *Dialogue*. It centers in her devotion to Christ crucified, especially to his precious blood, which played such an important role in medieval piety. Nearly all her letters open with formulas containing the words: "I, Catherine, write to you in his precious blood," and she exhorts her readers to "drink from the blood of the spotless Lamb," to fill themselves "like a vase, with the blood of Christ crucified." One of the most famous incidents of her life was concerned with the execution of a Perugian youth, Niccolo Tuldo, who had been condemned for a political crime against the Sienese government. Catherine had persuaded him to accept the capital sentence as the will of God and accompanied him to the scaffold, receiving his severed head into her arms while his blood flowed all over her clothes. She described this experience in a highly emotional letter to her confessor, the Dominican Raymund of Capua whom she wished to see "inflamed and drowned by that his sweetest blood" and continued to tell him how she "breathed the fragrance of his [Niccolo's] blood, and it was not without the fragrance of mine, which I wish to shed for the sweet Spouse Jesus." When Niccolo had been beheaded, she saw Christ, "and he stood wounded, and received the blood, and in that blood a fire of holy desire . . . When he was at rest, my soul rested in peace and quiet, in so great fragrance of blood that I could not bear to remove the blood which had fallen on me from him."

This mystical reverence for blood, which was as foreign to most Fathers as it is to the modern reader, is an outstanding feature of Catherine's spirituality and closely connected with her devotion to the sufferings of Christ which led her, like St. Gertrude before her, to the mystery of the Sacred Heart. She describes this especially in the *Dialogue*, so named because Catherine presented her teaching in the form of a conversation between her and God the Father. She connects the traditional three stages of the spiritual life with the Crucifix: the first is symbolized by the feet of Christ, which carry the affections up to the side, "which manifests the secret of his heart," where the soul tastes the love of this heart and is itself filled with love. This, however, is not the goal, for from the heart the soul will be led to the mouth, where it will find peace from the war against sin. In another passage God exhorts Catherine to hide herself in the cavern of Christ's side, where she will be given a taste of the divine nature through love of his humanity. For the heart of Jesus is given to the mystic "as a hostelry always open, that you might see and taste the ineffable love which I had for you."

But this love which the mystic feels for Christ is not mere emotion, it must express itself in love of one's neighbor. Catherine, whose own life was so full of charitable activities, was very explicit on this. "The soul," she makes God the Father say, "can in no way repay me for that pure love with which she feels herself loved by me, and therefore strives to repay it through the medium I have given her, that is to say her neighbour." Hence activity in the service of others is but a necessary outcome of the intense interior life of the mystic. But how can this interior life be lived to the full in a welter of activities such as Catherine herself lived it in her later years? She explained this in her doctrine of the inner cell. Catherine's whole teaching is permeated by a profound respect for knowledge, which she no doubt owed to her Dominican directors whose influence is unmistakable in her works despite her own originality. Hence, since she had no vocation to the cloister where she would have lived in a material cell, she developed the idea that one should construct an inner cell, the cell of self-knowledge, where one could withdraw at will from all the cares of the world and find God according to St. Augustine's word: May I know myself and may I know Thee. "Make two homes for yourself," she writes to a friend, "one actual home in your cell, and another spiritual home which you should always carry with you—the cell of true self-knowledge, where you shall find within yourself the knowledge of God's goodness." For self-knowledge and knowledge of God are interdependent; without the knowledge of God we would become discouraged, and without self-knowledge we would become pesumptuous; but the combination of both will lead to a properly balanced spiritual life, when the mystic will realize to the full the meaning of what Catherine believed God to have said to her: "I am he who is, and you are she who is not." This nothingness of the creature is experienced particularly in the periods of darkness and dryness, when God seems far away—a state in which the mystic must persevere with humility and withdraw ever more deeply into the cell of self-knowledge, "digging up the root of self-love with the knife of self-hatred and the love of virtue."

Like all authentic mystics, Catherine, too, does not esteem extraordinary experiences, even though her own life overflowed with them. She makes God say that "those who take great delight in mental consolations and seek for visions, place their end in the delight of these consolations rather than in me, hence they may be deluded." When she herself had an ecstasy during which she believed the stigmata would be impressed on her she asked that they should remain invisible—the perfect union of love and will between God and her rather than any outward signs was the goal of her life such as she describes it in her *Dialogue*. Those men who have died to themselves "can in no way be separated from my love, for by love they have arrived at so close a union. Every place is an oratory to them, every moment a time for prayer, their conversation has ascended from earth to heaven."

4. THE ENGLISH MYSTICS

The fourteenth century was also the mystical period of the English Church. But, unlike their Continental brethren, the English mystics were mostly solitaries. For side by side with monasticism there flourished in England an intense hermit life, though this was much less exaggeratedly austere than that of the Desert Fathers, as may be seen from the *Ancren Riwle*, composed probably in the early years of the thirteenth century. The best known of the English mystics were Richard Rolle of

Hampole (c. 1249–1349), the anonymous author of *The Cloud of Unknowing* (written probably about the middle of the fourteenth century), Walter Hilton (d. 1396), and Julian of Norwich (c. 1342–c. 1413).

The facts of Richard Rolle's life are somewhat uncertain. There exists still a liturgical office of Richard the Hermit that had been prepared in view of his future canonization which, however, never took place. According to this office he was born at Thornton, in Yorkshire, and studied at Oxford, but broke off his education at the age of nineteen and became a hermit. Recent investigation, on the other hand, seems to have proved that he went from Oxford to Paris, where he completed his studies and became a master and a priest, living as a hermit from about 1326, first on the estate of a friend and later at Hampole, as the spiritual director of a convent of Cistercian nuns.

Rolle wrote treatises on the spiritual life both in Latin and in English; he was much influenced by St. Bernard, Richard of St. Victor, and other earlier mystics. He shares with St. Bernard his intense devotion to Jesus, and his *Meditation on the Passion* is one of the most beautiful works in English on this subject. In his *Emendatio Vitae* (The Mending of Life) he describes the purgative way, demanding complete detachment from the world and a resolute fight against all obstacles, and describing, from his own experience no doubt, the great trials connected with this. For he speaks about them again in the first person in his *Incendium Amoris* (The Fire of Love), mentioning especially the opposition of trusted friends. But these sufferings will bear much fruit, for through them a man reaches that purity which is needed to "see God," as much as is possible in this life.

This painful period of purgation is followed by illumination, in which Rolle distinguishes three states which he describes as heat, song, and sweetness. Heat signifies the kindling in love, song the praise of the burning mind, and sweetness the effects in the soul of the other two. This imagery shows the emotional intensity of Rolle's spiritual life, which would often break out into real song, "when, for plenteousness of inward sweetness, I burst out singing before my Maker."

Rolle does not say very much on the actual unitive way; his description in *The Form of Perfect Living* (written in medieval English) is very sober. When men's love of God is perfectly purified they become contemplatives and are ravished in love, "and they see into heaven with their ghostly [=spiritual] eye," because contemplation is a sight. Nevertheless, they do not see into heaven perfectly, this they can do only after death.

The mystical teaching of *The Cloud of Unknowing* is totally different from the emotionalism of Rolle. It is profoundly influenced by the negative theology of the Pseudo-Dionysius. The anonymous author teaches a direct approach to God by forgetting all creatures, that is to say by purely contemplative prayer, which he frequently calls simply "this work." It consists in a "meek stirring of love," devoid of thought or any imaginary pictures. This leaving behind of all images and concepts is called the "cloud of unknowing," because when a man has forgotten all this he will enter the "cloud," to which he is led by "a sharp dart of longing love." The author is careful, however, to point out, that this unknowing does not take place at the beginning of the spiritual life. It follows after a man has meditated for some time on his own sins and the goodness of God. But this meditation, if practiced faithfully, is bound to lead to a period when God draws a man more directly to himself by introducing him into darkness. Once this stage has been reached, the author urges the contemplative to suppress all thought that might come between him and this darkness, a teaching that differs somewhat from that of the later mystics, especially St. Teresa and St. John of the Cross. For both teach that if at times the contemplative should still be attracted to meditation on special subjects he should do so and not actively suppress all thought, a doctrine meant to guard against the pseudo-mystical tendencies of the "illuminists" of their time. The author of the *Cloud*, on the other hand, advises his disciple to remain in the darkness as long as he can and to occupy himself with nothing but "a naked intent unto God" in his will, covering any definite thought "with a thick cloud of forgetting." This rules out even any thought about the Passion of Christ, which the Spanish mystics explicitly excepted even in the higher stages of contemplation.

The English author insists strongly that this "cloud" between God and man persists throughout this earthly life, however high the contemplative may ascend, because it is "the best and the holiest part of contemplation that may be in this life." Nevertheless, it may happen at times that God sends out "a ray of spiritual light, piercing this cloud of unknowing that is between you and him, and show you some of his secrets." But of this "work, that pertains only to God" he dares not speak—these are evidently the extraordinary mystical illuminations mentioned by such mystics as St. Paul or St. John of the Cross; for the principal aim of the author of the *Cloud* is to instruct and encourage a man in the ordinary ways of the mystical life. He strongly warns against the desire for strange experiences, which would lead only to illusions and keep a man back from true union with God, which is "nothing else but a good will unto God"; for the mystical union is essentially a union of wills. However, as man consists of body and soul, and God must be served with both, the happiness of the soul in the mystical union may at times overflow into the body "with wonderful sweetness and comforts." This physical enjoyment need not be rejected, nevertheless, it is only accidental and should not be consciously desired.

According to the author of the *Cloud*, ecstasy, which he calls "ravishing," is not essential to the life of union, which in many contemplatives will take a less violent form and have hardly any physical effects, whereas the Spanish mystics considered it a necessary stage on the way to the highest union, the "mystical marriage." But perhaps this divergence is due to a difference of temperament; for in the English the mystical life seems to take generally a less violent form than in the Latin races.

The Cloud of Unknowing has sometimes been ascribed to Walter Hilton, but his authorship of it is highly improbable, though the *Cloud* has undoubtedly influenced him. Hilton was an Augustinian Canon at a priory in Nottinghamshire, but no details are known of his life except that he directed an anchoress, to whom he addressed his most famous work, *The Ladder of Perfection.* This traces the mystical life from its beginnings in what he calls "the reforming in faith" to the various stages of the "reforming in feeling." The "reforming" concerns the image of God in the soul. The reforming in faith suffices for salvation, but for the contemplative and mystical life the reforming in feeling is needed, which has many degrees but reaches its perfection only in heaven. This life begins with feelings of great joy and devotion, but if a man is to progress in it he must be purified by what Hilton, like St. John of the Cross later, calls a dark night. In this night he becomes detached from all creatures and all the affections that still bind him to the world. This state may be either painful or soothing; it will be painful especially in the beginning, and Hilton counsels patience at this stage: when worldly thoughts occur at this time they should not be forcibly turned away, "but wait upon grace, suffer patiently and do not strain yourself too much." When the soul then becomes quite recollected and can think of nothing it is a good darkness. For Jesus (Hilton always speaks about Jesus, though this sometimes means God, or the Holy Spirit, or simply grace) will be in this darkness, "whether it be painful or restful." Nevertheless, he is there only by desire and longing; he is not yet there "resting in love, and showing his light." But when the soul gets accustomed to this darkness and begins to enjoy it, then it will very gradually be filled with spiritual knowledge, which is a light coming from the heavenly Jerusalem, Hilton's image of the fullness of contemplation. He describes its beginnings as the glimmerings of a great light seen through closed eyes, when something of the divinity of Christ is apprehended; as the soul becomes increasingly pure, this sight becomes clearer and more frequent, though it reaches its perfection only in the next world. Hilton insists that this is a purely spiritual sight, "not as some think that the opening of heaven is as if a soul might see by imagination through the skies above the firmament, how our Lord Jesus sits in his majesty in a physical light as great as a hundred suns. No, it is not so."

It seems that Hilton is writing against Rolle when he deprecates such physical signs of devotion as weeping, feelings of heat, and hearing of song. "These are not spiritual feelings," he says, "which are felt in the powers of the soul, principally in the understanding and love and little in imagination; but these feelings are in imagination, and therefore they are not spiritual feelings." The same applies to imaginary visions. The true mystical experience consists in an intellectual vision, in which there is no "fantasy," "but softness, meekness, peace, love and charity" and the mind is ravished from all earthly things. In this state the soul thinks that it touches God, "and by virtue of this ineffable touching it is made whole and stable in itself."

The little we know about Julian of Norwich comes from her own writings, in which she appears as the most lovable of women mystics. She lived as an anchoress in a cell that was attached to the Benedictine church of St. Julian in her home town, and at one time she had three fervent desires: she wished to realize more deeply the Passion of Christ, to suffer an illness while still young, about thirty years of age, and to receive the three "wounds" of contrition, of compassion, and of ardent longing for God. She had forgotten the first two wishes, when she became seriously ill at the age of thirty and a half years. When she was at the point of death the priest who attended her held up the Crucifix before her eyes. At this moment her sight began to fail and all grew dark about her except for the figure on the Cross; she became paralyzed from the waist downwards and could hardly breathe. But suddenly all her pains ceased, and then she remembered her desire to feel Christ's own Passion. At this point the figure on the Cross seemed to come to life and she had fourteen different visions which lasted from early morning till the afternoon.

These visions were of three kinds. She herself describes them as seen by bodily sight, by a word formed in her understanding, and by spiritual sight. The last and highest, she writes, "I cannot nor may not show as openly nor as fully as I would." In the technical language of modern mystical theology this description refers to imaginary visions, their interpretation by the understanding, and intellectual visions, in which a religious truth is impressed directly on the intellect.

Mother Julian's visions of the Passion conform throughout to the medieval artistic representations of the sufferings of Christ; despite their intensity, however, they are not the most significant part of her revelations. This is God's love for men, which is the very center of Julian's mystical doctrine. It is beautifully expressed in her vision of the world the size of a hazelnut, which despite its smallness lasts "because God loves it." In comparison with the Creator, the whole universe is as nothing; yet it is immensely important, because God himself loves it. And most of all he loves man, because he was made in God's own image and was redeemed by Christ.

For Julian God's love is not so much that of a Father but the more intimate and tender love of a Mother. So she calls Christ himself "our very Mother; we have our being in him, where the ground of motherhood begins, with all the sweet keeping of love that endlessly follows." She develops this theme in several ways: he is our Mother by nature and our Mother by grace, for "the mother's service is nearest, readiest and surest," and he feeds us with himself in the Blessed Sacrament as a mother feeds her children. Indeed, the word Mother is so beautiful that it should be said of no one but him.

This conception of God as a loving Mother explains also why Julian finds it extremely difficult to understand why he should have permitted sin, and to believe in the eternal punishment of hell. When she wondered about it Jesus answered her: "It behoved that there should be sin; but all shall be well, and all shall be well, and all manner of thing shall be well." But the problem remained with her, and she returns to it later in the book (itself the fruit of many years of meditation on what she had seen in the few hours of vision). There she admits that on

the one hand she was shown nothing but love and blissful salvation, on the other she believed in the teaching of the Church
on sin and punishment. Nevertheless, her own spiritual life was
evidently based wholly on an unshakable trust in God's motherly
goodness, which would not allow anyone to be lost. "Thus," she
writes, "our good Lord answered to all the questions and doubts
. . . saying full comfortably: I may make all thing well, I can
make all thing well, I will make all thing well, and I shall make
all thing well; and you shall see yourself that all manner of thing
shall be well."

B. The Eastern Church: Gregory Palamas and Hesychasm

It is a far cry from the simplicity of the English mystics to
the highly sophisticated mystical theology of Gregory Palamas,
(1296–1359) the greatest representative and leader of Hesychasm in the fourteenth century. His own life was agitated by a
bitter controversy with Barlaam, a Calabrian monk who used the
rational methods of Western Scholasticism in his theology,
whereas Palamas laid the greatest stress on supernatural illumination. In the West, Scholastic theology and mysticism could be
harmonized, since many of the great mystics, for example Tauler,
Suso, and later John of the Cross were themselves trained in
Scholastic theology; in the East such an harmonization was prevented by two factors: on the one hand the mystics emerged
from the monasteries, especially those of Mount Athos, where
Latin Scholasticism was unknown; on the other Barlaam, the
chief representative of a theology based on reasoning rather than
on the tradition of the Fathers, overemphasized the rational element while disregarding the supernatural factors in Christian
theology.

Gregory was the first-born of a very devout aristocratic family
of Constantinople; the grandson of the emperor, the future Andronicus III, was one of his closest friends. Being destined for
a court career, he received an excellent education and proved

himself a brilliant scholar. At the age of about twenty, however, he abandoned his studies and made his way to Mount Athos. Like St. Bernard, he did not go alone, but took his two younger brothers with him after placing his mother and his two sisters in a convent in the capital. Having spent three years in fasting, vigils, and constant prayer under the direction of an older monk, he settled in the Great Laura of St. Athanasius, which he left, however, about 1325, owing to the invasions of the Turks. He went to Thessalonica, where he was ordained priest, and afterwards retired with ten other monks to a hermitage on a mountain near Beroea. There he spent five days of the week in complete silence and uninterrupted prayer, practicing great austerities and leaving his solitude only on Saturday and Sunday to celebrate the liturgy and to converse with his brethren. In 1331 the invasions of the Servians forced him to leave and he returned to Mount Athos, where he continued his life of solitude in the hermitage of St. Sabbas. A few years later he began to write, among others, a long treatise on the *Presentation of the Blessed Virgin in the Temple*, which reflects his intense devotion to the Mother of God.

In 1337 Palamas received some writings of Barlaam, who ridiculed the method of prayer of the Hesychasts. This name derives from the Greek *hesychia*, which means both quiet and solitude. Now the Hesychasts believed that prayer is the activity of the whole man, both body and soul, hence they used methods employed especially in Eastern religions, such as a certain manner of breathing and a certain posture to aid them to concentrate, accompanied by the so-called Jesus prayer: "Jesus Christ, son of God, have pity on me." Barlaam considered this method heretical, called the monks "omphalopsyches," that is those whose soul is in their navel, and agitated against them in Thessalonica. Hence, Palamas went there in 1338 to defend himself and the Hesychasts and began his great work, the *Defence of the Holy Hesychasts*. He further drew up his *Hagioritic Tome*, approved by the monastic authorities of Mount Athos, which roundly condemned the ideas of Barlaam. A synod was called by the Emperor Andronicus III in June 1341 which pronounced itself in favor of Palamas and the monks. But Andronicus died immediately afterwards, and in the troubles that followed Palamas took the part of Cantacuzenus, the future emperor, against the Patriarch John Calecas, and was imprisoned, first in a monastery, and in 1343 in the palace prison. In 1344 he was also excommunicated. The Patriarch, however, overplayed his hand and came into conflict with the empress, Ann of Savoy, who called a council in 1347 which deposed him. Palamas was freed, and his friend Cantacuzenus became co-emperor with Ann's son, John V. Palaeologus. In the same year he was appointed bishop of Thessalonica, but he could not take possession of his see until 1350, when Cantacuzenus occupied the city. However, the controversy about his teaching still continued; hence in 1351 Cantacuzenus called a synod at Blachernae, outside Constantinople, over which he presided himself and which declared Palamas orthodox; since then his doctrine has been generally accepted by the Orthodox Church.

But Palamas was not allowed to administer his diocese in peace. He had to intervene in a quarrel between the two emperors, and on his way to Constantinople he was captured by the Turks, who treated him and his entourage well; he was released only in 1355, because the sending of his ransom had been delayed. His last years were devoted to writing and preaching. He was canonized in 1368 by the Greek Church.

Like the lives of St. Bernard, St. Catherine of Siena, and many other Western mystics, Gregory's life, too, proves that one can be a mystic and yet be deeply involved in the events of one's time. His mystical theology is firmly based on the Incarnation and the sacraments flowing from it. For the Son of God became man in order to create a new man and by assuming mortality bestow upon man immortality and "deify" him. This regeneration of man is realized in each individual Christian by the sacraments. The triple immersion of baptism signifies the three days Christ spent in the underworld before his resurrection—a favorite subject of the Eastern Fathers—from which the newly baptized emerges to the resurrection of his soul, having received the divine life which, given his generous co-operation, will lead to his deification. In this he is powerfully assisted by the Eucharist, through which Christ becomes one body with us and makes us a temple of the Divinity, because the fullness of the Godhead dwells in his body. Nevertheless, Gregory's mysticism differs in many respects from that of his Western contemporaries. For in the East the glorified rather than the crucified Christ is at the center of the mystical experience, and what the mystic desires is not so much a share in the sufferings of Jesus as a participation in his risen life, represented by the light that surrounded him at the Transfiguration on Mount Thabor. Palamas knows very well that both Gregory of Nyssa and the Pseudo-Dionysius described the mystical experience in terms of darkness and negation, but in his view behind and beyond the darkness is the divine light, which is perceived by the spiritual eyes the mystic has received. These are a gift of grace, the precondition for which is an ascetical life and the practice of the Jesus prayer, combined as has already been mentioned with certain breathing exercises and physical postures. For in the view of Palamas and the Hesychasts the whole man, both soul and body, has a part in the mystical life. Like Richard Rolle he affirms that prayer produces bodily heat, a view he supports by the evidence of such Old Testament prophets as Elijah and Jeremiah, the one ascending to heaven in a fiery chariot, the other speaking of his entrails being burned as by fire (Jeremiah 20:9). For the mystical life produces a transformation not only of the soul but also of the flesh. "For those," he writes, "who have raised their mind to God and lifted up their soul with divine longing, their transformed flesh, too, will be exalted and enjoy the divine communion and become the possession and dwelling place of God."

Those who are thus transformed will also have received a special knowledge, which is not procured by study—this he affirms against Barlaam—but by divine illumination and is accessible even to the senses, just as the light of Thabor was perceived by the apostles, even though this light itself was not sensible; it was made perceptible by a non-sensible power. For, he insists, the body, too, shares in the grace the spirit receives, "it enters into harmony with grace and senses in a certain way the ineffable mystery that is produced in the soul." Hence when in sustained prayer the soul is spiritually inflamed, "the body, too, becomes in a strange way light and hot," and the mystic tastes, through his spiritual senses, a divine joy without the slightest admixture of sorrow. For according to Palamas contemplation is not only renunciation and negation, it is a deifying union after all intellectual activity has ceased. For then both intellect and senses are replaced by the divine and incomprehensible Spirit himself. Hence in the opinion of Palamas this supernatural union of man with the divine light is the only source of a true theology—a teaching that is not without its dangers, because it may easily lead to illuminism, since the visionary himself is thus made the judge of his own experiences.

Now what exactly is the vision which the Hesychast aspires to see, "not through the intellect, nor through the body, but through the [divine] Spirit"? It is, first of all, the human spirit itself, "freed from the passions and resplendent with the divine light," because man was created in the image of God, hence the purified human spirit reflects this light like a mirror. But in the higher stages of the mystical life it sees the divine light, the light of Thabor itself, which is infinitely brighter than the sun. This light, however, is not God as he is in himself; for Palamas distinguishes between the incomprehensible Deity, which cannot be approached by men, and the divine energies—a difficult concept already found in some of the later Greek Fathers. In Palamas, the divine energies are inseparable from, though not actually identical with, the divine essence; they are the means by which the completely transcendent and incomprehensible God, in his goodness, makes himself known to us and gives us a share in himself. The light, then, which the mystic experiences in his vision, is this uncreated divine energy which manifests God. In it God communicates not his nature, but his glory and his splendor.

"Those," writes Palamas, "who are raised to this degree of contemplation know that they see a light with their intellectual sense [a paradox expressing that this 'sense' is neither sense nor intellect but something above either] and that this light is God who, through his grace, renders mysteriously luminous those who participate in the union." Nevertheless, the things the saints see in this light cannot be described in human words, for the mystical union with the divine light makes them realize that this light transcends everything, for it is a vision of the invisible.

Thus, in the mysticism of Palamas and the Hesychasts, there is no place for the visions of Christ and the saints who played such a considerable part in the mysticism of the medieval West; they aspired rather to the vision of, and union with, the divine light itself.

XI THE END OF THE
MIDDLE AGES

Though the fifteenth century still produced its quota of mystics it was nevertheless a period of decline. The so-called *Devotio moderna*, a spiritual movement that originated in the Netherlands and produced the Brothers and Sisters of the Common Life and the Canons Regular of the Congregation of Windesheim, was ascetical rather than mystical; its most famous literary product is the *Imitation of Christ*, generally attributed to Thomas a Kempis (c. 1380–1471), the most important exponent of the movement. The *Imitation* is a manual of the spiritual life intended for religious; but it became so famous that for centuries it has also been used by lay people. Though it cannot be said to be a mystical work properly so called, it nevertheless may lead to the mystical union, and mystical experiences seem to be mentioned in it. The author speaks, for example, of the voice of Christ heard within the soul and of his felt presence: "When Jesus is present, all is well, and nothing seems difficult, but when he is absent, everything is hard. When Jesus does not speak within, there is hardly any comfort; but when he speaks even only one word, great consolation is felt." It may, however, be questioned whether such expressions refer to actual "mystical" experiences or only to "consolation" and "aridity" in pre-mystical prayer.

A main characteristic of the *Imitation*, which has influenced much of the mystical literature for centuries to come, is its rigid separation of the supernatural from the natural life and its scorn for all human knowledge. The knowledge it recommends and to which it is intended to lead is an infused, mystical knowledge, for "he to whom the Eternal Word speaks is freed from many opinions . . . O God who is Truth, make me one with yourself in perpetual charity . . . Let all the teachers be silent and speak you alone to me." This individualism which relies only on personal experience, is noticeable throughout the spiritual teaching of the *Imitation;* it appears particularly also in the otherwise very beautiful Book IV, on the Blessed Sacrament, which is seen, however, only from a very personal point of view unrelated to the whole Mystical Body of Christ.

JEAN GERSON

The *Imitation* has also occasionally been attributed to Jean Gerson (1363–1429), at one time chancellor of the University of Paris, but on extremely slender evidence. He was a native of Rethel in the Ardennes, and studied theology in Paris. From the beginning of his career he was deeply concerned with the reform of the Church, torn at the time by the Great Western Schism. Many of his writings reflect this preoccupation, for, like Palamas, he took an active part in many of the controversies of his time. He attended the Council of Constance (1414–18) in 1415, approving the condemnation of the Bohemian reformer John Huss and opposing the defense of tyrannicide proposed by Jean Petit. Because of this opposition he incurred the enmity of the Duke of Burgundy, Jean sans Peur, who had ordered the assassination of the Duke of Orleans and in whose defense Jean Petit had developed his theory. Hence Gerson had to live the next years in exile in the Benedictine abbey of Melk near Vienna, returning to France after Jean's death in 1419. He spent his last years in retirement at Lyons, where he devoted himself to a life that combined writing and contemplation with apostolic activities, especially among the children.

Much of Gerson's mystical teaching is oppossed to the errors of his time which abounded in pseudo-mystical sects like the Beghards as well as in individuals claiming special mystical inspirations. Therefore he drew up rules for the discernment of spirits, some of which sound surprisingly modern. First of all, he demands a medical examination of visionaries, because visions and revelations may often be no more than hallucinations of a diseased mind. One should also be chary of the experiences of those newly converted to the spiritual life, because first fervor often leads to illusions. In fact, in appraising the value of mystical experiences the whole character and life of their recipients must be carefully weighed.

In his own mystical theology Gerson bases himself on earlier authorities, particularly Pseudo-Dionysius, St. Bonaventure, and the Victorines. Two powers of the soul correspond to the mystical life: the simple intelligence, also called the spiritual eye, and the synderesis, corresponding to the spark or ground of the soul which has been mentioned before. The first is the organ of contemplation, the second of mystical love. This love unites a man to God and fills him with supernatural joy. Against the false mystics Gerson insists that, however close the union, God and man always retain their identities, man is not as it were swallowed up in God. It seems that in 1425 he received a revelation in which it became clear to him that the mystical union is neither in the intellect nor in the affections, but above the activities of either in the ineffable and unknown union between the divine "Monad" (a Dionysian term) and the essence of the simplified and purified soul.

DIONYSIUS THE CARTHUSIAN

Though a prolific and very influential author in his own time, Dionysius the Carthusian (1402–71) cannot lay claim to much originality as a mystic theologian. He was a native of Rijkel in Belgium, and wanted to become a Carthusian when still only a boy. He was advised by the authorities of the order to study first at the University of Cologne, where he took his degree as Master of Arts in 1424. Soon afterwards he entered the Charterhouse at Roermund in Holland, where he combined a mystical life—he had frequent ecstasies—with his literary work, which in the modern edition comprises no less than forty-four volumes, largely scriptural commentaries but also commentaries on Pseudo-Dionysius and treatises on the contemplative and the mystical life and on the Blessed Virgin.

According to Dionysius the preconditions of the mystical life are an intense love of God, the detachment of the mind from all creatures, and concentration on God alone. But the mystical experience itself depends on the Holy Spirit, who is its principal cause, and especially on the gift of wisdom. He also teaches the negative way of the Pseudo-Areopagite, but not as the ultimate mystical experience. This is the contemplation of the Trinity. For after a man has been united to God as the unknown, he will ascend to the Three Divine Persons who give themselves to those who have been prepared for them by the gift of wisdom, intense charity, and a heroic life. In this state of mystical perfection the mystic will penetrate the mysteries of the faith and delight in their contemplation, he will understand their interconnection and the depth of the divine counsels and will often be rapt into ecstasy, wholly absorbed in God himself, the fount of infinite wisdom. For "the state of the perfect is to taste how sweet is the Lord through contemplation, and to attain to the secret of mystical theology through the intense fervour of charity." Like most other mystics before him, Dionysius situates this sublime contemplation in the fine point of the spirit (the ground or spark of the soul), which is itself wholly transformed in God through perfect love and the unitive life, without, of course, becoming identical with God.

ST. CATHERINE OF GENOA

St. Catherine of Genoa (1447–1510) inspired Baron Friedrich von Hügel's monumental work on mysticism, although she is not one of its outstanding figures. She belonged to a noble family who counted Popes Innocent IV and Adrian V as well as several cardinals among its members. According to her first biographer,

Cataneo Marabotto, who was her confessor in later life, she was inspired to do penance at the age of eight. When she was thirteen she wanted to enter the Convent of the Augustinian Canonesses of the Lateran, where her elder sister, Limbania, was a nun, but was refused on account of her extreme youth. Three years later she married Giuliano Adorni in obedience to the will of her parents. The marriage was not happy, for Giuliano was a very worldly man, who had fathered five illegitimate children before his marriage and spent money recklessly. The first five years Catherine tried to live like a nun, going out only to hear Mass and refusing to adapt herself to her station in life. When this conduct became impossible, and under the influence of her family's reproaches, she began to take part in the social life of her class and at first enjoyed this; she later reproached herself bitterly for these years of "dissipation," though like her namesake of Siena before her, she probably greatly exaggerated her sinfulness during this time. After a few years of worldly life, however, this began to disgust her, and in 1473, at the age of twenty-six, she had a conversion experience. At a visit to her sister, Limbania insisted that she should go to confession; Catherine complied, but when she was kneeling before the priest she suddenly received "a wound of love" in her heart and a clear vision of her own faults and miseries as well as of the goodness of God. Quite overcome, she fell to the ground unable to make her confession and had to come back next day.

From that day began her mystical life, in which genuine mystical experiences of a high order are combined with certain phenomena of manifestly neurotic origin. Her husband agreed that they should live together as brother and sister; and her own life is described in her biography in accordance with the traditions of medieval hagiography: she kept her eyes cast down, wore a hair shirt, fasted, slept on a bed made penitential by thorns and thistles, and even swallowed insects to overcome her disgust. She devoted six hours a day to prayer and received permission to communicate daily, a very rare practice in those days. She also visited the sick and later was put in charge of the women's ward of a large hospital. Her husband, whom she had converted, often joined her in her charitable visits and became a Franciscan tertiary. He died in 1497. The last ten years of her life she suffered from a very painful undiagnosed illness accompanied by strange phenomena.

Catherine's mystical experiences and teaching are contained in her biography, which reproduces many of her sayings and reflections, and in the *Treatise on Purgatory*, most of which was probably written by herself, whereas the *Dialogue* is the work of one of her disciples. The *Treatise on Purgatory* was inspired by her own experiences of mystical purification. It reflects her conviction that the total surrender of self-will and complete rejection of all earthly concerns is necessary to achieve union with God. In the purified soul there must be nothing of self; for perfect works are not accomplished by men, but by God. Thus Catherine considers the world as a prison and her body as chains which must be broken in order to reach God: resistance to all one's natural inclinations including spiritual consolations is the way to it. Then the soul will attain to the state of "pure love," where God takes complete possession of his creature in such a way that it can no longer act otherwise than as he wills. This is the annihilation of the human will, an annihilation which Catherine calls "queen of heaven and earth" and which causes a man "to remain like something entirely outside his own proper being," having no affection for any created thing. In this state the soul is so united to God that it says "my being is God, not only by participation, but by a veritable transformation and an annihilation of my own being"—a very exaggerated expression, but which probably means no more than an intense feeling of being united to God, which Catherine described in theologically inaccurate terms. For we cannot take the words of a mystic of her temperament, whose whole life was abnormal in many ways, at their face value; they are the outpourings of a woman whose experiences were intensified by broken health and colored by her disgust with her own bodily human nature.

For it is very difficult to distinguish in her life the authentically mystical from the pathological elements; she would, for example, temporarily lose her eyesight or her power of speech, have convulsions, lie immovable on the ground for many hours, and suffer from anesthesia (lack of feeling). Besides, her ecstasies usually lasted for three to four hours, a duration which seems to indicate abnormal physical debility. Nevertheless, her doctrine of the perfect annihilation of self and the pure love of God has had a great influence especially in seventeenth-century France, where it played a part in the Quietist controversy.

XII MYSTICISM IN THE AGE OF THE REFORMATION AND THE COUNTER-REFORMATION

1. THE REFORMERS' ATTITUDE TO MYSTICISM

The theology of the reformers, Luther (1483–1546) and Calvin (1509–64), was fundamentally inimical to the development of genuine mysticism, even though mystical trends made themselves felt at times. Luther himself was interested in mysticism in his early years, even for some time after he had started the "Reformation" by affixing his ninety-five theses to the door of the Schlosskirche at Wittenberg in 1517. He was attracted by the German mystics, Master Eckhart and Tauler, and especially by an anonymous late fourteenth-century treatise, the so-called *Theologia Teutsch* (German Theology), which he published himself in 1516. Of this he said that, except for the Bible and St. Augustine, no book had ever taught him more about God and Christ and the human condition. This is very significant, for though this book is fairly orthodox even if rather one-sided in its mystical teaching, it nevertheless emphasizes certain aspects which were later to be taken out of their mystical context and embodied in Luther's own doctrine.

These are above all an exaggerated insistence on the worthlessness of creatures and a very pessimistic view of nature, which the author occasionally even identifies with the devil, and further an opposition to reason and study. Moreover, the author considers the view that men can merit anything by their good works an affront to God. He also has the very strange view that man's will does not belong to man but to God, and ought to be exerted not by man but by God. There is no question of sanctifying grace, which is the foundation of the supernatural and hence also of the mystical life, and which builds on and transforms nature and thus gives value also to all man's natural actions—apart, of course, from sin—in the eyes of God. Add to the ideas of the *Theologia* the specifically Lutheran doctrine of justification by faith alone, without works, and you have the foundation on which Lutheran spirituality rests. It is a spirituality that tends fairly strongly towards Quietism, that deprecates human activity and opens up an abyss between God and man that can be bridged only by the legal fiction of God imputing the merits of Christ to man, who nevertheless remains as much a sinner as before. This "imputation" of the merits of Christ is brought about by faith, not in the Catholic sense of accepting certain doctrines, but in the sense of *fiducia* or trust, confidence. Now, since this acceptance has taken place once and for all, and as no further human activity follows from it, man's spiritual life allows of no progress, and so Luther's mysticism may well be called a mysticism, or perhaps rather a *mystique*, of justification. Man remains passive in gratitude for what Christ has done for him.

In later life Luther rejected mysticism increasingly and so did most of his followers, though experience taught both him and them that a Christian life simply could not dispense with human effort. This is quite evident, for example, in one of the most important later representatives of Lutheran orthodoxy, Johannes Gerhard (1582–1637), who wrote a book of meditations in which, while emphasizing faith in the sense of the reformer, he nevertheless extensively reproduced Catholic spiritual teaching, quoting St. Bernard and many other Catholic mystics, and insisting on moral effort and ascetical virtues such as chastity and self-denial.

The doctrine of the other great reformer, John Calvin, differed considerably from that of Luther in that it was activist rather than quietist. Where Luther stressed the justification that had taken place once and for all, Calvin wanted to lead his followers to a progressive santification. This, however, was restricted to those predestined to salvation; for Calvin taught a predestination to hell as well as to heaven. This doctrine necessarily led to grave anxiety: for how was a man to know to which of the two the inscrutable will of God had predestined him? From this dilemma evolved what today is called "the mysticism of consolation." Firmly convinced of his utter weakness and depravity, the Calvinist raises his mind to the mercy of God, the sole cause of his sanctification. This practice will gradually lead to a change in his image of God, who is no longer full of wrath but becomes increasingly gracious and loving. This processs culminates in a sudden illumination, through which a man feels with absolute conviction that God loves him and which assures him of his salvation. At this moment the divine image obscured by the Fall is restored.

Calvin, too, teaches the justification by faith, the word taken in the same sense as in Luther, but in the Swiss reformer's view good works are the necessary consequence of faith, for whomsoever Christ justifies, he also sanctifies. Even though he does not teach the real presence of Christ in the Eucharist, he is nevertheless convinced that the Holy Communion is a channel of grace which unites a man with his Saviour. He also encourages ascetical practices like fasting and watching. Despite these traits of Calvinist spirituality, however, its conception of a God whose main concern is his own glory and who inspires fear much more than love, as well as its teaching on a rigid predestination to heaven or hell prevented the development of mysticism in the Catholic (and Orthodox) sense, that is of the experienced loving union of man with God.

2. THE COUNTER-REFORMATION

a. Jesuit Spirituality

ST. IGNATIUS

While the Reformation—whatever its deeper causes—has been responsible for the unhappy division of Western Christendom, one of its more desirable effects was the renewal of Catholic spirituality and mysticism through the activity of some great saints. The first in the field was Ignatius of Loyola (1495–1556), best known as the very active founder of the Society of Jesus, but who was also a great contemplative and mystic. His early life, however, held out little promise of his later eminent sanctity. He was the descendant of a Basque noble family, who entered on a military career at an early age. He was an ambitious soldier, proud of his ancestry as well as of his own exploits, with no particular interest in his religion. The turning point of his life came on May 20, 1521, when he was wounded in his leg while defending the fortress of Pampeluna against the French. He was sent back to his family home at Loyola, and there spent long months of inactivity. The only books which his pious sister-in-law could procure for him were a *Life of Christ* by the Carthusian Ludolph of Saxony and the *Legend of the Saints* by Jacob of Voragine. He would have preferred fashionable romances of chivalry, but soon the deeds of the saints began to fire his imagination and he said to himself: "If St. Dominic and St. Francis of Assisi could do such things, why not I?"

By the time he was on his feet again his mind was made up: instead of remaining a soldier of his king he would become a soldier of Christ. Dressed in sackcloth he went on pilgrimage to the famous shrine of Montserrat near Barcelona, where he hung up his sword before Our Lady's image and stayed for some time with the Benedictines there, before going on to Manresa. There he remained for ten months, leading a life of extreme austerity and constant prayer, during which he received many mystic graces both of consolation and of the sufferings of the "dark night of the soul." The outcome of this period of retirement was the first draft of his famous *Spiritual Exercises,* a work which has influenced Christian spirituality throughout the following centuries. From Manresa he went to Rome to ask the Pope's permission for making a pilgrimage to the Holy Land, begging all the way, because he wanted to trust in God alone. The whole journey from Barcelona to Jerusalem took six months, but when he arrived at the Holy City the Franciscan Guardians told him to his dismay that he would not be able to stay there for the rest of his life, as he had intended, because of the hostility of the Turks.

After his return to Europe he resolved that, if he wanted to help others to find Christ, he would have to study; and so he went to Barcelona and, at the age of thirty-one, put himself to school with the children to learn Latin, still begging for his food, which consisted mostly of bread and water. In 1526 he left Barcelona for the University of Alcalà, where he attended the lectures, besides giving his *Exercises* and doctrinal instructions to a number of people who had been attracted by this extraordinary student. He was suspected of heresy and briefly imprisoned; after his release he left for Salamanca, where he suffered the same fate, so he decided to go to Paris, where he arrived early in 1528. During his time of study in Paris he made several journeys to collect alms for himself and his fellow students, which took him as far as England. In Paris he found the first six members of his future order, Peter Faber and Francis Xavier among them. In 1534 he took his degree as Master of Arts, and in the same year the seven companions made vows of poverty and chastity and resolved to go to Jerusalem if they could find a passage within a year, otherwise they would offer their services to the Pope to be sent wherever he chose.

Owing to the war between Venice and the Turks the former was not feasible, and so they went to Rome. On the way there Ignatius had a vision of Christ telling him that he would be favorable to them in that city. In Italy he also became aware of the dangers of Protestantism. He and his companions resolved to form themselves into a new order, making a special vow of obedience to the Pope; and in 1540 this was approved by Rome and a year later Ignatius was elected the first general of the Society. During the next years he worked out the constitutions of the new order, during which time he received many mystical graces. He was often in ecstasy during Mass and had many visions. He also conducted an immense correspondence; though he himself had led an extremely penitential life after his conversion, he always counseled prudence in his letters, urging, as he did for example to the later saint, Francis Borgia, that "since both body and soul belong to their Creator and Lord who will demand an account of them, you must not allow your natural powers to become weakened"—a view very different from that of many medieval mystics, who, as we have seen, regarded their body as their enemy.

Though St. Ignatius was himself a mystic, his main work, the *Spiritual Exercises*, is not a mystical treatise. In fact, it is no treatise at all, it may rather be called a book of instructions about how to make a truly successful retreat that will lead to a transformation of the whole man. For this purpose, intellect, senses, and imagination are all brought into play in order to influence the will to make the right decision and to order one's life according to God's purpose. The book breathes the spirit of the new age: it is profoundly concerned with human psychology and the inner springs of human action; meditation on the life and teaching of Christ is not an end in itself, but designed to spur the man who "makes" the *Exercises* (for this book must be "made," not read) to the most generous effort in the service of God, *ad majorem Dei gloriam*, to the greater glory of God, the motto of the order Ignatius had founded.

This is not to say, however, that the *Exercises* have nothing to do with the mystical life. The Jesuit Order has produced an impressive quota of mystics, and the way that led them, like their founder, to the heights of the mystical union was the way of the *Exercises*. At their end occurs a section called "Contemplation for Obtaining Love," which is really a description of the mystical life. For, in the words of Ignatius, "love consists in mutual interchange on either side, that is to say in the lover giving and communicating with the beloved what he has or can give, and on the other hand, in the beloved sharing with the lover." This sharing between God and man is the essence of the mystical union, in which man gives all he has to God and receives in return the divine life, so that he can say with St. Paul: "No longer I, but Christ in me." This awakening and development of the Christ-life in man as expressed in apostolic action is the whole purpose of the *Exercises*; but the way towards it is methodical, in keeping with the dawning age of science and technology.

ST. ALPHONSUS RODRIGUEZ

Though a lay brother and a late vocation, Alphonsus Rodriguez (1533–1617) is an impressive exponent of Jesuit mysticism. He had been married, but lost both his wife and his children and entered the Society of Jesus at the age of thirty-eight. After his novitiate, which, of course, involved making the *Exercises*, he was sent to the Jesuit house in Mallorca as a porter. Apart from a large number of vocal prayers which he recited as a priest recites his breviary, he spent much of his day in contemplative prayer. This prayer, however, was not an end in itself but was largely used by him to advance in virtue. For example, if some misfortune distressed him, he at once began to pray, "placing the pain between God and his soul." Then he made interior acts of the will rejoicing in the pain for the love of God and thus "turned bitterness into sweetness," and so "the way the soul must follow to reach sanctity is to mortify itself with the help of prayer." Thus even contemplative prayer becomes an instrument of overcoming oneself and is used as a means to achieve sanctity. Anything that does not have this sanctifying effect is of little value; hence Alphonsus, like so many mystics before him, attaches hardly any importance to visions and other phenomena. "Hence," he writes, "this person [referring to himself] behaves towards them as if he had to do with a shadow. He concentrates on the fear of God and forgets it all, except in so far as he must give an account [to his confessor] of what has happened to him. These extraordinary things seem to him to endanger humility and to be unnecessary for virtue. They ought to be feared and fled as much as possible."

Describing his own mystical union with God he uses precisely the terms of the *Exercises:* "Then the soul loves God and enjoys him, because it is so absorbed and as it were bathed in the divine love. The state at which it has arrived is that of a very perfect union with God, and, so to speak, of a transformation into God. At this point, *each gives to the other all he has and all he is*"—almost the exact words of Ignatius in the passage of the *Exercises* quoted above and of his famous prayer, *Suscipe.* This union, of course, is not achieved without great interior sufferings, during which the mystic feels himself abandoned by God and given over to all kinds of temptations. According to his order's emphasis on obedience Alphonsus practiced this religious virtue to a heroic degree, indeed he identified it with charity; for "the greatest charity," he writes, "is to obey God, the contrary would not be charity." This obedience is closely connected with perfect resignation or "abandonment" to the divine will, a high mystical state emphasized also by later Jesuit contemplatives. Through this perfect abandonment the mystic becomes truly a child in the sense of Christ's teaching, anticipating Teresa of Lisieux's later teaching on the spiritual childhood. "Provided the soul let itself be carried like a little child," he writes, "God visits it in proportion to its faith, humility, charity and purity of heart." Paradoxically, this state does not belong to the beginning, but to the end of the mystical way; for two years before his death, as a man of over eighty who had long been introduced to the heights of the unitive life, Alphonsus wrote of his attitude: "I behave as a child at the breast behaves to his mother."

3. THE CARMELITES

ST. TERESA OF AVILA

The latter half of the sixteenth century, so full of religious controversy especially in Central Europe, produced an amazing flowering of mysticism in Spain, represented above all by the two great Carmelites, Teresa of Avila and John of the Cross. It had been prepared by several influential spiritual writers such as the Dominican Louis of Granada (1505–88) and John of Avila (1500–69), both of them advisers of Teresa. Like St. Ignatius, Louis of Granada taught a method of meditation, though on simpler lines than the *Spiritual Exercises*, while John of Avila, himself a mystic, warned against the pseudo-mystical sect of the Alumbrados, then troubling the religious authorities in Spain. They were accused of favoring Lutheranism and persecuted by the Spanish Inquisition, so that even orthodox Catholic mystics became suspect. St. Teresa herself was to suffer from such suspicions.

Teresa de Cepeda y Ahumada (1515–82) came from a large, well-to-do family of Avila and spent a happy childhood with her eleven brothers and sisters. She grew up into a very attractive girl, fonder of romances of chivalry than of religious books and very concerned about her appearance. At the age of sixteen she was sent to a finishing school in her home town, run by Augustinian nuns, but the eighteen months she spent there did not give her an attraction to the religious life. She had to leave owing to a serious illness; after her recovery she visited an uncle, who gave her spiritual books to read which emphasized the sufferings of sinners in hell. She began to fear that she would have gone there if she had died during her illness, so she decided to become a nun, because "this was the best and safest state," as she writes in her autobiography.

The wrench from her home and her family cost her a great deal and soon after she had entered the Convent of the Incarnation at Avila she had a breakdown and was sent away to be given medical attention. But the strange cures of those times made her condition worse, and she returned to the convent, where she suffered a great deal from what seems mostly to have been nervous troubles, involving cataleptic states and paralysis. Nevertheless, she began to practice mental prayer and had made some progress in it, but having no understanding director and many distractions in her uninclosed convent she gave it up again. After the death of her father (in 1543), to whom she was deeply attached, her spiritual life deteriorated still more and she found it impossible to practice the recollection necessary for mental prayer; but since she was gay and attractive, she was much in demand in the parlor. In this way she continued to live for about twelve years.

The great change in consequence of which she was to turn from a very ordinary nun into the great mystic as which she is known throughout Christendom came in 1555, when she was in her fortieth year. She began to experience once more the presence of God and soon came also to see visions and hear voices. As the Jesuits had founded a house at Avila a short time ago, she consulted some of the Fathers who reassured her that her experiences came from God. About this time she also had her first rapture when she heard the words: "I will have you converse not now with men but with angels." From this moment she gave up her worldly friendships which had so far prevented her from devoting herself wholly to God.

There followed a time when Teresa suffered much from a number of priests, introduced by her regular confessor, who declared her experiences to be diabolic illusions and ordered her to cut down her Holy Communions and her prayer time. This threw her into a distressing uncertainty which lasted for two years, after which period her mystical experiences became more frequent, calming all her doubts. She had many visions of Christ on the Cross or in his risen glory, the best-known of them being the so-called transverberation of her heart, which seems to have taken place in 1559. She did not see it only once but "sometimes," as she writes herself. In this vision she saw an angel, "not tall, but short, and very beautiful, his face so aflame that he appeared to be one of the highest types of angel . . . In his hands I saw a long golden spear and at the end of the iron tip I seemed to see a point of fire. With this he seemed to pierce my heart several times so that it penetrated to my entrails. When he drew it out . . . he left me completely afire with a great love of God." The pain which this experience caused her was spiritual rather than physical, though her body had a share in it; but it was also intensely sweet. "During the days which this continued, I went about as if in a stupor. I had no wish to see or speak with anyone, but only to hug my pain, which caused me greater bliss than any that can come from the whole of creation."

This experience seems to have occupied the same place in St. Teresa's life as her mystical espousals in that of Catherine of Siena: it marked the end of her period of retirement and the beginning of greater activity. For soon afterwards she embarked on the chief enterprise of her life: the reform of the Carmelite Order. This she did also in obedience to several visions in which Christ commanded her to found a convent of Carmelite nuns following the original, not the mitigated Rule, a plan with which she had been toying for some time. She encountered violent opposition, especially from her own community, and had to shelve the project for the time being, but after many vicissitudes she finally succeeded in founding the first house of the Carmelite Reform (Discalced Carmelites), the Convent of St. Joseph at Avila in 1562. Her first years at the new convent she described as "the most restful years of my life"; she gave herself up completely to contemplation and also wrote her autobiography at the order of her confessor.

This peaceful time came to an end in 1567, when the general of her order gave her permission to found more houses. From that time onward she traveled almost ceaselessly, establishing one convent of the Reform after the other, often against great opposition and with hardly any money. Moreover, she was also instrumental in bringing about the reform of the men, John of the

Cross joining her in founding the Discalced Friars. Teresa had to interrupt her foundations in 1571, when she was appointed prioress of her original Convent of the Incarnation, which had become very relaxed and in which she was ordered to restore religious discipline—a difficult task, in which she was considerably helped by St. John of the Cross, who became confessor to the community in the following year. Her three-year term at the Incarnation was a complete success; after she had reformed the community she continued her foundations. Among them was the convent at Beas, a village just outside the political province of Andalusia. There she became acquainted with Jerome Gracián, a brilliant young Carmelite whom she esteemed so highly that she decided to make a vow of obedience to him. The extraordinary devotion of the aging foundress to this able but somewhat imprudent friar, far beneath her both in experience and in sanctity, is one of the aspects of her many-sided personality that is difficult to explain; though it must be admitted that she was not always right in her judgments. On his orders she undertook a foundation at Seville, which was made only under the greatest difficulties.

Towards the end of 1575 there began serious troubles connected with separating the reformed Carmelites from those of the Mitigation, the latter wanting to suppress Teresa's work altogether. She appealed to the King of Spain, and Philip II appointed a commission to examine the case. A few months later she went to Toledo, where on Gracián's orders she continued the *Foundations*, a book she had begun three years earlier, describing the events connected with the foundation of her convents. It was followed by her principal mystical work, *The Interior Castle*, which she wrote in three months, completing it at the end of November 1577.

Teresa's last years were saddened by anxieties about the fate of her reform, deaths of friends and relatives, and illness. In 1581 the order was finally divided, Gracián being elected provincial of the Discalced Carmelites. She had hoped that he would accompany her on her way to Soria, to make another foundation, and was deeply disappointed when he failed to do so. In January 1582, feeling very old and ill, she set out to make her seventeenth and last foundation at Burgos. She remained there for six months, organizing the new convent; she died on her way back to Avila.

St. Teresa's mystical doctrine is based on her own experiences; in *The Interior Castle* she traces the mystical life from its very beginnings to its heights in the transforming union. It is Teresa's great contribution to mystical doctrine that she described in detail the various stages of the mystical development of the individual. She had great powers of psychological observation and used them to give a remarkably clear picture of this evolution, which, if not applicable to other mystics in every detail, is yet true of most of them in its great guiding lines.

In her principal work on the subject Teresa represents the soul as a castle in which there are several mansions, leading into the interior. Outside the castle, in the courtyard, there are snakes and vipers representing worldly distractions and sins. Some of these will still be present in the First Mansions, the mansions of self-knowledge and humility, the very foundations fo the spiritual life. These lead on to the Second Mansions, when the soul begins vocal prayer, and from there to meditation and recollection, which will often be accompanied by dryness and difficulties. These must be faithfully endured if the Fourth Mansions are to be reached, which introduce the soul to the first stages of mystical prayer, which Teresa calls the Prayer of Quiet. In order to make it clear how it differs from the effects of meditation she uses the comparison or the various ways of filling a basin with water—her favorite element. In meditation the water of spiritual sweetness and satisfaction is transported by many conduits, built by human effort, till it reaches the soul; whereas in the prayer of quiet this water "comes direct from its source, which is God, and . . . its coming is accompanied by the greatest peace and quietness and sweetness within ourselves." This prayer already unites a man directly to God, but it does not yet do so perfectly, for only the will rests peacefully in God, whereas the other faculties of the soul, especially reason and imagination, are often left free to wander at will. In St. Teresa's view most contemplatives reach this stage but fail to ascend higher, because they do not become sufficiently detached from everything. If, however, they are generous enough to give themselves completely to God they will be led on to what Teresa calls the "prayer of union." This is described in the Fifth Mansion: "God implants himself in the interior of that soul in such a way," Teresa writes, "that, when it returns to itself, it cannot possibly doubt that God has been in it and it has been in God." This prayer lasts only for a short time, about half an hour, but during this time a man is quite dead to the world, his faculties and senses all being asleep. Teresa describes the contemplative who has reached this prayer under the famous simile of the silkworm which spins its cocoon and is hidden in it until it is transformed into a beautiful white butterfly: "Oh greatness of God," she exclaims, "that a soul should come out like this after being . . . closely united with him for so short a time . . . It has wings now: how can it be content to crawl along slowly when it is able to fly?"

She also compares this state of union to that of a human couple about to be betrothed, who meet frequently in order to get to know each other better. It is therefore an intermediary state, to be followed, in the Sixth Mansions, by another, the state of actual betrothal. This state is described at great length; for in it occur the many phenomena generally associated with the mystical life, such as trances, visions, locutions, and the like. The characteristic prayer of this stage is the prayer of ecstasy, which is an intensified form of the preceding prayer of union. For during ecstasy all normal human activities cease completely: a man can no longer speak, the body grows cold and becomes quite lifeless, hence Teresa says "complete ecstasy does not last long," but it "has the effect of leaving the will so completely absorbed and the understanding so completely transported—for as long as a day, or even for several days—that the soul seems incapable of grasping anything that does not awaken the will to love; to this it is fully awake, while asleep as regards all that concerns attachment to any creature." During this period a man has to endure great sufferings, both natural and supernatural, which cause great anguish and may even make the mystic cry out aloud with pain. In this context Teresa speaks of the "wound of love," caused by intense desire for God, as well as of all the various phenomena accompanying this state. She distinguishes—among others— imaginary from intellectual visions, the latter being directly impressed on the understanding, and ecstasy from what she calls the "flight of the spirit." This, she writes, "may be said to be of such a kind that the soul really seems to have left the body."

All these phenomena as well as the sufferings that accompany them prepare the mystic for the final stage, the "Spiritual Marriage," described in the Seventh Mansion, the innermost chamber, the dwelling place of the divine king. Here God "desires to remove the scales from the eyes of the soul," giving it an intellectual vision in which the Holy Trinity reveals itself. "Here all three Persons communicate themselves to the soul . . . and explain to it those words which the Gospel attributes to the Lord, namely that he and the Father and the Holy Spirit will come to dwell with the soul." This is no longer a transitory state like the spiritual betrothal, but here "the soul is always aware that it is experiencing this companionship." It is a state of great peace, for violent transports and ecstasies, which are really signs of the weakness of the soul which cannot yet endure the divine presence have almost ceased, and now "the soul remains all the time in that centre with its God." There is no higher state possible in this life, for it is the last stage before the direct vision of God in heaven.

ST. JOHN OF THE CROSS

St. John of the Cross (1542–91) was proclaimed Doctor of the Church in 1926. He received this honor for his mystical teaching which, like that of St. Teresa, was based on his own experience, but strengthened and systematized by his theological learning. He was born as Juan de Yepes in a small village about thirty miles distant from Avila. His father died when he was seven years old, and his mother, who made a living by weaving, moved with him and his brother to Medina del Campo. Having tried several trades without success, John was sent to school at the College of the Children of Doctrine, where he made such good progress that he attracted the attention of a wealthy retired businessman who had become warden of a hospital. He made himself responsible for the boy's education, while John had to help in the hospital. So from 1556 to 1562 John attended the classes at a school run by the Jesuits, and in 1563 he entered the Carmelite monastery at Medina. In the following year he was sent to study at the famous University of Salamanca; he was ordained priest in 1567.

In the same year he first met St. Teresa, who was just then looking for suitable Carmelite Fathers to extend her work of reform to the men of the order, while he was considering leaving the Carmelites for the more austere Carthusians. He agreed to join the Reform, and in 1568 he and a much older Father, Fray Antonio, moved to a miserable ramshackle little house of Duruelo, a tiny village near Avila, where they led a life of extreme austerity. Apart from the recitation of the Divine Office and long hours of contemplative prayer they went about preaching and hearing confessions in the neighborhood. The holiness of their lives made a great impression, and soon they received offers of better houses as well as novices. In 1570 they moved to another village, Mancera, and from there to Pastrana, where John held the office of novice master. In the next year the new branch of the order opened a house of studies at the University of Alcalá, where he was superior for a short time, before being sent as confessor to the Convent of the Incarnation at Avila. There he lived, together with another friar, in a small house near the convent for five years, from 1572 till 1577, St. Teresa being prioress of the convent during part of the time. She admired St. John tremendously, and the influence of his profound spirituality worked a transformation in the hitherto rather relaxed nuns.

His stay at Avila came to a sudden end, owing to the troubles that had arisen between the Carmelites of the Old Observance and the Discalced Reform. The former attempted to make John and several others return to them; when he refused, they employed violence. They kidnaped him on the night of December 3, 1577, and brought him to their own monastery in Avila, where he was flogged and otherwise ill-treated, and compelled to put on the habit of the Observance. He was then removed to the house of the Mitigation at Toledo and given the choice between abandoning the Reform with the promise of high office in the order and being severely punished for his refusal. John took the latter course. He was now imprisoned in a tiny dark cell and given only bread and water with occasionally some salt fish as his food. He was frequently flogged, and as he was allowed no change of clothing the clotted blood made his habit stick to his skin. This physical torture was aggravated by mental torment, for he kept being told that the Reform was practically finished, while he had no means whatever of finding out what happened to his fellow religious.

But this time of intense physical and mental suffering proved to be spiritually immensely fruitful; for in this prison cell in Toledo, St. John's first great mystical poems were written on a little paper he had been allowed to use, one on the night of faith ("How well I know the fount that freely flows") and the first thirty stanzas of *The Spiritual Canticle*.

After five months of intense suffering John's prison guard was changed, and the new man was horrified at the bad state of health of his charge and allowed him more freedom; the floggings, too, became much rarer. Nevertheless, he was not allowed to say Mass even on the Feast of the Assumption. Therefore St. John explored his chances to escape, and on the night of August 16, 1578, when the door of his cell had either been left open or he himself had picked the lock, he made his way to an open window, lowered himself into the courtyard by means of a rope he had made from his bedclothes, and walked as fast as he could to the convent of the Discalced nuns in the city.

After his escape he went south into Andalusia, where he first attended a chapter of the Discalced and then went to take up an appointment at the Carmelite house at Monte Calvario. On his way there he stayed for some days with the nuns at Beas, to whom he recited his poems; their request for an interpretation seems to have suggested the famous commentaries on these poems, which he began during his eight months stay at Monte Calvario. From there he went as rector to the Carmelite house of studies at Baeza, a place which, for all his detachment, he thoroughly disliked, because he detested Andalusians. He stayed there for two years and was then appointed prior of the Monastery of Los Martires near Granada, where he remained with some interruptions for six years. In Granada a convent of Carmelite nuns had been established with Anne of Jesus as prioress, who asked him for a commentary on *The Spiritual Canticle*; this, together with *The Living Flame of Love* and parts of *The Ascent of Mount Carmel* and *The Dark Night of the Soul* was written at Los Martires.

The last years of the saint were darkened by bitter controversies within the Teresan Reform itself. He had become Vicar-Provincial of Andalusia, an office which involved much traveling, and in 1587 Prior at Granada. A year later, during the first general chapter of the Discalced Carmelites at Madrid he was appointed prior of their house in Segovia and a member of the Consulta, the highest authority of the order after the vicar-general, Nicolas Doria, a very masterful personality. These offices left him very little time not only for writing but even for contemplation, so that he complained in a letter to one of his spiritual daughters: "my soul lags far behind." But he was relieved of all his offices at the general chapter of June 1591, because he protested against Doria's proposal of revoking Teresa's Constitutions of 1581. He was sent to the very poor and unimportant house of La Peñuela as a simple friar, where he was happy to give himself up completely to solitude and prayer.

In the meantime, however, his opponents in the order conducted a whispering campaign against him, accusing him of scandalous behavior and threatening even to deprive him of his habit. When John was informed of this by one of his friends he calmly replied that "they cannot take the habit from me save for incorrigibility or disobedience, and I am quite prepared to amend my ways in all wherein I have strayed, and to be obedient, whatsoever penance they give me."

In September 1591 he fell ill with erysipelas in the foot, and as there was no doctor available in La Peñuela he went to the house of his order at Ubeda. Its prior had once been reprimanded by him when John was his superior, and now revenged himself by forbidding him visitors and refusing him adequate nursing. This ill treatment came to an end when one of his friends informed John's old colleague Fray Antonio, then provincial of Andalusia, of the situation, who descended on the monastery in person and gave strict orders to do everything possible for the patient. But despite all the care and several extremely painful operations the erysipelas spread to his legs, and at midnight on December 14 he died, having told his brethern that he would "sing Matins in heaven."

The mystical doctrine of St. John of the Cross is to be found in the poems and the prose works mentioned before. He has been called the mystic's mystic, and he writes in the first place as a guide for those called to the heights of union with God, symbolized as the summit of Mount Carmel. To reach this, a person must leave behind not only all that attaches him to the world of sense but everything whatsoever that is not directly conducive to this union. Thus he enters into a "dark night of the senses" in which everything he had once appreciated disappears, so that he will be freed not only from sin, whether mortal or venial, but even from the slightest imperfection and from all attachment to creatures, however innocent it may seem, and which he compares to a cord by which a bird is held captive. It does not matter whether this cord be thin or thick—as long as it prevents the bird from flying away it is harmful to it. Therefore

St. John lays down certain principles which the novice in the contemplative life must follow if he wishes to make progress. He must always strive to choose not what is easiest, but what is most difficult, not what is pleasant, but what is repulsive, not what is comforting, but rather what brings discomfort, not what is best of the things of this earth but what is worst. This sounds very negative, but it is only the preparation for something quite positive; for by wishing to possess nothing a man will arrive at possessing everything, by desiring to know nothing he will know all. For the terrifying renunciations of St. John's principles are meant to lead only to the fullness of the mystical life, they are a means, not an end in itself.

These renunciations must be applied not only to all earthly attractions, but also to such phenomena of the spiritual life itself as visions, locutions, and the like, which St. Teresa had described in detail. St. John considers that none of them leads directly to God, because God is only apprehended here on earth by dark faith. And because they do not lead to him directly, they have to be completely disregarded. Other spiritual guides usually describe signs by which the origin of such phenomena may be distinguished, whether they come from God, from the devil or simply from man himself. St. John does not concern himself with them at all; he advises the contemplative to take no notice of any such phenomena, but to forget them as soon as possible. For if they come from God they will have their effect in any case, but if they derive from any other source they will only lead to dangerous illusions. The same applies to private revelations, so often greatly appreciated not only by the recipients themselves but by their confessors and even the general public, if they are made known. With regard to these St. John says: "The soul has its natural reason and the doctrine and law of the Gospel which are quite sufficient for its guidance, and there is no difficulty or necessity that cannot be solved and remedied by these means."

The Doctor of mysticism has certainly carried caution about extraordinary phenomena farther than any other spiritual teacher;

he rejects them all, because they can only be obstacles to the perfect union of the soul with its God to which he wishes to lead his readers. The purification necessary for this union is the work of God himself, again described under the image of the night, but no longer the night of the senses but the "Night of the Spirit," which is even more painful than the first night. In this night, when God assails the soul in order to renew and to divinize it, a man feels himself completely forsaken both by God and by all human beings, and enters most deeply into an agonizing realization of his own wretchedness. He feels himself completely annihilated and lives in an anguish that anticipates the sufferings of purgatory, very often not only unable to pray but even to perform his normal duties. The greater the height to which God intends to lead the mystic, the longer and the more painful this purification, which will normally last for several years. But all its sufferings will be forgotten when God finally leads the soul to the joys of the mystical union.

This St. John describes in *The Spiritual Canticle* and *The Living Flame of Love,* using, like many mystics before him, the imagery of the *Canticle* to analyze it. He begins his description with the "spiritual wounds of love" the soul has received from her Spouse, which cause her to seek him ever more ardently, practicing all the virtues to an eminent degree. The more deeply the soul is wounded the greater is her bliss, for in mystical love pain and joy are very close together. At this stage the union of God with the soul is not yet permanent; it becomes more complete when he calls her to "what is called spiritual betrothal with the Word, the Son of God." It is the time of dawn, when the dark night is past and the bride-soul is given marvelous knowledge of divine things and is confirmed in love. Nevertheless, even now the mystical life has not yet reached its perfection, for God still leaves the soul at times, and it is still occasionally troubled by the senses or by diabolic temptations.

These imperfections, too, will disappear in the last stage, the spiritual marriage. This brings about a total transformation of the soul into God (by grace, of course, not by nature), when

both surrender their possessions to each other in the consummation of the loving union, where the soul is deified and becomes
God by participation, as far as it is possible in this life. This is
the ancient concept of deification in the context of a psychological description of the unitive life. This last stage of the mystical life is presented by St. John of the Cross in the enraptured
language of the mystic who is both a theologian and a poet. It
is a state of the most perfect enjoyment, in which all the powers
of the soul are fully occupied: for the understanding drinks
wisdom and knowledge, the will sweetest love, and the memory
delights in the sense of glory. Man now is consciously united to
the divine Trinity in the very substance of his soul, "where
neither the devil nor the world nor sense can enter," while his
understanding is divinely enlightened by the wisdom of the Son,
the will is gladdened by the Holy Spirit, and the Father with his
power and strength absorbs the soul in the embrace of his sweetness. In this state the soul is habitually conscious of being indwelt by God who is "asleep in this embrace with the bride,"
though in rare moments he also "awakens," and then "the soul
is conscious of a rare delight in the breathing of the Holy Spirit
in God," which is a foretaste of eternal life, when this "breathing," which communicates both knowledge and love, will be
continuous.

With St. John of the Cross we have reached the heights of
Western mystical theology; to approach the seventeenth century
will mean a descent from the rarefied air surrounding the heights
of Mount Carmel to the lesser peaks of the mystical landscape.

XIII AN AGE OF DECLINE

Though the seventeenth century still produced some attractive mystics and a certain amount of mystical theology, it, and even more the eighteenth century of rationalism and "enlightenment," was a period of decline. The originality and mystical drive of a Catherine of Siena or Teresa of Avila as well as the theological and psychological penetration of a St. John of the Cross were no longer present in their successors.

ST. FRANCIS DE SALES

The importance of St. Francis de Sales (1567–1622) lies chiefly in the synthesis he achieved between Jesuit and Carmelite spirituality which he welded into a system, if this term be permitted, of his own. He was the eldest of ten children born to François and Françoise de Boisy at the Castle de Sales in Savoy. His education was supervised by the chaplain of the castle who accompanied him on all his journeys and later became canon of Geneva. From 1584 to 1588 Francis studied at Clermont under the guidance of the Jesuits; there he suffered an intense temptation to despair, lasting several weeks (from December 1586), which he finally overcame by an act of complete submission to the will of God, an experience that influenced all his later teaching. In 1588 he went to Padua to study law in deference to the will of his father, but also theology, returning to Savoy in 1592. By that time he had decided to become a priest; he was ordained in the following year and appointed Provost of Geneva. As such he devoted himself to re-

Catholicizing the Chablais, which had been forcibly converted
to Calvinism when it was annexed by the canton of Berne and
had been returned to Savoy in 1593. Francis made many converts, often at great risk to his own safety. In 1597 he was
appointed coadjutor to the bishop of Geneva, whom he succeeded in 1602.

His next years were occupied with his episcopal duties; but
he was also much sought after as a spiritual director. In 1604
he met Madame Jeanne de Chantal, together with whom he
was to found the Order of the Visitation (1610). For many
years he had followed the Ignatian form of meditation; but two
years before his meeting with Jeanne de Chantal he had made
the acquaintance of Madame Acarie, who had introduced the
Discalced Carmelites into France; through her he came to
know the works of St. Teresa of Avila and her teaching on mystical prayer, which he at first regarded with suspicion. He
visualized his own Order of the Visitation as mainly contemplative, too, but adapted to women not sufficiently strong to endure the austerities of Carmelites and Poor Clares. He also did
not want them to be strictly enclosed, but to be able to go out
to visit the sick and do other charitable works. In 1616, however, he agreed to the proposals of the archbishop of Lyons and
formed the Visitandines into a completely contemplative and
fully enclosed order, as which they were erected by papal brief
in 1618.

During the years of his episcopate Francis de Sales wrote his
two most important works, the *Introduction to the Devout Life*
(1608, last edition enlarged and revised by him in 1619) and
the *Treatise on the Love of God* (1616). The former work is
meant especially for people living in the world; it does not treat
of mysticism, but gives much practical advice on behavior and
teaches a simple form of meditation. The *Treatise*, on the other
hand, contains his theology of the mystical life. St. Francis'
doctrine centers in the love of God, the human response to
which may be summed up in the motto of his own life as well
as of the Visitation: "To ask for nothing and to refuse nothing."

He amplifies it in his teaching on "holy indifference" and religious obedience. St. Ignatius had likened the obedience required from his sons to that of "a corpse"; St. Francis uses the image of a statue. He desires his daughters to be like statues which, having been placed in a certain corner by their maker, remain there for no other reason than the will of him who has placed them there. They are content to be where the sculptor wishes them to be, even if he should never look at them again. This indifference is particularly necessary in times of dryness, when the contemplative feels himself abandoned by God. For the seat of the mystical life is not in the emotions, but in what St. Francis calls the "fine point of the will," which corresponds to the medieval spark or ground of the soul. This life itself is described somewhat differently from its presentation by the two great Spanish mystics. According to St. Francis de Sales, too, there are several degrees of prayer, but they are not worked out so clearly. He applies the term "mystical" even to meditation, which he calls "nothing else but mystical rumination . . . in order to find motives for love." This is succeeded by contemplation, defined as "a loving, simple, and permanent attention of the spirit to divine things," for "meditation is the mother of love, but contemplation is its daughter."

In the higher stages St. Francis speaks of "liquefaction," in which the soul "lets herself go out and flow into what it loves . . . This flowing of the soul into God is a veritable ecstasy by which the soul is all outside its natural being, all absorbed into God." However, the contemplative cannot as yet love God as much as he would like, and this unfulfilled desire produces in him the "wound of love." St. Teresa, too, uses this term; but there seems here, as in the meaning of ecstasy and later in the description of rapture, a subtle difference between the conceptions of St. Francis and those of the Carmelite. For in St. Teresa's account the wound of love is brought about by a truly mystical happening which takes place only in the fully developed ecstatic state, whereas in the description of St. Francis it is rather a psychological event, a subjective feeling of frustration in the soul who desires to love God more than she is actually capable of doing.

Later in the spiritual life, however, this love in increased and described by St. Francis as a "ravishment" by which "we go out and remain out of and above ourselves in order to unite ourselves to God." This is often brought about by the admiration of the understanding to which God shows "heavenly things." Here we are in a much more moderate climate, so to speak, than the red-hot mystical passion of the Spanish Carmelites. Besides, the human faculties are more active. Where St. John of the Cross, for example, speaks of the understanding drinking supernatural knowledge, St. Francis writes of its "application" to heavenly things; where St. Teresa writes that God communicates himself to the soul, the French saint says: "we . . . unite ourselves to God." In the Spanish mystics God overwhelms man, who is passive under the impact of his presence, whereas in St. Francis man retains the use of his faculties to a much higher degree.

On the other hand, according to St. Francis, human passivity is far more developed in his conception of "holy indifference"; for in the fully grown mystical life this should extend even to one's own salvation, and so St. Francis arrives at the impossible demand that the truly indifferent heart should "rather love hell with the will of God than heaven without it," and finally, "to imagine the impossible," as he himself admits, if the indifferent man "knew that his damnation would be slightly more pleasing to God than his salvation, he would abandon his salvation and run to his damnation." Here the saint's teaching on holy indifference would seem to overreach itself. For the mystical life is a life of love, and love must necessarily desire union with its object. In the teaching of the earlier mystics indifference extends to all that is not God, but never to God himself, and it may, indeed, be asked whether such speculations on "the impossible" are very profitable, even though they express a desire for the utmost generosity. Nevertheless, they are an expression of the saint's own personality, which was subtle rather than simple, as he himself admits in a letter to Madame de Chantal: "No, I certainly am not simple, but strange to say, I have a great love for simplicity."

This love of simplicity shows itself also in the use he makes of the image of childhood, when he advises the mystic to abandon himself to God as the small child hides itself in the arms of his mother, a teaching we have already found in Alphonsus Rodriguez and which is shared by many modern mystics, until it is finally popularized by Teresa of Lisieux. The influence of St. Francis on later spirituality has been tremendous, because his mystic teaching is more accessible to the modern mind which, like that of the bishop of Geneva, is not simple, but nostalgically seeking for simplicity.

LOUIS LALLEMANT

Louis Lallemant (1587–1635) carried on the mystical tradition of the Jesuits against much opposition. Born at Chalons-sur-Marne, he was educated by the Jesuits and entered their novitiate at Nancy at the age of eighteen. He followed the normal career of a gifted Jesuit, being successively professor of logic, physics, and metaphysics, and later novice master and instructor of the Third Year, the special last training period of Jesuit priests. There his mystical teaching was opposed by a number of his students, and he was relieved of his office in 1631 and sent to Bourges as prefect of studies.

Despite his many duties Lallemant gave much time to prayer and himself enjoyed mystical graces. He considered absolute purity of conscience as the necessary precondition of the mystical life, which itself is characterized by the direction of the Holy Spirit. This purity of heart involves detachment not only from all creatures, but also from all felt satisfaction in prayer and from extraordinary graces like visions; here Lallemant is in complete accord with St. John of the Cross. Far more important than such experiences are the sacraments of the Church, the virtues and the gifts of the Holy Spirit. Thus Lallemant coun-

seled frequent confession and Holy Communion, for "after a
good confession, one receives into one's soul a great light to
know one's own inner being . . . After a good Communion one
has a taste of God and new vigour to be employed in his service." But the action of the sacraments must be enforced by a
life of recollection, without which the virtues cannot grow and
activity loses its efficacy. This teaching was foreign to many of
his fellow Jesuits at the time, who thought that recollection
would hinder the apostolic activity to which the order was devoted. Lallemant told them that the exact opposite was the case
and "that it is certain that a man of prayer does more in a year
than another in his whole life." For to be fruitful external
activity must be founded on the theological virtues, especially
on faith, and this is strengthened not by an outwardly busy
life but by prayer.

The most effective form of prayer is contemplation, which
Lallemant defines as "a simple, free, penetrating, certain view
of God and of divine things, which proceeds from love and
tends to love." Unfortunately this was at that time often confused with total spiritual inactivity soon to be taught by the
Quietists, hence it was regarded with suspicion, whereas, on the
contrary, "contemplation carries souls to heroic acts of charity,
zeal, penitence, and other virtues." For it opens the soul to the
action of the Holy Spirit, which is the prime mover in the
spiritual life. Hence "the end to which we must aspire," says
Lallemant, "is to be so thoroughly possessed and governed by
the Holy Spirit that he alone guides all our powers and senses."

The most important of the gifts of the Spirit for the mystical
life is the gift of wisdom, because this unites most directly to
God and supplies a knowledge of him that is full of enjoyment.
This new knowledge may often throw a man into raptures and
ecstasies, but these are really imperfections, due to human
weakness, and "in proportion as a soul is purified its spirit becomes stronger and more capable of enduring the divine actions
without emotion or suspension of the senses"—a teaching in
complete correspondence with that of St. Teresa and St. John

of the Cross. When a person has arrived at this highest stage of the mystical way, he will imitate God himself in his trinitarian life, which is done "as much by the work of the understanding by which he is the principle of the Person of the Word as by that of the will by which he is the principle of the Person of the Holy Spirit . . . This should be our model: in the first place, we must have within us a very perfect life of continual application of our understanding and will to God. Then we shall be able to go forth from ourselves to serve our neighbour without harming our interior life."

Though Lallemant's teaching resembles so closely that of St. Teresa and St. John of the Cross, the goal he has in view is slightly different, according to the different purpose of his order: the Jesuit contemplative is not to rest in the joys of the mystical marriage but is to make them effective in his apostolate. For Lallemant holds that activity without close union with God is harmful to the soul itself; to preserve complete personal integrity as well as to give maximum efficacy to his work a man must be intimately united to God by mystical prayer.

ST. MARGARET MARY

In St. Margaret Mary Alacoque (1647–91) the chief seventeenth-century trends of spirituality meet; for she was a nun of St. Francis de Sales' Visitation and directed by the Jesuit Claude de la Colombière. However, her mystical experience differs from the teaching of either order, for it is inextricably mixed up with her own unusual psychological make-up, which was not without a neurotic streak. This is analyzed, for example, by Louis Beirnaert, S.J., in his essay in the *Etudes Carmélitaines* (*Le Coeur,* 1950) on the psychological background of her heart symbolism. According to him, wounds have always held a strange attraction for her, she would suck them and swallow the most repulsive matter. Moreover, she herself suffered for some time from pains in her side, and so her attention would have been riveted more and more upon the wound in the side of Christ.

Even as a child Margaret Mary often abandoned her play to retire into a "hidden corner"—a favorite expression of hers—where she could pray unobserved; for the relatives with whom her mother lived were not sympathetic to her pious exercises. As a young girl she had a mysterious illness, which the doctors did not know how to treat, and during which she could neither walk nor eat nor sleep—evidently a severe nervous complaint. She was suddenly cured after consecrating herself entirely to the Blessed Virgin. After a considerable interior struggle she entered the convent of the Visitation at Paray-le-Monial (Central France) in June 1670, at the age of twenty-three. Here her extraordinary experiences multiplied; on the day of her clothing Christ told her that this was her spiritual betrothal, and during her profession retreat he revealed to her, as she believed, that henceforth she would have no pleasure that would not be overshadowed by his Cross. "To love and to suffer blindly" became her motto; indeed, throughout her life she had an extraordinary and not altogether healthy love for suffering.

In the year following her profession she had her first great vision of the Sacred Heart, like St. Gertrude on the feast of St. John the Apostle. According to her account of the experience Christ made her rest for several hours on his breast and then told her that he had chosen her to reveal his heart to the world. He placed her own heart in his own burning one, then withdrew it as a tiny heart-shaped flame and restored it to its place. Since then similar visions occurred on each first Friday of the month. The second great apparition took place probably in 1674, again on a first Friday. Christ appeared to her in great glory, "his five wounds shining like five suns, his heart on fire in his open breast." He complained of the neglect with which men repaid his love and asked her to make reparation for this, specifying the devotions now known as the First Fridays and the Holy Hour. She herself was to rise for this purpose every Thursday night and spend the hour between eleven and midnight in prayer to appease the divine wrath and to soothe in some way the bitterness Christ had felt in the garden of Gethsemane when his apostles abandoned him. When she communicated these demands to her superior, Mère de Saumaise, she was forbidden to carry them out, a prohibition enforced by the advice of some theologians who considered that the visionary was having illusions. She suffered greatly from this opposition, but relief came when, in January 1675, she was visited by a young Jesuit, Père de la Colombière, who had just been appointed superior of the Jesuit residence at Paray-le-Monial. He reassured her and told her to abandon herself completely to the will of God. A few months later she received another revelation, the most famous of all, with orders concerning not only herself but the whole Church. It happened during the Octave of Corpus Christi, when she was praying before the tabernacle. Then Jesus showed her once more his heart saying: "Behold this heart, which has so loved man . . ." and complaining that the divine love, exposed on the altars in the Blessed Sacrament, received only insults and blasphemies in return for its condescension. Therefore a Feast of the Sacred Heart was to be instituted on the Friday following the Octave of Corpus Christi, and Holy Communion to be received on that day in reparation for the indignities to which the Blessed Sacrament had been submitted. When she asked how she, an insignificant nun, could establish a new feast in the Church she was told to go to Père de la Colombière for help.

After that Margaret Mary's life was wholly given to propagating the new devotion. There were practices in honor of the Sacred Heart to be recommended, pictures to be drawn, letters to be written, altars and oratories to be decorated. We are very far from the austere mysticism of St. John of the Cross, who shunned such concern with the externals of devotion. Two years after the last great revelation Christ commanded her to inform the community that she, Margaret Mary, was to be the victim for the expiation of their sins. It is not surprising that as a result of this extraordinary message she should have been regarded as possessed by the devil, and her fellow nuns threw holy water at her whenever they met her. For a long time afterwards she could hardly eat or sleep; she would feel ravenously hungry during prayer time, but have a violent aversion to all food as soon as she entered the refectory. At other times she was tempted to despair, fearing that she was deluded, the offices given to her in the community were extremely distasteful to her, even though as novice mistress she had excellent opportunities of propagating her devotion to the Sacred Heart.

Margaret Mary herself attributed her strange sufferings to her vocation of victim; but while not ruling out a supernatural element in them, her whole life shows certain neurotic features which may have contributed to their development. Mysticism and nervous complaints are not mutually exclusive; and when the Church approved devotion to the Sacred Heart in the terms of Margaret Mary's revelations, that is to say of reparation, this was done not because all the elements of her visions were considered supernatural, but because this devotion, which, after all, went back as far as the early Middle Ages (St. Gertrude) recommended itself as useful in an age of rationalism. For it was approved only seventy-five years after the saint's death, and she herself was beatified as late as 1864 (canonized 1920).

THE QUIETIST CONTROVERSY

Quietism is a kind of mystical heresy which can take various forms and which is not always easy to distinguish from authentic mysticism. The Alumbrados in Spain seem to have taught a quietist doctrine, but the name is usually restricted to a seventeenth-century school of spiritual authors, especially the Spaniard Miguel de Molinos and the circle round the French Madame de Guyon and Archbishop Fénelon. Indeed, in the second half of the seventeenth century Quietism had become almost the fashion, notably in the Latin countries, Spain, France, and Italy. Even St. Francis de Sales had required his contemplative nun to be like a statue, letting herself be moved wherever God willed and in a certain sense indifferent even to her own salvation. Now these tendencies came to be greatly exaggerated. Whereas the genuine mystics had restricted "passive" prayer, in which the human understanding and will are no longer active, to the higher stages of the mystical life, the Quietists held that such prayer was to be practiced by all devout Christians. They taught that everyone should suppress all thoughts, all considerations of whatever kind, any mental picture even of Christ; more, that there should be no conscious striving for virtue. For if a man had emptied his mind completely and thus entered what they called by such names as acquired contemplation, the interior way, inner recollection and quietude, this act of "self-annihilation" was all-sufficient; henceforth he remained in this perfect state and many Quietists held that in this state even what was sin in others ceased to be sin. It is not surprising that such teaching, rejecting all painful moral effort and advocating a "mysticism without tears," should have found a great following, nor that it should have been condemned by the Church, as it was bound to lead to the most undesirable consequences.

Miguel de Molinos (d. 1697) was its most celebrated exponent. He was a native of Muniesa near Saragossa in Spain, who went to Rome in 1663 after having become doctor of theology. He soon made a name as a much sought-after confessor and spiritual director, and his influence became even greater after he had published his *Spiritual Guide* (1675), in which he advocated the completely passive prayer and the soul's indifference to its own fate which were already in vogue in the spiritual circles of that time. Both Jesuits and Dominicans opposed the book, but the Quietists replied with quotations from St. Teresa, St. Francis de Sales, and others with such success that their adversaries were silenced. The situation changed, however, when the results of Molinos' spiritual direction became apparent and nuns and others who believed they had reached the state of perfect passivity refused to recite their office and their rosary, abandoned confession and all other normal religious practices, believing that they were no longer capable of sin. In 1685 Molinos was arrested by the Holy Office and two years later his teaching was condemned. He recanted, but was nevertheless sentenced to life imprisonment on charges of immorality. The documents on which these accusations are based have never been published, and as his conduct during his trial and later is said to have been in complete accordance with his own teaching on perfect indifference, it is difficult to judge how far he was in good faith.

The views of Molinos strongly influenced the famous Madame Guyon and her Barnabite director, P. La Combe. Jeanne-Marie Bouvier de la Mothe (1648–1717) was born at Montargis and seems to have suffered of nervous complaints from an early age. In 1664 she married Jacques Guyon, a sick man twenty-two years older than herself. The marriage was unhappy and increased Jeanne-Marie's taste for unusual spiritual experiences, in which she was encouraged by the Duchesse de Béthune-Charost, a very influential lady who considered her a saint and a mystic. Four years after the death of her husband in 1676 Madame Guyon left her family in order to travel, taking only her youngest daughter with her. In the company of Père La Combe she traversed a large part of France, propagating everywhere her teaching on the interior life. Owing to her natural eloquence and a certain spiritual charm she gained many disciples, mostly in high French society including the clergy. From September 1683 to May 1684 she underwent an illness—without doubt of hysterical origin—during which she was convinced that the Child Jesus had taken complete possession of her so that she herself did not exist any more. Moreover, she learned the secret of spiritual motherhood and believed that she was destined to bring forth a large number of "children of grace," among them La Combe himself, to whom she pretended to be mystically united in such a way that she could no longer distinguish him from God or from herself.

It is not surprising that this kind of language and the fact that Madame Guyon and her confessor were constantly traveling together should have given rise to rumors about their immoral relationship, always indignantly denied by her. These rumors have never been proved; but La Combe was arrested in 1687 on the charge of propagating the teachings of Molinos. He spent the rest of his life in various prisons, the last three years (he died in 1715) in the lunatic asylum at Charenton. Madame Guyon herself was interned at the Visitation convent in Paris from January to August 1688; after she had been discharged she resumed her mystical teaching in a very aristocratic circle, the most important member of which was François Fénelon (1651–1715, archbishop of Cambrai from 1695).

Fénelon, a son of the Marquis de Salignac, was educated first by the Jesuits, later in the seminary of Saint-Sulpice, being ordained about 1675. In 1678 he became superior of the Catholiques Nouvelles, a religious community founded to offer refuge to girls converted to Catholicism. Soon afterwards he became acquainted with Jacques Bénigne Bossuet, the famous bishop of Meaux, in whose diocese he frequently preached. In 1687 Fénelon published a treatise on the education of girls, and two years later he was appointed tutor to the Duke of Burgundy, the grandson of Louis XIV. A brilliant career seemed assured to him. But in the preceding year he had made the acquaintance of Madame Guyon, and this association proved a turning point in his life. Though his rather cold and reserved nature was at first shocked by her enthusiasm, he soon fell under her influence, because he believed to have found in her the personal experience of God which he himself had so far been seeking vainly. Indeed, in 1689 he placed himself under her direction and she taught him to accept the dryness which was the permanent state of his soul in the spirit of complete abandonment and spiritual childhood. He also began to read widely the spiritual works not only of his contemporaries, but of the medieval mystics and the Fathers. In the same year (1689) Madame de Maintenon, the wife of the King, introduced both Madame Guyon and Fénelon to Saint-Cyr, a religious house in which she was interested. Soon their Quietist teaching led to similar disorders as that of Molinos had done in Rome, and Madame de Maintenon turned against her former protégés. Fénelon sought an objective theological authority to decide the issue and addressed himself to Bossuet. But, to his great disappointment, Bossuet, who knew little of mysticism, judged his ideas very severely, and Fénelon asked for an official examination of his doctrine and morals. Thus, between July 1694 and March 1695 several discussions were held at Issy near Paris, the home of one of the members of the ecclesiastical commission appointed to judge the case. The conversations ended with the signing of the thirty-four articles of Issy by Bossuet, Fénelon, and Madame Guyon, condemning the Quietist teaching of the latter, especially that on the suppressing of all explicit acts of faith and the all-sufficiency of the one continuous act of contemplation.

In July 1695 Bossuet consecrated Fénelon bishop (of Cambria) in the chapel of Saint-Cyr, but soon afterwards a violent controversy broke out between the two bishops, sparked off by Fénelon's "Explanation of the Articles of Issy," his refusal to approve of Bossuet's "Instruction on the States of Prayer," and his own *Explication des maximes des saints sur la vie intérieure* (published 1697; Explanation of the Maxims of the Saints concerning the Interior Life), forty-five articles distinguishing between true and false mysticism and centered in the idea of pure love. They were approved by numerous experts, for they did not contain the heretical doctrines of Quietism proper. There followed a long drawn-out and bitter controversy between Bossuet and Fénelon. The latter appealed to Rome; but owing to the intrigues of Louis XIV inspired by Madame de Maintenon, twenty-three propositions taken from the *Maxims* were condemned, though not qualified as "heretical." Fénelon submitted and retired to his diocese, but he never changed his opinion on Madame Guyon. She had been imprisoned in 1695, first in a religious community, and from 1696 in the Bastille. She was released in 1712 and died five years later.

She was certainly a very unbalanced person, and her pseudo-mystical teaching, explained in a large number of voluminous writings, especially in *Moyen Court et très facile de faire oraison* (Short and Very Easy Method of Mental Prayer) and *Les torrents spirituels* (Spiritual Torrents) could easily lead to the same undesirable consequences as that of Molinos. For she writes, for example in the *Torrents*, of souls that have reached the "divine state" that "even the most evil actions, should they be obliged to perform them [i.e. by a strong temptation, which, Madame Guyon teaches, these "perfect" souls ought not to resist] cannot communicate their poison, since for them there exists no longer any evil in anything whatsoever, because of the essential unity which they have with God . . . so that such a soul is in complete ignorance of evil and as it were incapable of committing it." For this soul does not exist any longer, being completely lost in God, "and whoever does not exist cannot sin."

It is evident that such teaching, under the guise of mystical experience, must discredit true mysticism; and so it is not surprising that the Quietist errors, combined with the rationalism that sprang up towards the end of the seventeenth century, should have produced an anti-mystical atmosphere in the following period.

This, of course, does not mean that there were no more mystics in the eighteenth century. The Jesuit Jean-Pierre de Caussade (1675–1751), for example, was determined to defend the mystical tradition of his order against the anti-mystical trend of his time. He entered the Society at the age of eighteen, and from 1715 lived in various Jesuit residences as a preacher. In 1733 he became director of a retreat house at Nancy and was in close contact with the Visitation nuns in that city, several of whom placed themselves under his spiritual direction. He left Nancy in 1739 and subsequently became superior in several other Jesuit houses. His most famous works are his *Spiritual Instructions* and *Abandonment to Divine Providence*; indeed, the term "abandonment" may be said to sum up his mystical doctrine. The foundation of this teaching is the sovereign majesty of God emphasized in St. Ignatius' *Spiritual Exercises* and his infinite goodness, which shows itself clearly as soon as a man surrenders himself to him completely.

Now as abandonment means reliance on God in all things, and as men are creatures living in time, it can be practiced only from one moment to the other. Hence the present moment becomes a central concept in de Caussade's teaching, and he calls it "an ambassador who declares to us the order of God." Thus the present moment gains an almost sacramental significance, and if we give ourselves up to God's will in all the events of our life, then "every moment of our life is a kind of communion with the divine love and . . . will produce in our souls as much fruit as that in which we receive the body and blood of the Son of God." To see God's will in the present moment, through all the seemingly confused events of our lives, needs, of course, faith, which de Caussade calls "the interpreter of God." This faith is perfected in the "state of abandonment" which leads to the passivity of the mystical life and thus becomes pure. Like St. John of the Cross, de Caussade compares it to a dark night, through which a man is introduced to the very center of his soul, which is governed only by the will of God and thus is in profound peace, even though senses and emotions may be disturbed. These disturbances are inevitable, because the mystical life cannot develop without suffering. In his descriptions of them de Caussade is, however, much less dramatic than the Carmelite doctor. He stresses the weakness of human beings under the hand of God: "There is nothing in what they do or suffer save what is very small and humiliating; nothing dazzling in their existence; all is quite ordinary . . ."

As the feudal order of the Middle Ages and the colorful period of Renaissance and Baroque passed away to give place to the new age of the bourgeoisie, so mysticism, too, is presented in much more sober colors; in fact, almost two centuries before Teresa of Lisieux, the Jesuit director teaches the way of "spiritual childhood," though in a more adult manner than the famous young Carmelite. This way means being wholly abandoned to the divine action, giving up whatever God demands, our own ideas, inclinations, preferences, and so to die a "mystic death" to ourselves and become a martyr of divine providence.

A representative of the traditional type of the mystic was St. Paul of the Cross (1694–1775), the founder of the Passionists, who had frequent ecstasies and who believed that the habit of his order had been revealed to him in an intellectual vision. But eighteenth-century mystics were few and far between, and thus, as far as the history of mysticism is concerned, the eighteenth century is a rather uninteresting period; the mystical life had gone underground, as it were, and had to await a more favorable climate of opinion to rise to the surface.

XIV MODERN TIMES

This more favorable climate developed with the rise of the Romantic Movement in Europe. In opposition to the arid rationalism of the eighteenth century that would admit no supernatural realities, the Romantics stressed the claims of the heart and of religion, though in the latter they frequently over-emphasized the extraordinary phenomena such as miracles, visions, and revelations. At the same time mysticism began to be integrated also to a greater extent than hitherto into ordinary daily life.

One of the outstanding examples of this was Blessed Anna Maria Taigi (1769–1837), a simple Italian housewife, a native of Siena and a daughter of a spendthrift apothecary who took his family to Rome when Anna was six years old. After a few years at a convent school where she learned embroidery, she went into domestic service, and in 1790 she married Domenico Taigi, a valet in the Palazzo Chigi, who was considerably older than she. During the first year of her marriage she led the ordinary life of a pretty young wife; but after the birth of her first child she began to take her religion more seriously. Soon after this "conversion" she had a vision of the Blessed Virgin, who told her that it was to be her special vocation to show the world that sanctity can be attained in every walk of life and without extraordinary bodily austerities, the only condition for it being the mortification of self-will. And so Anna Maria was introduced to a mystical life in which the usual phenomena of ecstasies and visions were frequent, especially in the early stages, but which she lived in the midst of her growing family—

she had three boys and four girls—harassed by poverty and incessant work. She is also said to have had the gift of prophecy, and she was frequently consulted by such eminent personalities as Napoleon's mother, Madame Letizia, his brother Cardinal Fesch, and even by the Popes Leo XII and Gregory XVI. Like most other mystics, she, too, had to endure long periods of desolation, when she felt herself abandoned by God, as well as a good deal of opposition from her neighbors and also from priests, some of whom would even refuse her Holy Communion, because such a mystical life lived by a simple wife and mother seemed impossible to many.

The famous Curé d'Ars, John-Baptist Vianney (1786–1859) also combined a life of intense activity with high mystical experiences. He may well be called the mystic of the confessional, for his life was mostly spent reconciling sinners to God, and his penitents have testified to the supernatural enlightenment which showed him the most secret recesses of men's souls. Though a very simple man, who had found it difficult even to pass the ordinary examinations necessary for ordination, his wisdom soon attracted crowds from all over France to his confessional, who left him hardly any time for long prayers. His mystical experiences, of which he would not speak, seem to have taken place especially during his Mass and his thanksgiving afterwards, when he remained motionless in ecstasy, though usually only for a short time. Besides, he suffered much from feelings of desolation as well as from the attacks of the devil, though modern research has shown that many of these experiences, involving poltergeist phenomena such as strange noises and blows, may have been of psychological origin.

While Jean-Baptiste Vianney was a poor country priest overwhelmed with external activity, Charles de Foucauld (1858–1916) a French aristocrat, revived the life of the Desert Fathers. He had originally embraced a military career and fought in Algeria to suppress an insurrection. But early in 1882 he resigned his commission in order to explore Morocco, a very dangerous undertaking which won him the gold medal of the

French Geographical Society in 1885. A year later Charles, who had until then been an atheist, was converted by the Abbé Huvelin and decided to enter a religious order. After a visit to the Holy Land he entered a Trappist monastery in France in January 1890, and six months later was transferred to Akbès in Syria, where he was professed in January 1892. But the Trappist life did not correspond to his deepest desires: he wanted to found his own order, without the distinction between choir monks and lay brothers, without the divine office, and living entirely by manual work. In 1897 he left the Trappists and went to Palestine, where he found work as a servant of the Poor Clares at Nazareth, spending long hours of the day and night in mental prayer. Having decided, however, that he could serve God better as a priest, he returned to France and was ordained in 1901, having spent the night before his ordination in ecstatic adoration of the Blessed Sacrament. In the autumn of the same year he left for Algiers, for he had resolved to devote himself entirely to the conversion of Africa by a life of continual prayer and penance. He carried out this plan first in the oasis of Beni Abbès, and from 1905 in the even more lonely Hoggar Mountains and at the oasis of Tamanrasset.

Dressed like an Arab, he lived in a small hermitage, trying to follow a severe timetable of prayer and work which was, however, constantly interrupted by people coming to him for help and advice. He knew the dark night of the spirit when all his plans seemed to come to nothing and God himself seemed to have abandoned him, so that he could write: "Dryness and darkness: everything is painful: Holy Communion, prayers, contemplation, everything—even telling Jesus that I love him." And even on the very day of his death, before being shot during a revolt of the tribesmen, he had written: "One does not always feel that one loves, and this is another great suffering." It is the suffering of the mystic who cannot always live in the white heat of his love. Nevertheless, Charles de Foucauld, this Desert Father in the modern world, had long reached the heights of trinitarian mysticism, for he had written already in 1904: "I see all things in the light of the immense peace of God, of his infinite happiness, of the immutable glory of the blessed and ever tranquil Trinity. Everything loses itself for me in the happiness that God is God."

The spirituality of Carmel, too, was renewed in our time, especially through the tremendous influence of St. Teresa of Lisieux (1873–97), and, to a lesser extent, through Elisabeth of the Trinity (1880–1906).

The story of St. Teresa's short life is, of course, well known through her famous autobiography. She was the youngest and very spoiled daughter of devout middle-class parents. The studies of Ida Görres, *The Hidden Face*, of Father Etienne Robo, *Two Portraits of St. Teresa of Lisieux*, and others, have shown very clearly that there was a strong neurotic streak in her, which emerged after the death of her mother, when she was not quite five years old. It was aggravated after her sister Pauline, who had taken her mother's place, entered the Carmelite convent at Lisieux in 1882. A few weeks after this event, Teresa began to suffer from acute headaches, fits of catalepsy, and hallucinations, believing even that the medicines she was being given were meant to poison her. This "mysterious" illness was suddenly cured when she saw the statue of the Blessed Virgin smile at her, Mary now taking the place of her own mother and Pauline, and supplying the feeling of protection she needed.

Nevertheless, her intense nervous reactions, her headaches and her abnormal sensitivity continued, she was apt to burst into tears at the slightest provocation. She was made aware of this at Christmas 1886, when her father complained to her sister Céline that Teresa, then in her fourteenth year, still expected her shoe to be filled with sweets like the small children. Céline foresaw a flood of tears and told her not to go to her father till she had calmed down; but Teresa suddenly realized and overcame her weakness, swallowing her tears and behaving as if nothing had happened to upset her. It was the first great victory over her abnormal sensibility, even though it was by no means finally overcome. At this time she had already made up her mind to become a Carmelite like her sister Pauline and also decided on the date: Christmas 1887, when she was not yet fifteen years old. The authorities refused, and there was no reason why she should not have waited at least another year, especially as her father had already had his first stroke. Nevertheless, during a pilgrimage to Rome she made the well-known scene at the audience with Leo XIII. Despite the formal prohibition to address the Pope she threw herself at his feet, asking to be allowed to enter Carmel at the age of fifteen, and had to be forcibly removed by the Noble Guards. She finally had her way and was allowed to enter in April 1888. Her life in the convent was one long exercise in self-conquest, all the more remarkable for a spoiled girl of fifteen, even though the presence of her sisters must have made it a little easier for her.

The essence of her spirituality is the idea of "Spiritual childhood," her so-called "little way," and has had such tremendous success because it showed the life of perfection as accessible to all, without the need for extraordinary penances and the like. She was certainly not the first to have taught this; St. Francis de Sales and Père de Caussade, to name only two earlier authors, had done the same. But Teresa's influence was so strong because she not only presented her ideas in a very simple and popular form, but also because she herself, who died of tuberculosis at the age of twenty-four, was the personification of her own teaching. She wrote in her autobiography that she was "only a very little soul, who can offer the good God only very little things." The first part of this statement is true only in the sense that she was not an outstanding personality like the great St. Teresa; for her will power and determination were certainly not "little." The second is, indeed, true in every sense except that the Carmelite vocation in itself is not a "little thing." But within this vocation she certainly worked out her sanctity only by means of very small things: overcoming her irritation at hearing a nun rattling her rosary, or at finding her paint brushes in disorder because someone else had used them; folding up the mantles of sisters who had forgotten to do this, or treating a nun she disliked with particular friendliness. And, what is very revealing, these seemingly insignificant little "acts of virtue" cost her a great deal; for example, when she had once been wrongly accused of breaking a small jug she took the blame (incidentally, one might surely have expected the guilty nun to have owned up!) but found this so difficult that she "needed to think that all would come out at the Last Judgement"! The spoiled "little queen" of a doting father found these things evidently more difficult than others, but that she persevered in overcoming her defects day in and day out and that she gradually trained herself to meet all the pin-pricks that came her way with a smile constitutes her sanctity and makes it accessible, even though difficult, to all.

But in the context of this book the question has to be asked: Was she a mystic? It has been answered by the many authors who have written about her in diametrically opposite ways. All the customary signs of mysticism, such as the mystical union and ecstasy, are certainly absent from her life. More, during meditation she often was so tired that she simply went to sleep, but she did not consider this a fault, since "little children please their parents equally, whether they are asleep or awake"—and she constantly spoke of herself as a little child. Nevertheless, her spiritual life was not without severe trials, the worst of them occurring after her profession, and again in the months before her death. But from her own accounts it appears that these trials were really no more than a growing up and away from her childish beliefs; "Jesus . . . allowed my soul," she writes, "to be plunged in thickest darkness, and the thought of heaven, so sweet to me, to become for me only a subject of struggle and torment" and when she wanted "to be refreshed by the remembrance of the luminous country to which I aspire" she could no longer think of it. This is obviously no more than the inability of the adult to return to the happy, unquestioning belief in a poetic heaven such as it presents itself to the childish imagination.

She accepted these growing pains, presenting them under the

picture of Jesus asleep in her small boat. But were these the "dark nights" of the mystics? With great diffidence I can only give my personal opinion. As Teresa wanted so much that her teaching should be accessible to all, it seems to me that her spiritual life, too, did not attain to the heights of the mystical union, reserved only for a small minority. Her autobiography is full of "I thought," "I felt," "I hope," "I perceive"—which is not the language of the mystics who felt themselves to be passive under the divine inspirations and confessed to be unable to express in human language the mysteries God had revealed to them. Rather is it the language of the Christian who has to work out for herself the implications of her faith, but who does so in perfect dependence on the divine will. At the beginning of her spiritual life Teresa had often identified her own will with the will of God; towards its end she came to rely more and more on the divine will so that she could write: "Now abandonment alone is my guide." This is the union of wills which the great Teresa desired for all her daughters, in preference to all other forms of union; nevertheless it is not what is generally understood by "mystical union," which is the intensely felt and experienced union of God and man in the depths of the soul. It seems to me that just because her vocation was to live and to show the way to perfection in a form accessible to all, that these highest graces of the mystical union were withheld from her, and that precisely this was her own special grace which made her the most popular saint of our times.

Elisabeth of the Trinity (1880–1906), though as yet uncanonized and far less popular than her contemporary St. Teresa, was another exponent of modern Carmelite spirituality and is, as it were, a complement to her better-known sister-in-religion. While Teresa belonged to the petite bourgeoisie, Elisabeth Catez was the descendant of distinguished officers, and while Teresa was given to tears and self-pity, Elisabeth was subject to violent tempers, though she, too, was exceptionally sensitive. She dates her "conversion" from her first Holy Communion,

which she made at the age of eleven, when she decided to fight
resolutely against these two faults. Almost three years later she
believed she heard the word "Carmel" within her soul, and soon
afterwards she made a vow of virginity. But her mother was in-
flexibly opposed to her religious vocation, and, again unlike
Teresa, Elizabeth obeyed. She went unresistingly to all the
parties and festivities to which Madame Catez took her, smartly
dressed and seemingly enjoying herself. Several young men
asked for her hand in marriage, but she refused. During the
holidays she traveled with her family to the French resorts and
to Switzerland, making friends everywhere, but without ever
swerving from her determination to become a Carmelite. Her
prayer became increasingly contemplative, and on one of her
visits to the Carmelite convent of her native town of Dijon she
discussed it with a well-known Dominican theologian, Père
Vallée, whom she met there. She told him that in her prayer
she liked simply to give herself up to the divine presence she
felt within her. He assured her that she was on the right way,
because the soul was the dwelling place of the Holy Trinity. In
1899 her mother finally gave her permission to enter Carmel
when she was twenty-one, so she had still to wait two years,
during which she prepared herself by giving as much time as
she could to prayer and by frequent visits to the convent.

She finally entered Carmel in August 1901 and was clothed
with the habit on December 8 of the same year. She was given
the name Elisabeth of the Trinity, and her mystical life developed through the ever more deeply experienced realization of
this central mystery of the faith. This she combined with that
of the Mystical Body of Christ, which she found in the Letters
of St. Paul, her favorite spiritual reading. Hence, though she
belonged to a strictly enclosed contemplative order, she was
nevertheless deeply concerned with the needs both of the Church
and of the individuals with whom she was in correspondence.
For her greatest desire was to become to Christ "an additional
humanity" (*une humanité de surcroît*) in which—in the words
of St. Paul—he could fulfill what was lacking in his Passion. In

her famous prayer to the Trinity she asks of God that she may never leave him alone in her soul, "but may I always be wholly there, fully awakened in my faith, all adoring, totally surrendered to thy creative action." For her the mystical life was not anything extraordinary, but a "fully awakened faith," through which the indwelling of the Trinity in the soul is completely realized.

Like Teresa of Lisieux, Elisabeth, too, died young, at the age of twenty-six, of cancer of the stomach which she had to endure without any alleviation of its excruciating pains. But far from complaining, she called her illness "the sickness of love." "It is he who works in me and consumes me," she wrote, "I give myself up and abandon myself, happy in advance to accept whatever he will do."

As the nineteenth century wore on, more laymen and women combined mystical experiences with an ordinary family or professional life. There is for example Contardo Ferrini (1859–1902), a legal expert of international reputation, as well as a first-class mountaineer. For him the discipline of sustained intellectual work took the place of physical penances, and work and prayer were closely connected. Those who saw him kneeling, completely absorbed in God after he had received Holy Communion, realized his spiritual life had reached mystical heights: "Only our feet should touch the earth," he once wrote, "our soul should be absorbed in God. That calm and uninterrupted absorption ought to be an image of the Sabbath of the Trinity." He himself explained how one's daily work was to be combined with an intense prayer life: "Even in the daily occupations," he wrote, "there must be what I call the intimate communications between God and his creature . . . This will mean remembering the holy thoughts of the morning Mass, a remembrance that comes to us, consoling us in the course of our daily work. This will be a glance towards our Father in the midst of our daily cares," for "the end of Christian prayer is our transformation into Jesus Christ; this calm, tranquil absorption must reflect the union within the supreme Trinity," a description reflecting the trinitarian mysticism of the great Spanish mystics.

Another professional man, the German banker and member of the Prussian Landtag Hieronymus Jaegen (1841–1919) had not only himself mystical experiences but also wrote mystical treatises. He took an active part in the Catholic opposition to Bismarck's *Kulturkampf*, through which the Prussian chancellor tried to break the spiritual power of the Catholic Church over its subjects. Like Contardo Ferrini, Jaegen was a bachelor. In his book *The Life of Mystical Grace* he not only described the mystical life in its gradual ascent to the summit, but also inserted some of his own experiences. Explaining why he, a layman, wrote such a book, he said that the good, solid books on the subject were mostly in Latin and very difficult to understand, while those in the vernacular generally did more harm than good, "because they increase the desire for extraordinary experiences and hence may easily lead to deception and illusion"—thinking probably of such popular books as the revelations of Anna-Catherine Emmerick and others. As a professional man and a politician he could not indulge in conspicuous behaviour or poverty of dress so often associated with sanctity and mysticism, but led his life of union with God in the external setting corresponding to his position in society. For according to him a man aspiring to the mystical union ought "always to act according to the principles of Christian prudence and to avoid all extraordinary behaviour and offences against good manners. Everything at its time: external activity according to one's station in life and interior converse with God must peacefully progress together, helping one another until both reach the heights. This will then be a sure sign of authentic mysticism."

Another example for the fact that the mystical life is possible not only in the professions but also in a happy marriage and an active social life is Elisabeth Leseur (1866–1914). She was an attractive Parisienne, the eldest of five children, whose sister Juliette, six years her junior, was her special favorite. As a young girl Elisabeth was very devout; she kept a "rule of life" in which prayer, catechism lessons, and struggle against her faults played a considerable part, and her First Holy Communion which she made at the age of twelve was a deep spiritual experience.

When Elisabeth was twenty-one she met her future husband, Felix Leseur, who was immediately attracted by her beauty and elegance. He was a political journalist, who had completely lost his faith, and after his marriage in 1889 he also influenced Elisabeth in this direction. The young couple led a very worldly life, in which parties and exciting trips abroad were the order of the day. After having been married seven years Elisabeth gave up the practice of her religion altogether. But this period of complete unbelief did not last long; and her return to the Church was brought about by what would seem the most unlikely of books to have such an effect, the notorious *Life of Jesus* by the French atheist Ernest Renan. Renan, while admiring Jesus as a religious genius, completely denied his divinity and, of course, his miracles and his Resurrection. Renan's book had destroyed the faith of many Christians, but it revived the faith of Elisabeth Leseur. For she argued, whatever the truth about the founder of Christianity, it could not be that absurd medley of historical facts and improbable personal hypotheses that Renan had concocted. Hence she now began to make a serious study of the Gospels and of Catholic doctrine, and within a few months she not only returned to the practice of the faith but also sought to deepen it continually through prayer and reading, to the great disappointment of her husband, who had flattered himself that he had succeeded in estranging his wife from the Church for good.

Elisabeth's developing mystical life was built on sure foundations: she read St. Augustine and St. Thomas Aquinas, St. Teresa, and St. Francis de Sales. In 1903 she and her husband traveled to Rome, and there she had a mystical experience she describes in her diary: "I felt in myself the living presence of the blessed Christ, of God himself, bringing me ineffable love. His matchless Spirit spoke to mine, and for a moment all the infinite tenderness of the Saviour entered into me. Never will this divine trace be destroyed. In that unforgettable minute the triumphant Christ, the eternal Word . . . took possession of my soul for all eternity. I felt myself renewed by him to my very depths." Two years later her beloved sister Juliette died, a loss which left a permanent wound in her heart. Holy Communion, after which she often experienced a mystical union with Christ, was her great consolation; but she had frequently to deprive herself of it because of the objections of her husband, whom she dearly loved. The more deeply she entered into the mystical life, the less she tried to convert him by arguments. He should come to know her faith by its fruits and by the serene happiness of its expression. In her *Spiritual Testament*, written in 1905, nine years before her death, she foretold his conversion, and shortly before she died she predicted that he would become a religious. Her prediction was fulfilled, for her husband was reconciled to the Church three years after her death and later became a Dominican priest.

As we began the history of the Church's mysticism with the age of the martyrs, so we shall also end it with a martyr, for the persecutions of our own time have produced many martyrs, even though so far most of them have not yet become widely known. We select of their number one who was not only a mystic, but also a man in close touch with the industrial and technological problems of our time, the Polish Franciscan Father Maximilian Kolbe (1894–1941). He was the son of a poor and very devout weaver's family, and was educated at the minor Franciscan seminary at Lwow. His favorite subjects were science and mathematics; besides, he was very interested in questions of modern strategy, fortifications, and other subjects not normally associated with mysticism. So it is not surprising that, at the age of sixteen, he should have felt that he had no religious vocation and decided to ask his superior to release him. But just as he was about to do so his mother came to visit him and informed him that, since their youngest son had also decided to become a priest, she herself and his father were now able to realize a long cherished wish and to enter the religious life themselves. This caused Maximilian to change his mind; for if he were not to stay on at the seminary his parents would still be responsible for him and unable to carry out their desire for several years to come; so after his mother had left him he at once asked to be given the Franciscan habit.

In 1912 he was sent to Rome to study for the priesthood and three years later received his doctorate in philosophy. About this time a hitherto unperceived tuberculosis of the lungs began to show itself in several hemorrhages, and he had to restrict his activities. Two years later he conceived the idea of founding a Militia of the Immaculate Virgin in order to counteract the contemporary spirit of atheism which he had observed especially during the Freemasons' bicentenary celebrations in Rome. In 1918 he was ordained priest and in the following year he received his doctor's degree in theology. Soon after his return to Poland his health deteriorated, and he had to spend a year in a nursing home, where he converted many of his unbelieving fellow patients, whom he could meet on their own ground as he was well versed in modern science and philosophy. For he would have liked to see Catholics in the forefront of contemporary life, and far from deploring—like his fellow religious—such modern inventions as the cinema he saw their great possibilities in the service of the apostolate. After his return to Cracow his Militia began to grow rapidly, and despite a great deal of opposition from his brethren who did not consider his activities consonant with Franciscan principles, he founded a publishing house to produce a periodical for his Militia, and other religious literature. He collected a number of lay workers for the printing, whom he formed into Franciscan brothers and treated in the same way as his fellow priests, for he would accept no class distinctions: they were all "working brothers in a working world."

In 1926 his health broke down again and he had to go back to the nursing home for eighteen months. It was a time of intense suffering, both physical and spiritual, for God and the Blessed Virgin seemed to have abandoned him and he felt like a broken tool fit only to be thrown away. More, without his presence his publishing house ran into grave difficulties, and he finally decided to return, even though he was not yet completely cured. Under his direction the work once more began to flourish; the circulation of his periodical went up by leaps and bounds, and in 1930 he went to Japan and began to publish his review at Nagasaki. Though he hardly ever mentioned his mystical experiences, he admitted under persistent questioning that while in Japan he had had a revelation in which he was promised heaven. After two years at Nagasaki he went to India to prepare yet another foundation, and as his health had once more deteriorated he went back to Poland and became superior of Niepokalanow, the publishing community of six priests and over seven hundred brothers he had founded, and which was now responsible for a number of publications. But despite ever increasing work, both he and his men gave several hours each day to prayer and meditation, for Father Maximilian held that God would not speak to them in noise and excitement. He also prepared them for the war he knew was imminent, urging on them the sanctifying power of suffering and the glory of martyrdom that would open heaven for them. He himself was arrested by the Gestapo in February 1941, cruelly ill-treated, and transferred to the concentration camp at Auschwitz in May. There he was often brutally beaten, but he told his fellow sufferers that the Immaculate Virgin was helping him. And indeed it seems impossible that he, whose tuberculosis had never been really cured, should have survived his sufferings without supernatural help. For not only did he frequently give away his own starvation rations, but he gave conferences and heard confessions in the prison "nursing home" to which he was transferred for a while to recover from the beatings.

Soon after he had been considered fit to go back to the normal camp routine a prisoner escaped from the block to which he belonged. As a punishment a number of the other inmates of the camp were condemned to the horrible death of starvation in the hunger bunker. As those chosen for it were lined up, one of them began loudly to bewail his family. Suddenly Father Kolbe stepped forward and asked to be allowed to die in his place, and to the amazement of all the brutal Nazi actually granted his request. And so Father Maximilian went into the hunger bunker with his companions, comforting them and praying with them; but when all others had died he was still alive and was given the syringe with its lethal poison that brought an end to his sufferings.

It may have struck the reader that in these last pages there has been much less said of ecstasies and visions than in other parts of this book. But it seems that in our time the mystical life, though present, is far more hidden than in what is sometimes called "the ages of faith"; spectacular ecstasies are rare, and the mystical union with God is often lived even in the turmoil of the modern world as well as in the convent. For, as the greatest mystics never weary telling us, the external phenomena are not the most important aspects of mysticism; what constitutes mysticism in the Christian sense is the experienced union with God in the depths of the soul, and this is possible in the world as well as in the cloister. It is especially necessary in our time, as men like Thomas Merton have so clearly seen, to counterbalance the all-pervading materialism of the Western world and to provide centers of energy from which to recharge its spent spiritual batteries.

SELECT BIBLIOGRAPHY

1. EDITIONS

St. Catherine of Genoa, ed. Charlotte Balfour and Helen D. Irvine. Sheed & Ward, New York, 1946.

St. Catherine of Siena, The Dialogue, ed. Algar Thorold. Newman Bookshop, Westminster, Md., 1943.

The Cloud of Unknowing and Other Treatises, ed. Justin McCann. The Newman Press, Westminster, Md., 1952.

Master Eckhart and the Rhineland Mystics, ed. Jeanne Ancelet-Hustache. Harper & Brothers, New York, 1958.

St. Francis of Assisi, Writings of, tr. Benen Fahy and ed. Placid Hermann. London, 1964.

Walter Hilton, *The Scale of Perfection*, ed. Evelyn Underhill. Allenson & Co., Ltd., London, 1948.

Julian of Norwich, ed. Roger Hudleston. The Newman Press, Westminster, Md., 1952.

Complete Works of St. John of the Cross, trans. and ed. E. Allison Peers. The Newman Press, Westminster, Md., 1953 (3 vols.).

The Collected Works of St. John of the Cross, trans. and ed. Kiernan Kavanaugh and Otilio Rodriguez. Doubleday & Company, Inc., Garden City, N.Y., 1964.

Raymond Lull, *The Book of the Lover and the Beloved*, tr. E. Allison Peers. The Macmillan Company, New York, 1923.

Raymond Lull, *The Tree of Love*, tr. E. Allison Peers. The Macmillan Company, London, 1926.

Raymond Lull, *Blanquerna*, tr. E. Allison Peers. The Macmillan Company, London, 1926.

Mechthild of Magdeburg, *The Revelations*, tr. Lucy Menzies. Longmans, Green & Co., Inc., New York, 1953.

Complete Works of St. Teresa of Avila, tr. and ed. E. Allison Peers. Sheed & Ward, New York, 1946 (3 vols.).

The Autobiography of St. Thérèse of Lisieux, trans. John Beevers. Doubleday & Company, Inc. (Image Books), Garden City, N.Y., 1957.

English translations of many of the Fathers are easily accessible in the *Ancient Christian Writers Series*, The Newman Press, Westminster, Maryland.

2. GENERAL BIBLIOGRAPHY & SUGGESTED READINGS

Abelson, J. *Jewish Mysticism*. The Macmillan Company, New York, 1914.

D'Aygalliers, A. Wautier. *Ruysbroeck the Admirable*. E. P. Dutton & Company, New York, 1925.

Balthasar, Hans Urs von. *Elizabeth of Dijon*. Pantheon Books, Inc., New York, 1956.

Baumgardt, David. *Great Western Mystics*. Columbia University Press, New York, 1961.

Bedoyère, Michael de la. *Greatest Catherine: The Life of Catherine Benincasa, Saint of Siena*. The Bruce Publishing Co., Milwaukee, 1947.

Bedoyère, Michael de la. *The Archbishop and the Lady*. Pantheon Books, Inc., New York, 1956.

Bergson, Henri. *Two Sources of Morality and Religion*. Doubleday & Company, Inc. (Anchor Books), Garden City, N.Y., 1954.

Bordeaux, Henry C. *St. Francis de Sales*. Longmans, Green & Co., Inc., New York, 1929.

Brodrick, James. *The Origin of the Jesuits*. Doubleday & Company, Inc. (Image Books), Garden City, N.Y., 1960.

Burnaby, John. *Amor Dei: A Study of the Religion of St. Augustine*. Allenson & Co., Ltd., London, 1960.

Butler, C. *Western Mysticism*. E. P. Dutton & Company, New York, 1951.

Chadwick, Owen. *John Cassian: A Study in Primitive Monasticism*. Cambridge University Press, Cambridge, 1950.

Chambers, Percy F. *Julian of Norwich*. Harper & Brothers, New York, 1955.

Clark, J. M. *The Great German Mystics*. The Macmillan Company, New York, 1949.

Conze, Edward. *Buddhism: Its Essence and Development*. Philosophical Library, Inc., New York, 1951.

Curtayne, A. *St. Catherine of Siena*. Sheed & Ward, New York, 1931.

Daniélou, Jean. *Origen*. Sheed & Ward, New York, 1955.

Dasgupta, Surendra N. *Hindu Mysticism*. Frederick Ungar Publishing Company, New York, 1960.

Eliade, Mircea. *Myths, Dreams and Mysteries*. Harper & Brothers, New York, 1960.

Fremantle, Anne, ed. *Protestant Mystics*. Little, Brown & Company, Boston, 1964.

Garrigou-Lagrange, Reginald. *Christian Perfection and Contemplation*. B. Herder Book Co., St. Louis, 1937.

Ghéon, Henri. *The Secret of St. Margaret Mary*. Sheed & Ward, New York, 1937.

Gilson, Etienne. *The Mystical Theology of St. Bernard*. Sheed & Ward, New York, 1940.

Gobry, Y. *The Nature of Mysticism*. Hawthorn Books, Inc., New York, 1964.

Goerres, Ida F. *The Hidden Face* (A Study of St. Thérèse of Lisieux). Pantheon Books, Inc., New York, 1958.

Goodier, Alban. *Introduction to the Study of Ascetical and Mystical Theology*. The Bruce Publishing Co., Milwaukee, 1946.

Graef, Hilda. *The Light and the Rainbow*. The Newman Press, Westminster, Md., 1959.

Graef, Hilda. *Mystics of Our Times*. Doubleday & Company, Inc., Garden City, N.Y., 1962.

Happold, F. C. *Mysticism*. Penguin Books, Inc., Baltimore, 1963.

Hodgson, G. E. *English Mystics*. Morehouse Publishing Co., Milwaukee, 1922.

Hodgson, G. E. *The Sanity of Mysticism: A Study of Richard Rolle*. Morehouse Publishing Co., Milwaukee, 1931.

Hügel, Friedrich von. *The Mystical Element of Religion as Studied in St. Catherine of Siena and Her Friends*. E. P. Dutton & Company, New York, 1909.

Hyma, A. *The Christian Renaissance: A History of the Devotio Moderna*. The Century Company, New York, 1924.

James, Edwin O. *Prehistoric Religion*. Barnes & Noble, Inc., New York, 1961.

Little, Katharine D. *Francis de Fénelon*. Harper & Brothers, New York, 1951.

Lossky, Vladimir. *Mystical Theology of the Eastern Church*. Allenson & Co., Ltd., London, 1957.

Nugent, Rosamond. *Portrait of the Consecrated Woman in Greek Christian Literature of the First Four Centuries*. Catholic University of America Press, Washington, D.C., 1941.

Otto, Rudolph. *Mysticism East and West*. Meridian Books, Inc., New York, 1964.

Peers, E. Allison. *Spirit of Flame, A Study of St. John of the Cross*. Morehouse-Gorham Co., Inc., New York, 1944.

Peers, E. Allison. *Mother of Carmel, A Portrait of St. Teresa of Avila*. Morehouse-Gorham Co., Inc., New York, 1946.

Pistorius, Philippus V. *Plotinus and Neoplatonism*. Bowes & Bowes, Ltd., Cambridge, 1952.

Rice, Cyprian. *The Persian Sufis*. Humanities Press, New York, 1964.

Richardson, Cyril C. *The Christianity of Ignatius of Antioch*. Columbia University Press, New York, 1935.

Robo, Etienne. *Two Portraits of St. Teresa of Lisieux*. The Newman Press, Westminster, Md., 1957.

Saudreau, A. *Mystical Prayer According to St. Francis de Sales*. Benziger Brothers, Inc., New York, 1929.

Spencer, S. *Mysticism in World Religion*. Penguin Books, Inc., Baltimore, 1963.

Suzuki, D. T. *Mysticism: Christian Buddhist*. Harper & Brothers, New York, 1957.

Thurston, Herbert. *The Physical Phenomena of Mysticism*. Henry Regnery Company, Chicago, 1952.

Underhill, Evelyn. *Essentials of Mysticism*. E. P. Dutton & Company, New York, 1957.

Underhill, Evelyn. *Mysticism*. Meridian Books, Inc., New York, 1955.

Zaehner, Robert C. *Mysticism, Sacred and Profane*. Oxford University Press, London, 1957.